LEARNING
JAPANESE
TEXTBOOK FOR BEGINNERS

First Edition

A Step-by-Step Approach to Learning Japanese Effectively

We recommend this book to those who haven't yet learned about Hiragana, Katakana, and basic Kanji characters. This workbook is designed to teach Hiragana, Katakana, and basic Kanji to beginners. It includes practice exercises and writing drills to help learners master the writing systems. The book has received positive reviews on Amazon, and it may be a helpful resource for those who prefer a workbook-style approach to learning Japanese.

Learning Japanese Workbook for Beginners: Hiragana Katakana and Kanji

by Just Reality

There are free Online audio files available on justreality1.com, recorded by a native Japanese speaker. These audio files cover Hiragana, Katakana, Kanji characters, vocabulary, and lessons, and you can download them for free.

Learning Japanese

Textbook for Beginners

First Edition: Jan 19, 2024 Mie - Japan
ISBN-13: 978-4991267222 (Paperback)
Website: www.Justreality1.com

IMPORTANT NOTICE

Considering that the book is in black and white and includes various patterns or images that might cause discomfort for individuals with visual sensitivities, we have simplified the patterns and images in this edition to accommodate readers who experience such sensitivities.

Limit of Liability / Disclaimer of Warranty

The author and publisher make no representations or warranties with respect to the accuracy or completeness of the contents of this work and expressly disclaim all warranties, including, without limitation, warranties of fitness for a particular purpose. No warranty may be created or extended by sales or promotional materials.

The advice and strategies contained herein are not suitable for every individual. By providing information or links to other companies or websites, the publisher and the author do not guarantee, approve or endorse the information or products available at any linked websites or mentioned companies or persons, nor does a link indicate any association with or endorsement by the publisher or author.

This publication is designed to provide information with regard to the subject matter covered. It is offered or sold with the understanding that neither the publisher nor the author is engaged in rendering legal, accounting, or other professional service. If legal advice or other expert assistance is required, the services of a competent professional should be sought. Neither the publisher nor the author shall be liable for any loss or loss of profit or any other commercial damages, including but not limited to special, incidental, consequential, or other damages.

TABLE OF CONTENTS 1-3

TABLE OF CONTENTS 2-3

TABLE OF CONTENTS 3-3

10. Section 3

Free Bonus Materials

Download

As a bonus, we've included some extra materials for you to download along with the audio files these resources will help you deepen your understanding of the content and apply the insights in practical ways.

1 **ONLINE AUDIO RECORDINGS**
All the vocabulary words and sentences were recorded by a native Japanese speaker.

2 **250 ESSENTIAL JAPANESE VERBS**
(Irregular, Godan, Ichidan verbs) Learning is essential for proper verb conjugation and effective communication.

3 **JAPANESE VERB CONJUGATION TABLES**
Mastering the Japanese language often involves understanding and practicing Japanese verb conjugation tables.

4 **VERBS PRACTICE REFERENCE WORKSHEETS**
Helpful for practicing and comparing plain and polite verb tense forms.

SCAN ME

www.justreality1.com

How to Download Audio Files

Follow these five simple steps to download audio files:

1. Using your computer, smartphone, iPhone/iPad, or tablet, either scan the QR code provided or visit www.justreality1.com/audiofiles.

2. To download the audio files for free, enter your name and email address.

3. Within a few seconds, check your email for the download link.

4. If you haven't received the email, please check your spam or junk folder.

5. We have included multiple links for you to download the audio files. Please select the one that is most convenient for you to initiate the download process.

We hope you find these materials useful in your language-learning journey!

This textbook is designed to help beginners master the Japanese language and culture quickly and easily. It provides straightforward grammatical explanations without unnecessary complexities, making it easier for you to achieve your Japanese language learning goals in conversational skills, vocabulary, and everyday expressions. You will learn many things about Japanese culture, language patterns, and grammatical structures that actual Japanese people use daily, so you can use them to form sentences and interact with those around you.

Learning new concepts and making time to study can be difficult. Moreover, studying with inadequate materials can make the process very complicated and boring, which makes you lose interest in learning the language. So this book aims to make language learning simple.

To facilitate learning this language, we have covered all the main topics and provided zipped audio files that can be downloaded from our website for free. This book will enable you to speak Japanese within a few months. However, learners have to clearly understand their goal in learning Japanese (e.g., for travel, work, meetings, etc.), based on which they can decide whether they want to learn only conversation and daily expressions, or both speaking and writing.

For whom is This Book Designed?

This book is intended for beginners new to the Japanese language and culture. It suits students, travelers, and anyone interested in Japan who wants to learn more about the culture and language. Whether you are interested in learning for personal or professional reasons, This book will provide you with the necessary skills to effectively communicate in Japanese.

Upon Completion of This Book

■ Read and write essential Japanese texts and simple stories, and understand the main points of short news articles and essays Including the grammar structures and vocabulary of everyday speaking, and having the foundational literacy skills to read and write short phrases and hold rudimentary discussions.

■ You will gain an understanding of Japanese culture, and the customs you've embraced will be invaluable in comprehending how Japanese people think. Persistently studying and practicing will further enhance your skills and fluency.

■ You will become able to understand spoken vocabulary and use it in everyday communicative situations. Also, your listening skills will improve, allowing you to easily understand most words in anime and movies.

Points of Difficulty in the Japanese Language

There are several different elements of Japanese, including grammar, pronunciation, reading, and writing the characters. A foreigner who wishes to learn Japanese may wonder why even native Japanese people sometimes find their language difficult to understand.

This is partly because it's challenging to use a variety of honorifics and grammar styles. A particularly difficult aspect of communication is the fact that words that are similar in meaning can convey different implications.

 ## Kanji

There are also multiple ways to read each kanji character, and even Japanese people find it difficult to memorize all of them correctly. For example, 店, which means "shop" or "store" has two readings: (てん) ten and (みせ) mise.

 ## Honorifics

Honorifics (謙譲語 "kenjou-go") are used to show respect, and using them can be polite, deferential, or humble. While the honorific is a form of expressing simple regard for other people, this form of speech may also have the purpose of showing reverence and humbling yourself when talking to someone of a higher status. When you talk to a "superior" someone older than you, someone higher ranking in your company like your boss or manager, or a customer, client, etc. to whom you must show respect you must use polite Japanese.

When conversing with different people, adjusting your level of politeness is essential. It is considered rude to use improper honorifics, so it is crucial to learn how to use them correctly.

 ## Grammar

Grammar is the set of rules used for creating sentences. Grammar has different forms, such as particles and parts of speech. In particular, if you make a mistake in using particles such as "〜は" 〜が" or "〜を" the sentence will be completely different from what was intended.

- The usage of particles in a sentence has the potential to alter its meaning.

- Don't worry we've covered the fundamental concepts and techniques to start communicating effectively in Japanese (reading, writing, grammar, and speaking).

Japanese Language Proficiency Test (JLPT)

The JLPT has three sections: vocabulary, grammar, reading, and listening. The vocabulary and grammar sections are multiple-choice, while the reading and listening sections consist of multiple-choice and fill-in-the-blank questions.

The JLPT is widely recognized by Japanese language schools, companies, and government agencies as a reliable measure of Japanese language proficiency. Many people take the JLPT to improve their job prospects, study at a Japanese university, or challenge themselves and track their progress in learning Japanese. To pass the JLPT, you must have a solid understanding of hiragana, katakana, kanji, and grammar and be able to read and write them accurately. The JLPT is offered at five levels, and the number of required kanji increases with each level.

Level	Total Test Time	Test Time by Section		Listening
		Language Knowledge. Reading		
N1	170 minutes	110 minutes		60 minutes
N2	155 minutes	105 minutes		50 minutes
N3	140 minutes	30 minutes	70 minutes	40 minutes
N4	115 minutes	25 minutes	55 minutes	35 minutes
N5	90 minutes	20 minutes	40 minutes	30 minutes

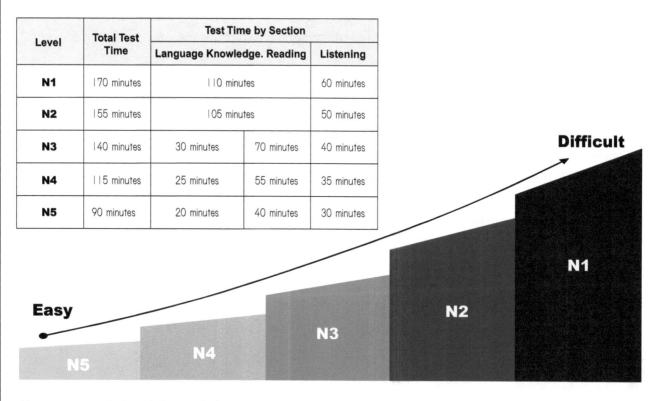

Here is a rough breakdown of the kanji and vocabulary words required for each JLPT level:

JLPT	Hours	Vocabulary	Kanji	Levels
N5	150-200	800	100	Beginner
N4	250-300	1,500	250	Upper beginner
N3	450-500	3,000	650	Intermediate
N2	600-800	6,000	1,000	Advanced
N1	800-2,150	10,000	2,000	Proficiency

Characteristics of Japanese textbooks

Most Japanese language textbooks are like this:

文型　わたしは たなかです。	Grammar: I'm Tanaka.	
例文　「あなたは」たなかさんですか。	Sentences：Are you Mr./Mrs./ Miss/ Tanaka?	
はい、「わたしは」たなかです。	Yes, I'm Tanaka.	

As shown in the above example, this textbook type focuses on grammatical patterns rather than communication. They help understand sentence structure, but unfortunately, these sentences are unnatural. Real people don't talk like that.

■ First, you must understand how to use Japanese particles so you can build sentences correctly.

Kanji ← 私は、寿司を食べる。 → **Romanized Script**

わたしは、すしをたべる。

Particles ←

watashi wa sushi wo taberu.

Grammar Note

Translation ← I eat sushi.

を Indicates object of action
は indicates the main topic of a sentence

These are not grammatical patterns or model conversations but a list of expressions. Don't worry if they look complicated. We use these expressions during lessons while greeting each other for the first time. You will learn them in context and come to understand their meaning and usage instantly and instinctively.

■ Some Japanese textbooks may not strongly emphasize speaking or listening skills, leaving students unprepared to communicate with native speakers.

How This Book is Structured

This book has been arranged systematically to make it easy to learn from. Split into four sections and 20 units, it will give you knowledge of Japan's past, culture, and traditional way of life, as well as the unique idiosyncrasies of the Japanese people and fascinating facts about modern-day Japan.

Culture and Customs

The book provides a comprehensive exploration of Japanese culture and traditions, covering topics such as social norms, etiquette, cultural expressions, historical and cultural context, an overview of Japan, religion, beliefs, and the warriors of Japan. Exploring these cultural aspects deepens learners' comprehension of the Japanese language and provides valuable insights into its people.

Approach to Reading, Writing, and Grammar

Comprehensively covers the basics of grammar and vocabulary and delves into advanced topics like reading and writing. You'll swiftly enhance your sentence structure, vocabulary development, particles, and pronunciation skills through clear explanations and a wealth of practice tasks. Additionally, the book provides conversation practice exercises and commonly used phrases so you'll quickly learn to speak, read, and write Japanese.

Headings and Subheadings

Throughout the book, headings and subheadings are used to break up the text and guide the reader. They are often formatted differently (e.g., bold, larger font) to make them stand out.

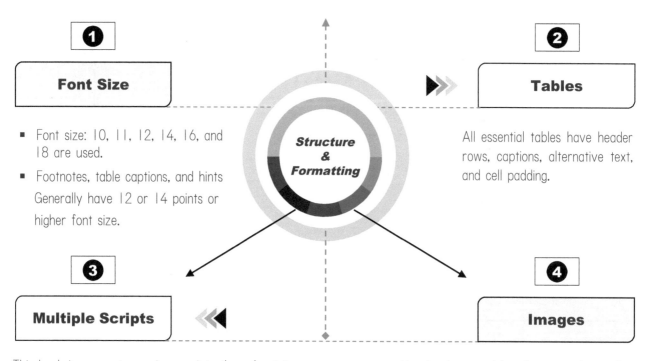

❶ Font Size

- Font size: 10, 11, 12, 14, 16, and 18 are used.
- Footnotes, table captions, and hints Generally have 12 or 14 points or higher font size.

❷ Tables

All essential tables have header rows, captions, alternative text, and cell padding.

Structure & Formatting

❸ Multiple Scripts

This book incorporates various scripts throughout its pages, including intricate characters or scripts with multiple potential interpretations.

❹ Images

- Meaning is not solely reliant on color in the conveyed information through images.
- The images are aligned with the text content.

Preview the book's contents and familiarize yourself with its layout and organization.
Look for sections or units that seem interesting or relevant to your goals.

Culture and History

Learn about Japanese culture, history, and customs. It will help you understand why and how the language is being used, and will also help you to connect more with the people you meet.

Reading

Start with basic vocabulary and sentence structures. Begin by practicing simple reading exercises and gradually progress to more complex texts. Reading aloud can significantly contribute to improving your pronunciation and rhythm.

Writing

Start writing simple words and phrases, gradually increasing in difficulty. Write simple sentences and practice using the grammar structures you have learned. Use writing exercises from the book or create your own.

Listening

Improve your language proficiency by listening intently to audio recordings from a native Japanese speaker. These recordings provide comprehensive coverage of all the book's units and offer accurate pronunciations, conversational vocabulary, grammar, and phrases to learn.

Speaking

Practice speaking Japanese with a tutor or language exchange partner. Use the dialogues and exercises from the book to practice conversational skills. Start with simple phrases and move on to more complex sentences.

Basic Kanji

Trying to memorize the Kanji mentioned in this book can be difficult initially, but with practice and repetition, you will gradually become more comfortable with them. As you progress through the book, practice and apply your learning. It can include writing out sentences in Hiragana and Katakana and practicing new vocabulary words and grammar rules.

 Exercises

You can use the exercises provided in the book to assess your understanding and measure your progress. If you find that you're having trouble with a particular section, make sure to re-read it and review the related exercises until you feel comfortable moving on.

 Be Patient

Learning a language takes time and effort, so don't get discouraged if progress seems slow at first, and do not try to study all of the characters at once, as you will probably have a lot of trouble remembering them.

 Answer Key

Checking the answer key for the exercises is crucial to validate your answers. The answer key is included at the book's end and organized according to lesson numbers. It allows you to access and refer to the corresponding answers easily.

 Audio Files

This book comes with Online audio recordings featuring pronunciations of all the vocabulary words and sentences by a native Japanese speaker. Free audio recordings for the book's units are available on the **justreality1.com** website. Be sure to download them.

 www.justreality1.com

The book's contents are tailored to cover essential vocabulary, grammar, and patterns necessary for passing the Japanese Language Proficiency Test at Level N5. The vocabulary and scenarios presented in this book have been designed for beginner levels associated with the JLPT Level 5. It also incorporates advanced-level examples that are highly beneficial.

To provide the correct reading of Kanji, Hiragana will be placed above them. This practice, known as Furigana, is commonly used in comic books and other publications, ensuring accurate Kanji pronunciation for readers.

Example:

← *Furigana*

にほんご　まな
日本語を学びたいです。(Nihongo wo manabitai desu.) I want to learn Japanese.

Just Reality team

The Just Reality team consists of experienced Japanese teachers who employ a straightforward approach to teaching language and culture effectively.

We truly value this book and see it as a valuable resource for your learning journey. Whether you're interested in the culture, considering studying or working in Japan, or want to visit, mastering Japanese is the key to discovering all the wonders of Japan.

Your thoughts matter!
Would you kindly share your thoughts by leaving a review on our Amazon page?
Your feedback is invaluable and helps us grow. Thank you for your time and support

頑張ってください。
DO YOUR BEST

Let's get started, and take the first step towards fluency today!

Currency: Yen (¥)
Emperor and Empress: Naruhito and Masako
Prime Minister: Fumio Kishida
Government: Constitutional Democracy Official
Language: Japanese
Religion: Shintou, Buddhism, Christianity, Other
Population: 125.8 million (as of 2020) Writing
Systems: Hiragana, Katakana, Kanji
National Sport: Sumou
Popular Sport: Baseball and Soccer

HOKKAIDOU
北海道

SAPPORO

PACIFIC
OCEAN

SEA OF JAPAN

AOMORI

AKITA

IWATE

YAMAGATA

SENDAI

KYOTO
京都

FUKUSHIMA

HYOGO
兵庫

OSAKA
大阪

IBARAKI

CHIBA

HIROSHIMA
広島県

TOKYO
東京都

KANAGAWA
NAGOYA

FUKUOKA

ISE SHIMA

NAGASAKI

MIE

NARA
奈良

OKINAWA

Japan is an island nation, consisting of an entire archipelago of 6,852 islands. Despite this huge number, it consists of five major islands (Hokkaidou, Honshuu, Shikoku, Kyuushuu, and Okinawa) that account for about 97% of its total area.

The island of Honshuu, the mainland of Japan, is a very large residential area. Japan has been divided into 47 administrative prefectures, spread over eight traditional regions.

Each prefecture has its own unique culture, history, and attractions. For example, Hokkaidou is known for its beautiful natural landscapes and outdoor activities, while Osaka is known for its food and lively·atmosphere. Tokyo, the capital of Japan, is a highly populous city renowned for its bustling streets, advanced technology, and rich cultural heritage.

Kyoto is famous for its temples, shrines, and traditional architecture, and Hiroshima is known for the tragic atomic bombing during World War II, and its Peace Memorial Park.

The word "Japan" in Japanese is pronounced in two ways: "Nihon" and "Nippon". Both of these readings are often translated as "Land of the Rising Sun". Although "Nippon" has a more patriotic connotation, "Nihon" is more commonly used in everyday speech.

Other Names Used to Refer to Japan

Wa (和)

Japan and its populace were once referred to as "Wa" in ancient Chinese writings. The initial instance of this name appears in the 3rd century AD, within the document records of the three Kingdoms (Sanguozhi).

Yamato (大和)

While "Yamato" served as a government district in Nara long ago, its modern association is generally linked to the "Yamato" battleship – the premier vessel of the Imperial Japanese Navy's Yamato class utilized during the Second World War.

Japanese National Flag

Kyokujitsuki   **Hinomaru**

Kyokujitsuki (きょくじつき)

The Rising Sun Flag, as it's commonly known, is a Japanese national symbol. It prominently displays a vibrant red disc with sixteen rays of red colour emanating from its centre. The flag has a long history and was originally used as a crest for samurai. During the Meiji era in 1889, the Rising Sun Flag was formally embraced as the naval ensign of the Imperial Japanese Navy.

Hinomaru (ひのまる)

The national flag of Japan, known as the Hinomaru, is a rectangular white banner featuring a crimson-red circle at its center. It is officially called the Nisshouki and was adopted on August 5th, 1854. The Hinomaru has been in use since at least the 14th century and recalls the name of Japan, the "Land of the Rising Sun". In 1999, the Japanese government formally adopted the Hinomaru as the modern flag of Japan. The move was controversial due to the flag's association with Japanese imperialism in the middle of the 20th century.

Mount Fuji

Mount Fuji, or Fuji-san, is the highest point in Japan, standing at 3,776.24 meters (12,389 feet). Its summit is always covered in snow. Its exquisite shape has captured the hearts of people from Japan and all over the world, and it has been a prominent symbol of Japan from ancient times to the present. Many people from around the world visit Japan in the summer to climb Mt. Fuji and reach the country's highest point.

The Climbing Season

Every year, the climbing season spans from the beginning of July to the start of September, offering a specific window for enthusiasts to embark on mountainous adventures.

Five Lakes

Mount Fuji is surrounded by a picturesque landscape known as the Five Lakes region. Five lakes leave a beautiful impression on the landscape around the mountain, particularly Lake Kawaguchi. In 2013, Mount Fuji was registered as a UNESCO World Heritage site.

Worshiping Mt. Fuji

Mount Fuji worship is deeply rooted in Shintoism, Japan's indigenous religion. Shintoism teaches that all natural objects, such as mountains, rivers, and trees, possess divine spirits known as "Kami". One of Shintoism's most significant "Kami" resides on Mount Fuji – "Konohanasakuya-hime" a goddess of fertility and Mount Fuji itself.

Throughout history, pilgrims have traveled to Mount Fuji to worship and honor the mountain and its "Kami". Ascents to Mount Fuji's summit are considered acts of worship during summer. Mount Fuji's beauty, power, and spiritual significance are integral to Japanese culture and religion.

Mount Fuji（富士山）

The Japanese Islands have been continually inhabited by humans since the Upper Paleolithic era this means there is a treasure trove of artifacts and other evidence that archaeologists can use to piece together an accurate account of Japan's rich cultural and political history. To help categorize their findings chronologically, historians have divided Japanese history into distinct periods, starting from about 14,000 BCE and going up to the modern day. This book will provide a brief primer on these periods, including what technological or social advancements.

Jomon Period (14,000 BCE – 300 BCE)

Although there is evidence of human habitation in Japan as far back as 40,000 years ago, the emergence of a cohesive Japanese culture didn't start until the end of the last ice age in what is called the Jomon Period. Like their ancestors, the Jomon people were largely hunter-gatherers whose diet was predominantly comprised of fish and wild plants. Unlike the pre-historic era, however, the Jomon people built permanent villages comprised of pit-dwellings (circular or rectangular domiciles dug into the ground and covered in natural roofing materials). The Jomon also began to develop cultural artifacts like ceramics, stone tools, jewelry, and small figurines, indicating a complex culture borne from food security and a lack of external threats.

Yayoi Period (300 BCE – 300 CE)

The development of agriculture, especially rice farming, ushered in what is known as the Yayoi Period. The largely disparate small villages of the Jomon people began to consolidate into more complex social groupings governed by powerful landowners. New technologies like the potter's wheel, loom, and iron tools were invented, allowing the Yayoi people to develop art and textiles that were more refined than those of the Jomon. As Japanese society grew more complex, new religious ideas emerged, which would eventually serve as the basis for the Shinto faith system. The Yayoi Period also saw an increase in migration from mainland Asia, mostly of Korean and Chinese people, who introduced Buddhist philosophy and a new writing system to Japan.

Kofun Period (250 – 538 CE)

Kofuns are keyhole-shaped burial mounds that range in size from a few meters to nearly half a kilometer in length. Similar to other grand tombs like the pyramids of Egypt or mounds of the Mississippi Valley, these monuments were specifically built for elite members of Japanese society, indicating a significant consolidation of power into a centralized government. The Kofun Period is marked by the development of the Yamato State, a complex system of law and order with an administrative center and imperial court located in the Nara Prefecture. Historians note that the Yamato State had similar features to the Chinese government at the time, and it is likely that the continued migration of people from mainland Asia brought new political ideas and technology to Japan during this time.

Nara Period (710 - 794 CE)

In 710, an imperial decree declared the city of Nara as the new capital of Japan, kicking off what historians refer to as the Nara Period. This era was characterized by advances in philosophy and storytelling that helped lay the groundwork for the modern Japanese identity. Nara Period emperors were strict adherents to Buddhism and established the religion as the official "guardian of the state". They reformed political institutions to be more in line with Buddhist teachings and welcomed Buddhist priests into the imperial court. Scholars also developed Kanji during this time a logographic writing system based on Chinese characters. Authors and poets used Kanji to pen two of the quintessential works of Japanese literature, the Kojiki and Nihon Shoki.

Heian Period (794 - 1185 AD)

The imperial court was relocated to Heian-kyou (modern-day Kyoto) in 794, marking the start of the Heian Period. The aristocracy began to isolate itself from broader society, preferring instead to focus on courtly rituals, poetry competitions, and appreciation of nature. By the latter half of the Heian Period, the imperial court had disengaged so thoroughly from their political and military duties that a new class of warrior chiefs, called samurai, emerged to fill the power vacuum.

Commoners of this era continued to adopt Buddhism as their religion. Novel sects developed during this time, and a distinctly Japanese-flavored Buddhism emerged.

Edo Period (1603 - 1868 CE)

In 1603, a powerful warlord named Tokugawa Ieyasu consolidated power and established a new imperial capital in Edo (modern-day Tokyo), marking the beginning of the Edo Period. Under the Tokugawa Shogun, literally "military government", Japanese society was reorganized into strict social hierarchies. The samurai had their power significantly curbed, and the borders were almost entirely closed to foreign trade and diplomacy.

The stability and peace ushered in by these policies allowed Japan's economy and arts to flourish Japanese theatergoers would enjoy Kabuki performances, Ukiyo-e woodblock printing allowed artisans to mass produce art, and poets began composing Haiku, all of which remain touchstones of Japanese culture today.

The Meiji Restoration in 1868 ended the Edo period, ushering in a period of rapid modernization and Westernization in Japan.

Meiji Period (1868 - 1912)

As the world outside of Japan began to industrialize, internal pressures on the shogun to modernize began to mount. The last shogun tendered his resignation in 1867, and the following year Emperor Meiji was declared to be the new ruler of Japan, ushering in the Meiji Period. This marked the first time in nearly seven centuries that political power rested primarily in the imperial court.

The Emperor set about a series of reforms aimed at rapidly modernizing Japanese society and bringing it in line with the Western powers. The Meiji government abolished the samurai class and built a modern military. Its industrialization program revitalized the Japanese economy and helped grow a middle class comprised of businessmen and other professionals. In 1889, the Japanese government reorganized into a nominally constitutional monarchy based on the German government at the time. This marked the first time in Japanese history that any form of democratic rule was established. The social and economic reforms of the Meiji period fostered a creative renaissance in Japan. Artists took full advantage of their expanded rights to express themselves in new, thoroughly modern ways.

Emperor Meiji also reformed how Japan engaged with the world. He threw open the borders for trade, welcoming new technologies that had been rejected under the shogun. Relationships with Western nations were formally established. Japan engaged in a colonization program, conquering the island of Formosa (modern-day Taiwan) as well as parts of Korea. Japan also engaged in its first foreign wars in many centuries, fighting and defeating both China and Russia.

Emperor Meiji -1888

Japan is prone to several sorts of characteristic disasters, including seismic tremors, tsunamis, tropical storms, and volcanic ejections. The country is found on the "Ring of Fire" a region of heightened seismic and volcanic movement, and is additionally influenced by the seasonal typhoons that are created within the Pacific Sea.

1. Earthquakes:

- 2011 Touhoku earthquake and tsunami, which resulted in over 15,000 deaths and caused noteworthy harm to the north-eastern parts of the country.

- 1995 Great Hanshin earthquake, which killed over 6,000 people.

- 1923 Great Kanto earthquake, which had a magnitude of 7.9, resulted in over 100,000 deaths and caused widespread damage in the Tokyo area.

2. Tsunamis:

Japan's coastal locales are vulnerable to tsunamis, which are frequently caused by earthquakes.

- 2011 (Touhoku) earthquake, a tsunami of considerable magnitude ensued, with heights reaching up to 40 meters (130 ft.) in certain regions. This devastating tsunami inflicted substantial harm upon Japan's north-eastern coast, leading to the loss of thousands of lives.

- The Tokyo area was also affected by a tsunami resulting from the Great Kantou earthquake of 1923, leading to significant damage.

3. Typhoons:

Japan is additionally influenced by tropical storms, which are violent weather systems that form over the Pacific Sea. These storms can bring solid winds and overwhelming rain, causing flooding and avalanches. In recent years, Japan has been hit by several major typhoons, including one in 2019 which caused widespread flooding and landslides and resulted in over 80 deaths.

4. Volcanoes:

There are many volcanoes in Japan that are still active, the highest of which is called Mount Fuji. It is 3,776 meters (12,389 ft.) tall. While most volcanic eruptions in Japan are relatively small, the country has had many big explosions in recent years, including the eruption of Mount Unzen in 1991, which resulted in 43 deaths.

5. Preparedness and Response:

Japan is ready to handle natural disasters with a good alert system. The government has different groups that watch and take action during natural disasters, like the Japan Meteorological Agency and the Japan Coast Guard.

The country has a plan to protect people in case of a disaster. They have systems to warn people ahead of time and ways to get them to safety. Additionally, lots of households and businesses in the country are prepared for emergencies. They have supplies and plans ready in case something happens.

Earthquake warning

緊急地震速報
千葉南方沖で地震発生。強い揺れに
備えて下さい（気象庁）

Once an earthquake is detected, the JMA quickly issues an alert message to the public via television, radio, and cell phone notifications.

Known as the J-Alert, the system is a nationwide emergency warning system that provides rapid information on disasters and other emergencies.

The early warning system of Japan has garnered acclaim for its precision and efficacy in mitigating fatalities and casualties resulting from seismic events. It's important to recognize that alert notifications on mobile devices aren't effective for protecting people from severe seismic events or tsunami, as the temporal gap between the alert and the ensuing impact may prove insufficient. Hence, it is imperative for citizens to possess awareness of their surroundings and acquaint themselves with the emergency evacuation routes as a contingency plan.

Conclusion

Japan faces the constant threat of natural disasters because of its geographical position along the Pacific Ring of Fire. Additionally, its susceptibility to typhoons and tsunamis further increases the risk it encounters. However, robust disaster response systems and a culture of preparedness mitigate their impact.

In Japan, the religious landscape is shaped by two major faiths: Shinto and Buddhism.

1. Shinto (神道) (The Way of The Gods)

Shinto, also known as "The Way of the Gods" in Japanese, holds deep roots in Japanese culture and stands as the oldest ongoing indigenous religion in the country. Shinto started in Japan and is usually considered Japan's original religion. Historians have several theories regarding when Shinto first appeared in Japanese history.

Some believe that Shinto derives from a form of religion that was practiced a very long time ago, from 13,000 BC to 300 BC. The gods of Shinto are called "kami" 神.

The Japanese people believe deeply in the presence of gods within every aspect of existence, including living beings and the forces of nature such as wind, rain, mountains, trees, rivers, forests, and oceans. In the Shinto religion, people also become kami when they pass away, and their loved ones honor and respect them. However, Shinto does not have a particular deity that is the subject of worship, and it does not have a founder or sacred scriptures.

The places of worship in Shinto are called shrines (jinja) 神社 and are usually found in beautiful natural settings or high mountains.

The Most Sacred Shrines in Shinto:

- Ise Jingu 伊勢神宮 (Ise Grand Shrine) located in Mie prefecture.

- Meiji Shrine is devoted to honoring the spirit of Emperor Meiji. (Tokyo).

Amaterasu-Omikami

In Japanese mythology, the Sun Goddess Amaterasu holds a paramount position as the most significant Kami (deity) in the Shinto belief system. Shinto followers believe that more than eight million deities exist, who manifest themselves in various ways in facets of daily life.

Despite the existence of over eight million gods, religion isn't a significant aspect of daily life for the majority of Japanese people. However, most Japanese people visit Shinto shrines to pray, asking for blessings from their deities during important celebrations such as holidays and New Year's and important life occasions including births, weddings, or funerals.

In Japanese homes, it's common for every member to have a "Kamidana" 神棚, which is a small home altar typically placed on a well-lit shelf. The family can provide offerings such as rice, sake, water, beer, fruits, and salt as they pray to the Kami and the spirits of their ancestors.

2. Buddhism

Since its introduction around the 6th century CE, Buddhism has enjoyed a prominent position within Japanese society. Buddhism was quickly adopted by the imperial court, and its core tenets were used as the philosophical underpinnings for new government institutions. Laypeople and clan leaders were slower to adopt Buddhism, due to its esoteric theories and the influence it was having on Japanese politics. As time passed, Buddhism and Shintoism began to borrow from one another's beliefs and were soon coexisting as the primary religions in Japan.

The Japanese practice all three branches of Buddhism to some extent, but the most prevalent by far is Mahayana. Mahayana Buddhism was developed in China under the Han Dynasty and spread throughout Eastern Asia due to migration and trade. The Japanese school of Zen Buddhism is considered a subsect of Mahayana teachings.

Buddhist monasteries, called tera (寺), can be found all over Japan. The most widely known "Tera" is probably the Toudai-ji temple, located in Nara, which is recognized by UNESCO as a World Heritage Site. The Toudai-ji Temple houses the Great Buddha statue, an immense bronze relic that serves as the symbol of Japanese Buddhism.

Major Buddhist Temples in Japan

- Toudai-ji Temple (Nara) The Great Buddha
- Kiyomizu-dera Temple (Kyoto)
- Kinkaku-ji Temple (Kyoto)
- Sensou-ji Temple (Tokyo)
- Houkoku-ji Temple (Kamakura)
- Sanjusangendou Temple (Kyoto)
- Shitennou-ji Temple (Osaka)

Toudai-ji Temple (Nara)

3. Christianity

Christianity was introduced to Japan by Portuguese missionary Francis Xavier in 1549. However, it was later forbidden by the Edo government, and most missionaries were expelled.

With the revival of Christianity in the 19th century, a splendid Catholic church called Oura Church (Oura Tenshudou) was erected in Nagasaki. This magnificent architectural gem, crafted by a French missionary in 1864, marked the end of the Edo Period.

Oura Church-Nagasaki.

4. Islam

There are no historical sources documenting the date of the entry of Islam into Japan. It is suggested that the Japanese may have first become aware of Islam in 1877 when a translated version of the Prophet's biography was made available to them.

This work helped Japanese intellectuals to know about Islam, but this was part of their knowledge of the history of civilizations. The Japanese gained a deeper understanding of Islam when a friendship mission was sent to Japan by the Ottoman Sultan Abdul Hamid in 1891. The mission was led by Lieutenant General Osman Pasha, and the ship, Al Tughrul, had a crew of over 600 people. Following Osman Pasha's meeting with the Emperor of Japan, it was decided that the ship would return home.

This encounter allowed for a more meaningful exchange and interaction between the Japanese and Islamic cultures. While the ship was still on the Japanese shores at Wakiyama Prefecture, a severe hurricane hit it, causing it to crash and kill 550 people, including Osman Pasha, on September 16, 1890 AD. The dead were buried in the area, and two Japanese ships took the survivors to Istanbul.

Japan currently has approximately 80 mosques, varying in size from large buildings to small rooms, mostly located in large cities. These include Tokyo Mosque, Kobe Mosque, Yokohama Mosque, and Fukuoka Mosque. Kobe Mosque, built in October 1935 in Kobe City, is the first Muslim mosque in Japan.

Kobe Mosque -Kobe City
The First Muslim Mosque in Japan

The Samurai

The samurai (or bushi) 武士, despite heavily influencing Japanese culture and heritage, no longer exists. Emerging as formidable warriors within feudal Japan, they belonged to a mighty military caste and initially served as provincial soldiers. Their influence steadily grew from the 12th century until their eventual dissolution in 1876. Samurai were known for their strict code of conduct called **bushido**, which stressed loyalty, honor, and self-discipline. They were expected to be skilled in combat and trained in a variety of weapons, including the sword, bow, and spear.

Samurai served the nobility and held a high social status. In Japan's Edo period (1603-1868), the samurai class held a pivotal position in both the government and society.

The Edo period was a time of peace and stability in Japan, and the samurai were no longer needed as a military force. Instead, they served as administrators and officials in the government, and many also became artists, scholars, and teachers.

After the Edo period, the samurai no longer fought on the battlefield, but their descendants inherited their ideology and code of conduct, now known as bushido. While each samurai family may have had their interpretations of etiquette and rules, there were some common principles that they shared, such as "I will risk my life for my actions and responsibilities", "I will serve my lord, even if it costs me my life", and "When I make a mistake, I must be prepared to give up my life". What they all had in common was the willingness to risk their lives, and the custom of seppuku, or ritual suicide by disembowelment, was born from this idea.

The End of the Samurai Era

In 1868, Shogun Yoshinobu Tokugawa handed over Imperial rule to Emperor Meiji, marking the end of the samurai's rule over Japan and the beginning of the Meiji Restoration era.

The class system that categorized peasants, farmers, craftsmen, and merchants was abolished, and the classes were reorganized into peers and commoners.

Although some upper-class samurai became peers, many were forced to earn their own living expenses and live as commoners. Despite losing their status as samurai, many former samurai continued to value their spirituality and the samurai way of life.

The Greatest Samurai Warrior in History

It is difficult to determine who the greatest samurai warrior in history was, as this would depend on individual opinions and criteria for what makes a warrior "great". There were many famous samurai warriors in Japanese history, each of whom was known for their skill and bravery in combat. Some of the most well-known samurai warriors include:

- **Miyamoto Musashi:** Musashi was a famous swordsman and martial artist who wrote "The Book of Five Rings", a classic text on strategy and tactics. He is considered one of the greatest swordsmen in Japanese history.

- **Minamoto no Yoritomo:** Yoritomo was the first shogun of Japan and founded the Kamakura Shogun, which ruled Japan for over 150 years. He was a skilled military leader and is remembered as a strong and just ruler.

- **Takeda Shingen:** Shingen was a powerful daimyou (feudal lord) who was known for his military strategy and tactics. Renowned as a skilled and strategic commander, he stood among the most celebrated samurai warriors of his era, leaving a lasting legacy.

- **Oda Nobunaga:** Nobunaga was a powerful daimyou who played a key role in the unification of Japan in the 16th century. He was known for his military prowess and innovative use of firearms in battle.

Where Were the Samurai Located in Japan?

The central and eastern parts of Japan, particularly the Kantou region, which encompasses present-day Tokyo, and the Kansai region, which includes Osaka and Kyoto, were where the samurai held the most sway. These regions were the abodes of several powerful samurai clans that played a pivotal role in politics and governance.

The Touhoku region in the north and the Chuugoku region in the west also had a considerable samurai presence. Nonetheless, the samurai's influence in these areas was relatively lesser compared to the Kantou and Kansai regions. It is worth noting that many samurai resided in these regions during that period.

The term "ninja" derives its etymology from the Japanese words "nin", which means "endurance", and "ja" which represents "person". Collectively, the term is interpreted as "one capable of bearing hardships while accomplishing assignments". This description highlights ninjas' impressive resilience and capacity to persevere even in challenging situations.

Training and skills of Ninjas

Feudal lords in Japan often sought out ninjas, hiring them to perform tasks such as espionage and to carry out sensitive missions such as reconnaissance and target eliminations. Thanks to their remarkable skillset, ninjas became renowned for circumventing obstacles, accessing restricted areas, and amassing coveted data before vanishing without leaving a trace. Ninjas were experts in multiple areas of knowledge, possessing abilities in stealth and concealment tactics like disguise and trickery. They had expertise in combat arts using tools such as throwing stars called **shurikens**, swords named **katana**, and smoke bombs.

For approximately four centuries, spanning from the 15th to the late 19th century, the legendary ninjas thrived in Japan. Their prominence was particularly notable during the tumultuous **Sengoku** period (1467-1603), a time characterized by intense power struggles between regional warlords, commonly referred to as **Daimyous**, who fiercely vied for control over land and authority.

A lot about the ninjas remains unknown since they chose not to leave many written records, given how secrecy was essential to their profession. Still, experts presume that the ninja tradition emerged from the mountain settlements of **Iga** and **Kouga** in Mie prefecture, nestled amidst the rugged peaks of central Japan. However, their legacy remains an integral part of Japanese history.

Variety of Ninja Weapons

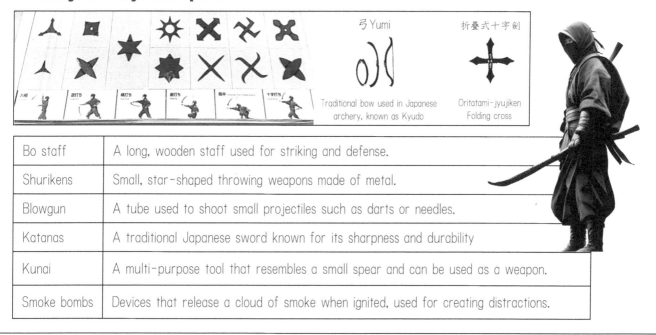

弓 Yumi
Traditional bow used in Japanese archery, known as Kyudo

折畳式十字劍
Oritatami-jyujiken
Folding cross

Bo staff	A long, wooden staff used for striking and defense.
Shurikens	Small, star-shaped throwing weapons made of metal.
Blowgun	A tube used to shoot small projectiles such as darts or needles.
Katanas	A traditional Japanese sword known for its sharpness and durability
Kunai	A multi-purpose tool that resembles a small spear and can be used as a weapon.
Smoke bombs	Devices that release a cloud of smoke when ignited, used for creating distractions.

Female Ninjas

Women also participated in the Japanese world of the ninja, playing vital roles throughout history. Many scholars argue that the ladies had a special gift for cunning and were often hired as secret agents and saboteurs. There was a group of elite female ninjas called **Kunoichi** (クノイチ), trained in the same hand-to-hand combat skills as their male counterparts, and tasked with covert operations such as reconnaissance and target elimination. They made full use of their charm and charisma in the performance of their duties, obtaining valuable data, or achieving undiscovered goals.

Do Ninja Exist Today?

There is no historical ninja alive today, as ninjas were only active in Japan from the 15th to the 19th century. Ninjutsu, the traditional martial art associated with the ninjas, thrived in feudal Japan. Although the historical ninja is but a memory, their place in Japanese culture and folklore remains strong due to the lasting impact of their legendary status and reputation.

The imagination has translated ninjutsu and the ninja into numerous forms of media such as literature, film, and television productions. Many contemporary individuals practice martial arts styles based on or influenced by the ninjas' techniques, striving to uphold the rich heritage of this once secretive profession. Even though they walk among us only in spirit now, interest in the ninja lives on as new generations encounter their enthralling legacy.

Modern-day practitioners who study ninjutsu may not always accurately represent the skills and tactics used by historical ninjas. They often focus on specific martial arts techniques and don't receive training in the complete set of strategies employed by past ninjas. For example, the historical ninja had expertise in spying, destroying property, and assassination missions, which aren't commonly taught in today's martial arts schools. However, there are several ninja museums located in Japan that are dedicated to preserving the history and traditions of the ninja.

1. Kimono

Kimonos are beautiful traditional Japanese garments that consist of a long, loose, dress-like robe with wide sleeves and a belt that ties at the waist. People usually make kimonos out of smooth silky fabric, and they pair them with an obi (a decorative sash). People typically put on kimonos for fancy get-togethers, like weddings or traditional tea gatherings.

Different designs and styles can be worn, and the choice of what to wear depends on the event type and the person wearing it. Overall, kimonos are essential in Japanese culture and are admired for being stylish.

The word "kimono" means "something one wears" in Japanese. If you break down the word into its two components —"ki", which means "wear", plus "mono" ("thing"), referring to an object, that's how you end up with a garment named kimono! They primarily come in silk, but you may see versions crafted out of cotton or artificial substances. Various kinds of kimonos exist, and each serves a distinct purpose depending on the event.

Types of Kimonos and Their Uses:	
Uchikake	A formal kimono worn by brides, typically over a traditional white shiromuku kimono.
Iromuji	A solid-colored kimono, for formal events, and can be worn by both men and women.
Houmongi	A kimono worn by women for formal occasions, such as tea ceremonies and weddings
Yokohama-fuku	A Western-style kimono worn by women in the port city of Yokohama during the Meiji period.
Furisode	Worn by unmarried young women, typically for formal occasions such as coming-of-age ceremonies and weddings
Tomesode	A significant kimono style in Japan, is primarily worn by married women on formal occasions. It is renowned for its elegance and is commonly seen at weddings, tea ceremonies, and formal receptions, symbolizing tradition and refinement.

■ And many more, depending on the occasion, age, and gender are also worth noting that kimonos are not just worn on formal occasions, they can be worn casually as well.

振袖 - Furisode

2. Yukata

A yukata is a lightweight version of the traditional kimono. It is a breathable cotton robe with a casual appearance. This attire is commonly worn during the summer months, particularly at festivals and other outdoor gatherings.

The yukata is worn with a decorative "obi" belt and complementary shoes — either narrow sandals or ancient wooden clogs called "geta". Despite its casual nature, this flexible outfit has gained immense popularity among both males and females who cherish comfort and style.

> ■ Modern yukatas come in many new designs inspired by pop art, anime, and manga. They're getting popular, not just in Japan, but worldwide. You can find the perfect yukata for any occasion with all the different styles.

Yukata

3. Haori and Hakama

In Japan, both men and women wear the traditional outfit of haori and hakama. The haori is like a shorter version of the famous kimono worn on top of the kimono or regular clothes. It's usually made from nice fabrics like silk or wool, and there might be a differently colored lining inside. To complete their look, people may pair a haori with hakama, a type of loose, wide-legged pants worn over a kimono or other traditional clothing.

Haori and hakama are worn in Japan for formal events, including weddings and other important cultural gatherings, and by practitioners of traditional Japanese arts, such as flower arranging (ikebana) and tea ceremonies. Interestingly, both men and women who practice certain martial arts like kendo, iaido, and aikido may also choose to wear hakama during their training sessions. In Japan, pairing a haori jacket with hakama pants is considered to be formal attire, and many people continue to do this impressive combination on significant occasions even today.

4. Montsuki and Hakama

Montsuki are traditional Japanese garments worn by men. The montsuki is a type of silk kimono with a crest on the back and front chest and is worn with hakama, a wide-legged pleated pant. They are worn for formal occasions and by practitioners of traditional Japanese arts, such as martial arts and tea ceremonies.

Montsuki and Hakama

Noh is a traditional style of Japanese theater that has been around since the 1400s. It features the use of masks, ornate costumes, and distinctive acting techniques. These dramatic productions tend to reenact significant moments from history or mythology at a leisurely tempo, inspiring deep reflection among audience members.

Theatrical Characters

Performers include a choral ensemble, instrumentalists (hayashi), and multiple actors, most notably the primary figure (shite) who dons a mask and enacts characters via subtle movements and gestures, aided by a supporting player (waki). Music serves as an integral component of each act, heightening emotional intensity through melodies played on various instruments like the flute, the shoulder drum, and smaller drums. Additionally, vocals furnished by the chorus contribute to the overall ambiance of each scene.

Ko-omote Mask

Hannya Mask

Five Acts

Noh plays are typically divided into five acts or primary segments. Each part holds significance, serving unique functions in advancing the story. The first act, called "jo", introduces the play's premise and characters. The second phase, known as "ha", encompasses most of the production's drama. This section showcases the bulk of the activity within the story.

The third phase "kyu" bridges the gap between sections three and four. Part four "shimai" highlights the climax of the tale, and lastly, the fifth act, called "kyougen", is a comedic interlude that provides a contrast to the more serious nature of the Noh play.

Noh is still performed today and is considered an important part of Japanese cultural heritage. It can frequently be witnessed at classic venues like the National Noh Theatre in Tokyo, and celebrations nationwide.

Noh masks are made of lightweight and durable cypress wood with intricate designs and motifs corresponding to the character's role. The mask's eye, mouth, and eyebrow shapes express emotions, while a black hole aids with breathing and vision. There are two hundred and forty unique types of masks, each representing unique characters like ghosts, gods, demons, old men, and women.

Kabuki is a captivating traditional theater art form originating from Japan, characterized by its striking attire, intricate stage makeup, and exaggerated acting styles.

The artists themselves, referred to as "kabuki-ya", are predominantly male. They perform a variety of roles, including those of men, women, and even ghosts. The performances often include music, dance, and acrobatics, all while narrating mesmerizing tales of folklore and events of historic significance.

Kabuki Origins

This unique genre of entertainment finds its origins in the works of "Okuni", a talented dancer who introduced her innovative fusion of music, dance, and drama on the bustling streets of Kyoto during the early 17th century. As her unconventional approach gained traction amongst the masses, rival performers emerged, eventually paving the path towards kabuki's evolution into a full-fledged theatrical format steeped in customs and legacy by the latter part of the same era.

Costumes and Makeup

Kabuki theatre is known for its extensive use of makeup and costume design, which is one of its defining characteristics. Kabuki performers don elaborately decorated, vibrant outfits and intricate facial paint that amplifies facial expressions and conveys meaning through color and pattern.

Makeup motifs can signify characters' attributes like age, sex, or caste; this allows audiences to more easily follow storylines and immerse themselves within scenes. Shows consist of three stages, punctuated by lively musical accompaniments performed using classical Japanese instruments.

Kabuki Masks

In kabuki theater performances, actors wear masks called "noumen" to depict various characters, emotions, and sentiments. The word "kabuki" comes from three Japanese terms "ka", meaning song; "bu", referring to dance; and "ki", representing talent or technique, which combine to mean "song, dance, and skill".

The ancient tradition of kabuki theatre continues to captivate audiences today, serving as a vital connection to Japanese heritage while attracting new fans worldwide.

Kuma dori
Mask

Kitsune
Mask

The Traditional Art of Writing

Shodou is the traditional art of writing Japanese characters, also known as Japanese calligraphy. In shodou, the characters written in Japanese kanji or Chinese hanzi are treated like works of art, because they often have incredibly beautiful designs.

Shodou was first introduced by Buddhist monks, who used Chinese script before developing their unique Japanese style of shodou. In fact, the oldest extant piece of shodou dates back to roughly AD 600! During the Meiji era in Japan, specifically in 1894, efforts were made to standardize shodou (Japanese calligraphy) to promote widespread accessibility to learning. Following World War II, the Ministry of Education established an enduring official grade system that continues to be implemented to this day.

The Way of Writing

Each character is written with a brush and ink on paper or silk. The brushstrokes are made with fluid movements, and the brush is held vertically to the paper. The characters are written in a specific order, with the brushstrokes done in a certain way. Shodou is considered a form of self-expression and is often used in art, tattoos, and other forms of Japanese culture.

Shodou Today

Shodou is taught in schools and is considered an important part of Japanese culture and heritage. It is also a popular hobby and many people attend classes and workshops to learn the art. In addition, there are many resources available Online to study classical forms of Shodou, which can take years to master.

What is Origami?

Origami is the traditional Japanese art of paper folding. It involves folding one sheet of paper into different shapes, which creates intricate designs without using scissors or adhesives. This method of paper crafting started in Japan but now spans the globe due to its simple tools yet highly creative results. Origami paper usually measures square dimensions, boasts thin thicknesses, and can come in multiple types including traditional Japanese washi and standard options such as light crepe papers and printer paper.

Designs

Origami can be relatively straightforward, and numerous classic designs are simple to master, such as the crane, the boat, and the frog. But patterns can also be very complex. Some artists and origami enthusiasts create intricate and impressive designs replicating animals, buildings, and even mechanical models.

Develop Creativity and Thinking

Origami is a versatile activity that offers artistic expression and fun for all ages. It has practical uses as a learning tool and for preventing dementia. From simple designs for children to complex shapes, origami is a cultural and creative pursuit with endless possibilities. It challenges the mind and fosters creativity beyond just paper folding. Origami also enhances working memory and spatial cognition. As a result, it is an effective teaching tool for brain training and is commonly incorporated into school education.

Types of Origami

Traditional Origami: This is the most common form of origami, and it typically involves folding a single sheet of paper without cutting or gluing it. Traditional origami models include animals, flowers, and other simple shapes.

Modular Origami: his type of origami involves folding multiple sheets of paper and then assembling them to create a larger and more complex model. Modular origami models can include geometric shapes, such as cubes and spheres, as well as more complex structures like polyhedral.

Action Origami: Also known as "kirigami", this type of origami involves folding and cutting the paper to create models that can move or change shape. Action origami models include things like flapping birds and jumping frogs.

During the Edo period (1603–1868), which was a time of relative peace and prosperity in Japan after centuries of civil warfare, the nation's stability allowed for the flourishing of artisanal crafts. A new type of art called Ukiyo-e, or woodblock printing, arose at this time. This involved making pictures by carving images onto wooden printing blocks and then pressing paper onto them to make copies.

The Flourishing of Woodblock Printing in Edo

Woodblock printing became a major industry in Edo (present-day Tokyo). Woodblock printers worked with artists who created designs for mass production; these designs were then carved onto blocks made of cherry tree wood and printed using watercolors made from natural pigments and vegetable dyes. The finished products were sold as single sheets or bound into books.

Ukiyo-e Prints: Depicting Transience and Diverse Subjects

One key characteristic of Ukiyo-e prints is their focus on ephemeral beauty—capturing the transience of fleeting moments and fads. Artists often portrayed famous actors, courtesans, geishas, sumo wrestlers, and other celebrities in the entertainment scene. These characters tended to be associated with luxury and decadence, but they also represented the possibilities of upward mobility through talent and entrepreneurship. Other common motifs included seasonal scenery, landmarks, city views, domestic interiors, genre vignettes, wildlife studies, bird-and-flower arrangements, shunga erotica, and occasional supernatural horror tales.

Ukiyo-e Prints: A Cross-Cultural Influence on the Art World

Ukiyo-e prints had a significant impact on the art world, not just in Japan but also internationally. The works of famous ukiyo-e artists such as Hokusai and Utamaro became particularly well-known and popular among Western artists and collectors. Many Western artists have been inspired by ukiyo-e, including Vincent Van Gogh, Claude Monet, and Mary Cassatt. They were captivated not just by the style and design principles, but additionally by the printing methods used in creating these artworks. Their work has at times drawn inspiration directly from the original Japanese ukiyo-e pieces.

In traditional Japanese culture, a geisha is a highly skilled female entertainer specializing in performing various arts, including music, dance, games, and conversation, primarily to entertain male customers in designated areas. The term "geisha" can be translated as "artist" or "performance artist". They originated in the pleasure districts of Japan during the Edo period and have since become symbols of that era.

Traditional Japanese Female Entertainer

To become a geisha, women undergo extensive training in traditional Japanese arts such as music, dance, tea ceremony, and ikebana (flower arrangement). These artists must also master the ability to carry out engaging conversations and build proper patron relations. Their appearance plays a significant role in conveying professionalism, so they adhere to strict standards regarding clothing, hairdos, makeup, and accessories.

A geisha's attire typically includes a standardized kimono dress paired with an elaborate belt called an obi. She wears her hair in specific traditional styles decorated with ornate hairpieces called kanzashi, as well as heavy white makeup on her face and red lipstick. The white makeup is said to symbolize the traditional ideal of feminine beauty, and the red lipstick represents a woman's social status.

Geisha are not prostitutes, but rather highly trained and respected female entertainers. They occupy a unique niche in Japanese culture as elite women who spend countless hours honing intricate skills that enchant admirers.

Preserving Japan's Geisha Tradition

Despite changing societal norms and the dwindling number of geishas, with only a few hundred remaining in Japan, the tradition still perseveres in some regions like Kyoto, and measures are being taken to conserve this vital aspect of Japanese cultural heritage.

Can Geisha Girls Marry?

While the traditional role of a geisha is to entertain men, they are not considered to be prostitutes and are free to pursue personal relationships. However, becoming a geisha is a significant commitment and many women choose to remain single to focus on their careers.

■ Geisha leads a demanding life that leaves little time for personal pursuits. However, some opt to retire from the profession to start families. Fortunately, the cultural stigma surrounding leaving the geisha community has decreased, allowing individuals to depart if they choose to do so.

Sakura (桜) is a beautiful word meaning "Cherry blossoms" in Japanese. It is also a well-known name for girls and families in Japan. During spring, cherry blossoms are celebrated all over the country. People gather under the cherry blossom trees to admire the beautiful flowers, celebrate the coming of spring, and take some pictures with family and friends.

Flower Viewing - 花見"Hanami"

Flower Viewing, known as "Hanami" in Japanese, is a lovely tradition where people gather to appreciate the beauty of flowers, especially cherry blossoms "Sakura". Each year, countless individuals flock to parks and gardens throughout Japan to take part in "Hanami". Beneath the ethereal branches adorned with fragile buds, families and friends congregate to indulge in merriment, savor scrumptious eats, imbibe refreshing libations, and simply soak up the enchantment of the moment. Hanami is a well-loved tradition in Japan that has been carried on for many generations and has become a fundamental part of Japanese culture.

Cherry Blossoms in Culture and Art

Cherry blossoms appear in many works of art and literature, and they are often used in tattoos such as "irezumi" (Japanese traditional full-body tattoos) and other forms of body art. Recently there has been increased interest in them, and the trees themselves have become more prevalent abroad as symbols of traditional Japanese culture. This cultural tradition holds special meaning not just in Japan, but also in other East Asian countries like South Korea and China.

The Kanji "桜" is used to represent the cherry blossom tree and its beautiful flowers, while the hiragana characters "さくら", pronounced "sakura", can also be used as a representation of the word in more casual or informal writing.

Different Types of Cherry Blossom

Cherry blossom trees come in many different varieties and hues. The Somei-Yoshino cherry tree, a hybrid species notable for its enormous, white blooms with five petals, is one of the most well-known varieties of cherry blossom trees. It is a highly popular type in Japan, where it is commonly used for decorative planting and cherry blossom watching.

Japan has a traditional culinary style and cuisine that has developed over the centuries. It is characterized by the use of fresh, seasonal ingredients, minimal use of spices, and a focus on simplicity and presentation. "Umami" a savory flavor often associated with meatiness or brothlike tastes, is highly prized within Japanese cuisine.

Essential Components

The primary components incorporated into Japanese recipes may consist of rice, fish, and other seafood, algae, fermented condiments like soy sauce and miso paste, herbs such as wasabi, green tea leaves, and alcoholic drinks like sake. The cuisine also features various cooking techniques such as grilling (yakitori), deep-frying (tempura), boiling (nabemono), and steaming (mushi).

Popular Japanese Dishes

Sushi is a famous Japanese food, made with rice flavored with vinegar and usually served with many types of raw fish, vegetables, or eggs. Ramen, udon, and soba are popular types of Japanese noodles. People like to eat them in a hot soup with different ingredients on top, like sliced pork, green onions, and soft-boiled eggs.

A wide selection of sushi variations exists, such as onigiri sushi, made of a compacted handful of rice adorned with raw fish; maki sushi, which incorporates sushi rice and additional components that are encased in seaweed and sliced into bite-sized portions; and temaki sushi, that takes the form of a cone filled with sushi rice and other ingredients.

Other Popular Japanese Dishes

Other popular Japanese dishes include lightly fried seafood or vegetables known as tempura; grilled chicken skewers called yakitori; and savory pancakes called okonomiyaki is a Japanese savory pancake made with a batter of flour, cabbage, and other ingredients like meat or seafood.

Traditional Food for New Year's Eve

Japanese cuisine also has a strong cultural significance, with certain dishes and ingredients being associated with particular regions or occasions. During the New Year celebrations people eat mochi, a sweet glutinous rice cake, and soba noodles, also osechi is a traditional Japanese New Year's meal with carefully prepared dishes served in lacquer boxes.

It symbolizes luck, prosperity, and health. It includes dishes like a sweet rolled omelet, herring roe, steamed fish cake, sweet black soybeans, candied dried sardines, and boiled shrimp, mashed sweet potatoes with chestnuts, and simmered vegetables or seafood.

1. Polite

The most common personality trait that Japanese people are told about is their politeness. All foreign tourists say this. Japanese people tend to be polite in everything, and that is considered natural in Japan. Even the greetings used in everyday life are seen as especially respectful by outsiders.

2. Obey the Rules

Many Japanese people always obey the rules. They feel bad when they don't follow them or almost do the wrong thing. Even though many people in other countries break the rules without hesitation, the Japanese tend to be very loyal to their regulations.

3. Punctuality

In Japan, being punctual and diligent is a matter of course. Trains in Japan are known for their punctuality. There was even a time when a Japanese railway company made headlines internationally for apologizing when a train left a few seconds ahead of schedule.

4. Shy and Quiet

Foreigners have a strong impression of Japanese women as shy and modest. In Western countries, particularly in the US, people are usually straightforward when expressing their thoughts, regardless of their gender. Japanese women are especially quiet even at school and at work, and they rarely express their own opinions. It seems that they naturally have that kind of image. When a man from another country feels attracted to a Japanese woman and tries to initiate a conversation, she may feel shy or embarrassed and the conversation may not last long. She may also lack confidence in speaking or understanding correct English.

5. Cute

The cuteness of Japanese women is often cited as one of their main characteristics. The Japanese word "kawaii" has become popular even overseas. In Japan, women prefer cute accessories decorated with lace and glitter over the simple patterns that are popular elsewhere. Conversely, Japanese women seem to prefer clothes with lace and very flashy prints that emphasize cuteness and a little bit of bubbliness. Japanese women also do not mind wearing short skirts and exposing skin even in the middle of winter.

6. Hard-working

Japanese employees are renowned for their diligent work ethic, often referred to as "hataraki-mono", which signifies hard workers. However, this culture of dedication can be quite demanding, as evidenced by the existence of the term "karoshi", meaning "death from overwork". Many employees endure long hours of work without sufficient sleep or rest. Consequently, they may experience heightened levels of anxiety, exhaustion, and, in extreme cases, mental health challenges such as feelings of sadness and even suicidal thoughts, commonly known as "karoshi suicide".

7. Respectful

Japanese people are deeply ingrained with a strong sense of respect. From a young age, they learn to respect and value their family as well as strangers. Polite behavior towards elders is emphasized, and as teenagers, they are taught "Keigo", a polite form of speech. Respect for age and hierarchy is significant in social and business settings, where seniority traditionally determines higher rank. This emphasis on respect contributes to the overall harmony and orderliness of Japanese society.

8. Harmony and Conflict

Harmony is deeply rooted in Japanese society, it emphasizes the importance of peaceful coexistence, cooperation, and consensus-building. Japanese people tend to avoid confrontation or conflict, seeking to find a balance and compromise that preserves the overall harmony of the group. This cultural value influences various aspects of Japanese life, including relationships, decision-making processes, and social dynamics.

9. Strong Sense of Responsibility

Indeed, Japanese people exhibit a strong sense of responsibility both at the personal and social levels. They prioritize fulfilling their obligations and duties toward their family, work, and community. There is a deep sense of pride in carrying out these responsibilities diligently and contributing positively to society. This mindset is reflected in their work ethic, commitment to quality, and dedication to their roles and relationships. Japanese individuals often take their responsibilities seriously and strive to make meaningful contributions to their immediate circles and the broader society as a whole.

Summary

Japanese people are extremely polite, value harmony and etiquette, and have a highly structured and traditional society. They are honest in dealing with others and show respect for their elders. Japanese people exhibit diverse characteristics in areas such as customs, eating habits, religion, and thinking patterns.

1. Vending Machines

In Japan, vending machines are commonly referred to as "jidou hanbaiki," 自動販売機 which translates to "automated selling machines" (vending machines) in English.

The abundance of vending machines is one of the most notable features that tourists in Japan will encounter as they wander around the metropolis. Numerous machines are available that vend an array of products, ranging from beverages and snacks to cigarettes, fresh produce, umbrellas, ice cream, hot ramen, soup, eggs, face masks, and a lot more.

Vending Machines: Two Payment Options

Cash or IC cards. For cash payments, those machines accept denominations of 1,000 yen, 500 yen, 100 yen, and 10 yen, but take note that they do not accept anything below 10 yen. On the other hand, IC cards, such as "Suica" and "Pasmo" are widely used in public transportation, allowing users to pay for fares on trains and buses in major metropolitan areas like Tokyo. These IC cards also serve for making purchases at vending machines, convenience stores, and various other locations.

2. Extreme Cleanliness

Japanese cleanliness is renowned worldwide. The cleanliness is not maintained in personal areas only but is also extended to public spaces like streets, train stations, and restrooms. You'll hardly see any trash scattered around these areas. It's also uncommon to come across trash cans on the streets, as people are encouraged to carry their garbage back home with them.

Japanese schools are a testament to the country's cleanliness standards as well. The students are responsible for cleaning the schools themselves, rather than relying on janitors. They are divided into teams and assigned cleaning duties in a roster that they follow strictly, ensuring that the school is cleaned every day. The students even take turns sweeping and wiping the floors, making sure that their school is always spotless.

It is normal to see people cleaning not only their own houses but also their neighborhoods. They make sure to keep their surroundings clean and tidy. Furthermore, volunteers also participate in cleaning up busy areas, further reinforcing Japan's commitment to cleanliness.

3. Safety and Security

Japan ranks among the top 10 safest countries globally. The incidence of crime in Japan is lower compared to many other countries, and its large cities are generally considered safe compared to others. Even if you lose or forget something in Japan, it may be found at a later date.

4. Convenience Stores

Japanese convenience stores, commonly referred to as "Konbini", are an integral aspect of the daily fabric of life in the country. The stores provide a diverse range of products and services that go beyond basic groceries, making them indispensable to the Japanese lifestyle.

In addition to food and drink items, customers can find daily necessities like magazines and even clothing, making Konbini stores a one-stop shop for all their needs. These stores also provide various services like ATMs, bill payments, ticket reservations for shows and museums, and copy machines. Moreover, customers can send mail from these stores, making them a reliable and easy option for sending letters or parcels. With such a comprehensive range of products and services, Konbini stores have become a valuable part of Japanese society.

5. Face Masks

In Japan, it is common to see people wearing face masks. Even before the COVID-19 period, it was not unusual to observe individuals wearing white masks while waiting for trains, socializing with friends, or going about their daily routines at work or in public places. The primary motivation behind wearing these masks is often related to allergies or illness. By wearing a face mask when feeling unwell, individuals aim to prevent the spread of contaminants to their colleagues, friends, or family members. The purpose is not solely to protect oneself from germs or viruses, but rather to avoid transmitting them to others. Nevertheless, there exist additional reasons for wearing face masks in Japan.

- Concealing physical imperfections

Some Japanese individuals opt to wear masks as a means of concealing any physical imperfections they may have or simply on days when they prefer not to use makeup.

- Fashion

Face masks have become an integral part of Japanese fashion. Modern masks are now designed in various colors and shapes to align with fashion trends.

Three-dimensional masks known as (立体マスク "rittai masuku") that contour to the face in an aesthetically pleasing manner have emerged, serving both functional and fashionable purposes.

6. Hot Springs (Onsen)

Japan has many hot springs, including hidden ones deep in the mountains, open-air baths facing the sea with spectacular views, and free-flowing ones filled with healing energy. Hot spring resorts offer healing waters, delicious dishes made with local ingredients, and various recreational activities that both children and adults can enjoy.

7. Temples and Shrines

In Japan, there is an extensive number of shrines and temples, totaling more than one hundred thousand. Approximately half of these belong to the Shinto religion, while the remaining half belong to Buddhism, which was introduced by Korean and Chinese monks to Japan in the sixth century during the Nara period. The magnificent architecture and serene landscapes within these spiritual places attract countless travelers from across the world.

8. Bullet Train (Shinkansen)

The "Shinkansen" bullet train stands out among other high-speed railways as the inaugural line created exclusively for quick and efficient transportation around Japan. Capable of reaching speeds up to 320 km/h (199 mph), the Shinkansen makes trips noticeably faster, and passengers may choose between six categories of service based on stopover locations: Nozomi, Hikari, Mizuho, Kodama, Hayabusa, and Sakura. By having alternatives tailored to specific routes, the railway system ensures flexibility and convenience for riders.

9. Capsule Hotels

Capsule hotels offer convenience and affordability for various scenarios like sightseeing and business trips. These establishments feature stylish interiors and clean, comfortable units equipped with amenities like high-speed Wi-Fi, outlets, TV, radio, alarm, and dimming systems for comfort. However, it's important to note that capsules don't include toilets or bathrooms. Typically, shared toilets are available at the end of the hall, along with a Japanese-style bathing area in the building. Capsule hotels are favored by budget-conscious Japanese business travelers and those needing a temporary resting place after missing the last train home.

10. Free Tissues Handed Out on the Street

It is common for packets of tissues or handkerchiefs to be handed out on the street in Japan, especially near tourist attractions or busy shopping districts. Local businesses or organizations frequently sponsor these tissues as a means to promote their products or services. The tissues may be imprinted with the sponsor's logo or message, and they are usually provided for free

11. Maid/Butler Cafes

Maid and butler cafes, commonly located in Tokyo's Akihabara district, epitomize the unique and quirky side of Japan. These establishments offer a one-of-a-kind experience where impeccably dressed Japanese maids and butlers provide not only exceptional service, but also entertainment through songs, dances, and engaging performances. Patrons can immerse themselves in this fascinating blend of dining and live entertainment, creating unforgettable memories of their visit to these extraordinary cafes.

12. Cat Cafes

Japanese cat cafes (猫カフェ, neko cafe) have rapidly grown in popularity due to their singular and tranquil atmosphere, where customers can spend time with cats while sipping on drinks like coffee or tea. Visitors appreciate the welcoming and snug setting where they can unwind and playfully engage with gentle kitties. These cafes serve as peaceful havens away from bustling urban areas, offering an immensely pleasing experience for pet enthusiasts and those who may not have pets of their own. As such, cat cafes stand out as a beloved spot worth visiting when coming across them during one's journey through Japan.

13. Rental Family or Girlfriend Services

There are services in Japan that offer the option to rent family members or companions for various purposes. These services cater to specific needs, such as attending social events, practicing language skills, or experiencing traditional activities with a simulated family or girlfriend/boyfriend.

It's important to understand that these services offer temporary companionship and are primarily focused on providing a social experience rather than forming genuine relationships. The individuals hired for these roles are typically professionals who are trained to fulfill specific roles and serve as company during the designated time.

Summary

Apart from its vibrant cities, Japan is home to stunning natural beauty. You'll find magnificent mountains, peaceful lakes, charming islands, beautiful waterfalls, winding rivers, lush rice fields, and enchanting forests. What's even more magical is that you can often discover temples and shrines nestled in these picturesque settings, creating a serene and captivating atmosphere.

The Japanese writing system comprises three scripts: Hiragana, Katakana, and Kanji. Hiragana and Katakana are syllabic scripts, also known as Kana, and are used to write words of Japanese origin and grammatical elements and provide a phonetic reading for Kanji. Kanji is a logo-graphic script used to write words of Chinese origin and is often combined with Hiragana or Katakana. The intricacy of the Japanese writing system is widely recognized, positioning it as one of the most complex in the world.

1. Hiragana（ひらがな）

Hiragana, a phonetic alphabet created in the ninth century, aimed to simplify the writing system. Today, it predominantly serves to represent native Japanese words. Derived from the more intricate Kanji, each Hiragana character corresponds to a syllable. The Hiragana script consists of 46 fundamental characters and some Hiragana characters feature modifications called Dakuten and Handakuten, indicating alterations in the pronunciation of the syllables.

2. Katakana（カタカナ）

Katakana, an alphabet designed to represent the same syllable range as Hiragana, encompasses a set of 46 unique characters. Notably, it features modifications known as Dakuten and Handakuten, which serve to indicate changes in the pronunciation of the syllables. The primary purpose of Katakana is to transcribe foreign loanwords, and on occasions, it takes the place of Kanji or Hiragana to add emphasis to specific elements. Its development can be traced back to the ninth century, originating from a more intricate Kanji script.

3. Kanji（漢字）

Kanji is a logographic script that is used in the Japanese writing system, along with Hiragana and Katakana. Kanji characters are derived from Chinese characters and are used to write words of Chinese origin. A Kanji character represents a word or concept and can have different meanings and pronunciations. Kanji characters are more complex than Kana characters and often have multiple strokes.

In Japan, the number of Kanji characters that are considered to be in common use is around 50,000. The Japanese government has established a list of 2,136 Kanji characters, known as the "Joyo Kanji" that is considered to be necessary for basic literacy in Japan. Kanji characters are often used in combination with Hiragana or Katakana to indicate the pronunciation of the word. This is known as Furigana, and it is often used in text to help readers understand the pronunciation of difficult or obscure kanji characters.

- ## Tategaki（縦書き）Traditionally

Tategaki is a style of writing Japanese text that is read from top to bottom and from right to left. It is the traditional way of writing Japanese and is still used in certain contexts such as in traditional books and documents, poetry, street signs, and menus, as well as in some personal communication such as letters, postcards, and calligraphy.

Tategaki was used in the Heian period (794-1185) in Japan, particularly in literature and poetry. It was also used in official government documents and in religious texts, During the Edo period (1603-1868), Tategaki became more widely used particularly in the popularization of novels and the printing of books.

Tategaki Vertical Writing

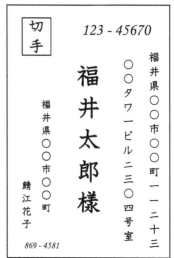

- ## Yokogaki（横書き）Modern

Yokogaki is a writing style in Japanese where text is read horizontally from left to right and vertically from top to bottom, resembling the writing and reading direction of English text. It is the most common way of writing Japanese today and is used in most forms of modern literature, newspapers, and other types of writing.

This style was introduced to Japan during the Meiji era and it became widely adopted as it was easier for foreigners to read and for Japanese people to learn foreign languages. It was also more efficient for printing and typesetting.

Yokogaki is the standard writing style for most forms of modern Japanese writing, is easier to read and learn for most people, and it's widely used in day-to-day writing as well as in books, newspapers, and other forms of modern literature.

Yokogaki Horizontal Writing

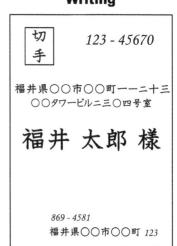

Rōmaji

Apart from the three Japanese writing systems, the Roman alphabet is employed to represent sounds in Japan. **Rōmaji** (ローマ字), or Romanized letters, are utilized in Japanese text aimed at non-Japanese speakers, including street signs, dictionaries, textbooks, and passports.

Rōmaji is also commonly used when typing on computers. Despite Japanese keyboards having the ability to type in Kana, many individuals prefer using the Latin script to input sounds and characters in **Rōmaji**. When initially learning the characters, **Rōmaji** proves helpful in reading Japanese.

Furigana

Furigana is a Japanese writing system in which the readings of Kanji characters are written in small Hiragana or Katakana characters above or beside them. This is used to indicate the pronunciation of difficult or obscure Kanji characters for people who are not familiar with them. It is often used in children's books, manga, and other materials to make them more accessible to a wider audience.

Uppercase and Lowercase

There are no upper and lower case letters in the Japanese writing system emphasis can be done by including font styling, putting dots over letters, and putting them in quotes 「」『』.

Question Marks

In Japanese writing, question marks are represented by particle か (ka?) or " ？ " (Full-width question mark). The use of " か？ " is more traditional and used in informal writing like a conversation, while " ？ " is more modern and used in formal writing like an article or news.

Examples:

これは何ですか。(kore wa nan des **ka.**) What is that?

あなたは食べましたか。(anata wa tabe mashita **ka.**) Did you eat?

In both these sentences above, the か at the end indicates a question, which ends with the normal Japanese full stop (。).

Logographic Kanji

Kanji are Logographic symbols that represent words or concepts and are made up of various strokes and components. There are over 2,000 commonly used Kanji in Japan, although some estimates put the total number closer to 50,000. Kanji is often grouped by their radicals or the basic components that make up the character.

Here are some examples of logographic Kanji and their meanings:

(ki) tree 	This kanji represents a tree, with the horizontal line at the top indicating the trunk and the three lines underneath indicating the branches.	
(hi) fire	This kanji represents fire, with the lines at the top indicating flames and the line underneath indicating the ground.	
(yama) mountain	This kanji represents a mountain, with the two lines at the top indicating the peaks and the two lines underneath indicating the slopes.	
(kawa) river	This kanji represents a river, with the horizontal line at the top indicating the riverbank and the two lines underneath indicating the flow of water.	
(mon) gate	The usual kanji for "door" is 門 (pronounced "mon" or "kado"). It represents a gate or entrance and is made up of two parts meaning "door" and "to enter." This kanji is commonly used in words related to gates or entrances.	

■ While many Kanji are derived from pictographs, over time they have evolved and changed, making it more difficult to recognize their original form, some Kanji are a combination of different components or radicals, making it difficult to identify their pictographic origins.

Basic Hiragana

あ **a**	い **i**	う **u**	え **e**	お **o**
か **ka**	き **ki**	く **ku**	け **ke**	こ **ko**
さ **sa**	し **shi**	す **su**	せ **se**	そ **so**
た **ta**	ち **chi**	つ **tsu**	て **te**	と **to**
な **na**	に **ni**	ぬ **nu**	ね **ne**	の **no**
は **ha**	ひ **hi**	ふ **hu**	へ **he**	ほ **ho**
ま **ma**	み **mi**	む **mu**	め **me**	も **mo**
や **ya**		ゆ **yu**		よ **yo**
ら **ra**	り **ri**	る **ru**	れ **re**	ろ **ro**
わ **wa**				を **wo**
ん **n**				

Dakuten

が **ga**	ぎ **gi**	ぐ **gu**	げ **ge**	ご **go**
ざ **za**	じ **zi(ji)**	ず **zu**	ぜ **ze**	ぞ **zo**
だ **da**	ぢ **di(ji)**	づ **du**	で **de**	ど **do**
ば **ba**	び **bi**	ぶ **bu**	べ **be**	ぼ **bo**

Handakuten

ぱ **pa**	ぴ **pi**	ぷ **pu**	ぺ **pe**	ぽ **po**

Youon

きゃ **kya**	きゅ **kyu**	きょ **kyo**
しゃ **sha(sya)**	しゅ **shu(syu)**	しょ **sho(syo)**
ちゃ **cha(tya)**	ちゅ **chu(tyu)**	ちょ **cho(tyo)**
にゃ **nya**	にゅ **nyu**	にょ **nyo**
ひゃ **hya**	ひゅ **hyu**	ひょ **hyo**

みゃ **mya**	みゅ **myu**	みょ **myo**
りゃ **rya**	りゅ **ryu**	りょ **ryo**

ぎゃ **gya**	ぎゅ **gyu**	ぎょ **gyo**
じゃ **zya(ja)**	じゅ **zyu(ju)**	じょ **zyo(jo)**

びゃ **bya**	びゅ **byu**	びょ **byo**
ぴゃ **pya**	ぴゅ **pyu**	ぴょ **pyo**

Sokuon

つ **tsu**
Pause (no sound, small "tsu")

THE BASIC 46 HIRAGANA CHARACTERS

SPECIAL GROUPS OF CHARACTERS

HIRAGANA - ADDITIONAL SOUNDS YOUON

SMALL つ

Basic Katakana

ア **a**	イ **i**	ウ **u**	エ **e**	オ **o**
カ **ka**	キ **ki**	ク **ku**	ケ **ke**	コ **ko**
サ **sa**	シ **shi**	ス **su**	セ **se**	ソ **so**
タ **ta**	チ **chi**	ツ **tsu**	テ **te**	ト **to**
ナ **na**	ニ **ni**	ヌ **nu**	ネ **ne**	ノ **no**
ハ **ha**	ヒ **hi**	フ **hu**	ヘ **he**	ホ **ho**
マ **ma**	ミ **mi**	ム **mu**	メ **me**	モ **mo**
ヤ **ya**		ユ **yu**		ヨ **yo**
ラ **ra**	リ **ri**	ル **ru**	レ **re**	ロ **ro**
ワ **wa**				ヲ **wo**
ン **n**				

Dakuten

ガ **ga**	ギ **gi**	グ **gu**	ゲ **ge**	ゴ **go**
ザ **za**	ジ **zi(ji)**	ズ **zu**	ゼ **ze**	ゾ **zo**
ダ **da**	ヂ **di(ji)**	ヅ **du**	デ **de**	ド **do**
バ **ba**	ビ **bi**	ブ **bu**	ベ **be**	ボ **bo**

Handakuten

パ **pa**	ピ **pi**	プ **pu**	ペ **pe**	ポ **po**

Youon

キャ **kya**	キュ **kyu**	キョ **kyo**
シャ **sha(sya)**	シュ **shu(syu)**	ショ **sho(syo)**
チャ **cha(tya)**	チュ **chu(tyu)**	チョ **cho(tyo)**
ニャ **nya**	ニュ **nyu**	ニョ **nyo**
ヒャ **hya**	ヒュ **hyu**	ヒョ **hyo**

ミャ **mya**	ミュ **myu**	ミョ **myo**
リャ **rya**	リュ **ryu**	リョ **ryo**

ギャ **gya**	ギュ **gyu**	ギョ **gyo**
ジャ **zya(ja)**	ジュ **zyu(ju)**	ジョ **zyo(jo)**

ビャ **bya**	ビュ **byu**	ビョ **byo**
ピャ **pya**	ピュ **pyu**	ピョ **pyo**

Sokuon

ツ **tsu**
Pause (no sound, small "tsu")

一	二	三	四	五
六	七	八	九	十
百	千	万	水	火
木	天	土	北	東
西	南	左	右	日
月	花	魚	空	山
川	雨	本	目	口
耳	手	足	人	母
父	女	男	子	小
中	大	上	下	何
行	見	言	語	食
飲	会	学	休	買
聞	来	立	生	話
出	読	入	書	後
古	高	安	多	新
少	長	白	分	時
間	週	年	今	先
前	午	半	店	外
電	道	毎	友	名
金	円	車	駅	気
国	社	校		

■ The book contains some of the Kanji mentioned above for the Japan Language Proficiency Test N5. We specifically focus on the most critical Kanji for beginners.

In Japanese, you'll come across two types of "tsu" characters: the regular "tsu" つ and the smaller version, known as small "tsu" っ. You can see this difference in both hiragana and katakana. For instance, "mittsu" みっつ means "three," and "nattsu" ナッツ means "nuts."

➤ So, what's the deal with small "tsu"? How does it work, and what's it called?

Small "tsu" (っ) is a little Kana used in Japanese to show that the consonant before it is said twice as long. You might also hear it referred to as "Sokuon" or "Chiisai tsu," which means "small tsu." It helps make the consonant sound more emphasized. Small tsu (っ) is a small kana that is used in the Japanese language to indicate that the preceding consonant is pronounced in a geminated or "double" manner. It is also known as a Sokuon or Chiisai "tsu" 小さい「っ」.

Unlike most other Kana characters, the small tsu doesn't stand for a whole sound in a syllable. Instead, it helps create a unique effect known as a "clogged sound" or a "double consonant." When you spot a small tsu before another Kana in a word, it makes Kana's consonant sound twice as long. Some of these double consonants come with a quick pause at the start, almost like a tiny throat closure, making the sound distinct.

If you find a small tsu at the end of a word or sentence, it signals a quick pause in the sound, abruptly ending the word's pronunciation instead of gradually fading away.

Examples:

Kekkon	Married	けっこん
Motto	More	もっと
Happa	Leaf	はっぱ
Gakkou	School	がっこう

Hiragana
Example of regular "tsu"

Hiragana
Example of small "tsu"

hatto	Hat	ハット
nattsu	Nuts	ナッツ
poketto	Pocket	ポケット

Katakana
Example of regular "tsu"

Katakana
Example of small "tsu"

In Japanese, there are only 5 vowel sounds, and they are always pronounced consistently. Even if your grammar and vocabulary aren't perfect, if you speak clearly, Japanese people will understand you. Pronouncing Japanese is easier than English, as it has fewer vowels and consonants.

❑ **Normal Vowels**

あ a	as in Ah!	Example: あめ	ame	Rain
いi	as in See!	Example: いす	isu	Chair
う u	as in Moon!	Example: うさぎ	usagi	Rabbit
え e	as in Get!	Example: えんぴつ	enpitsu	Pencil
お o	as in Oh!	Example: おちゃ	ocha	Tea

❑ **Long Vowels** (Chouon 長音)

Long vowels in Japanese, they are pronounced for twice the duration of short vowels. ああ、いい、うう、ええ、おお、These words have longer sounds, and whether a vowel is short or long can actually change the word's meaning.

1. ああ long vowel ああ (aa) for two beats.
   Examples: お母さん okaasan おかあさん mother, お・か・あ・さ・ん
   Its written か・あ. don't read them separately — read them all together.

2. The sound "いい" is pronounced twice as long as "い". When a sound ends with "い" (i), you simply add another "い" after it. For example, "おじさん" (Uncle) becomes "おじいん" (Uncle) → おじいさん (Grandfather).

3. うう is twice the length of う. すうじ (Numbers) す・う・じ、すうじ

4. ええ oneesan お姉さん・おねえさん (older sister). For sounds ending in a え e sound add either a え or い. It might seem unclear, but as you learn new vocabulary words, memorize which pronunciation to use for each.

5. When a long vowel with an "o" sound (お) comes at the end of a word, you add an extra う (u) sound. For instance, "ohayou" (おはよう) means "good morning." However, some words have two "o" sounds together, like "ookii" (大きい・おおきい), meaning "big."

55

It's very important to master long vowels because the meaning of a word can change depending on whether the vowel is long or short.

Example 1:

おじさん　　(ojisan) "o-gee-san"　　Means: "uncle"

おじいさん　(ojiisan) "o-geeee-san"　　Means: "grandfather"

おじさん　　　　おじいさん
↓ ↓ ↓ ↓　　　↓ ↓ ↓ ↓ ↓
O ji sa n　　　O ji i sa n

Example 2:

おばさん　　(obasan) "o-ba-san"　　Means: "aunt"

おばあさん　(obaasan) "o-baa-san"　　Means: "grandmother"

おばさん　　　　おばあさん
↓ ↓ ↓ ↓　　　↓ ↓ ↓ ↓ ↓
O ba sa n　　　O ba a sa n

❑ Long Vowels in Katakana

This is much easier than Hiragana. Instead of adding another vowel simply add a dash after it. ー.

コーヒー	Coffee	ニュース	News
アパート	Apartment	メニュー	Menu
バター	Butter	サーモン	Salmon
ビール	Beer	サッカー	Soccer
カード	Card	テーブル	Table
スーパー	Supermarket	スイーツ	Sweets
デパート	Department	フォーム	Foam

In Japanese, you'll notice that some words appear identical, but the only distinction is that one has a long vowel while the other doesn't.

It's important to note that in some cases, you may also encounter a repetition of the same vowel character to represent a long vowel sound. For instance:

エ (e) → エエ (**ee**)

オ (o) → オオ (**oo**)

Note: If you pronounce a word incorrectly, it can completely change its meaning.

UNIT 1

<ruby>挨<rt>あい</rt>拶<rt>さつ</rt></ruby>

Greetings

- Lists of very common Japanese greetings.
- The difference between "kudasai" and "o-negaishimasu".
- How to use kudasai in a sentence.
- How to use o-negaishimasu in a sentence.

■ LESSON 1

❑ In this lesson, you will practice using greetings that you can apply in various situations.

1.	おはようございます。	O-hayou go-zaimasu.	Good morning.

EXPLANATION
Typically used in the morning hours before noon. However, the kanji word is "hayai"(早い), which means "early" "o-hayou" can be said casually or "o-hayo go-zaimasu" to be polite.
Kanji: お早うございます。o-hayou go-zaimasu.

2.	こんにちは。	Konnichiwa.	Hello.

EXPLANATION
Translated as "hello", and can be used at any hour. However, you most commonly use it during the daytime. Kanji: 今日は。konnichiwa.

3.	こんばんは。	Konbanwa.	Good evening.

EXPLANATION
Translates as "good evening" and is used in the evening or sunset. Kanji: 今晩は。konbanwa.

4.	おやすみなさい。	O-yasuminasai.	Good night.

EXPLANATION
Supposed to be used before going to bed or taking a rest. "o-yasuminasai" is the formal way of saying this phrase, informal version is oyasumi. Kanji: お休みなさい。o-yasuminasai.

5.	ようこそ。	Youkoso.	Welcome.

EXPLANATION
Greeting given upon someone's arrival.

6.	さようなら。	Sayounara.	Good bye.

EXPLANATION
Goodbye (for a long period of time).

■ **LESSON 1** 🔊

7.	いってきます。.	Ittekimasu.	See you later!

EXPLANATION
Used when someone is leaving the house or office. Kanji: 行ってきます。

8.	いってらっしゃい。	Itterasshai	Please go and come back.

EXPLANATION
Used daily, but only at the home or office or somewhere where people are based since it only makes sense when they will go and come back. Kanji: 行ってらっしゃい。

9.	ただいま。	Tadaima	I'm back.

EXPLANATION
The phrase you can say when person returns home. Kanji: 只今。

10.	おかえり。	O-kaeri.	Welcome home.

EXPLANATION
"O-kaeri"（おかえり）is a shorter way of saying "o-kaerinasai," which means "welcome home" or 'welcome back' in Japanese. The Kanji for "o-kaeri" is お帰り。

11.	ひさしぶり。	Hisashiburi.	Long time, no see.

EXPLANATION
A person whom you have not seen in a long time. Kanji: 久しぶり

12.	おつかれさまです。	o-tsukaresama desu.	Thanks for your hard work.

EXPLANATION
Does not have a particular meaning and expresses the appreciation of your co-workers' hard work. Kanji: お疲れ様です。

LESSON 1 🔊

| 13. | はじめまして。 | Hajimemashite. | Nice to meet you. |

EXPLANATION
To someone, you meet for the first time. Kanji: 初めまして。

| 14. | どうぞ, おさきに。 | Douzo, o-sakini. | Go ahead. / After you. |

EXPLANATION
Translates to "Please, go ahead" or "After you" in English. It's a polite way to let someone know that they can go ahead or proceed before you.

| 15. | じゃあまた。 | Jyaa mata. | See you. |

EXPLANATION
A casual phrase that can be used by both women and men, and it translates to "See you later"

| 16. | またあした。 | Mata ashita. | See you tomorrow. |

EXPLANATION
Friends say it at the end of a school day or the end of the evening to mean "See you tomorrow".
Kanji: また明日。

| 17. | がんばって。 | Ganbatte. | Do your best. |

EXPLANATION
Good Luck!, do your best, try hard. Kanji: 頑張って。

| 18. | きをつけて。 | Ki wo tsukete. | Be careful. / Take care. |

EXPLANATION
To be careful, to take care, to watch out. Kanji: 気をつけて。

■ LESSON 1 🔊

19.	ごめんなさい。	Go-mennasai.	I'm sorry.

EXPLANATION

I'm sorry; Casual expression of apology. Kanji: 御免なさい。

20.	すみません。	Sumimasen.	Excuse me.

EXPLANATION

Excuse me, Sorry; In daily conversation, "suimasen" is overwhelming often used and it is also used as a light apology. The polite form is sumimasen. Kanji: 済みません。

21.	おめでとうございます。	O-medetou go-zaimasu.	Congratulations.

EXPLANATION

A polite form of congratulations on a favorable occasion such as a birthday, wedding, etc.

22.	おたんじょうび おめでとう。	O-tanjoubi o-medetou.	Happy birthday.

EXPLANATION

"o" is the polite form "tanjoubi"(たんじょうび) means "birthday" and "o-medetou" means "congratulations" polite version would be "o-tanjobi o-medeto go-zaimasu".

23.	ありがとうございます。	arigatau go-zaimasu.	Thank you very much.

EXPLANATION

In formal situations, expressing gratitude can be done by using "ありがとうございます" for the present tense and "ありがとうございました" for the past tense, which translates to "Thank you."

However, when your relationship with the person is more familiar and casual, "ありがとう" can be used for both present and past tense. It is a way to thank someone for what they have done.

LESSON 2

"Kudasai" and "Onegaishimasu" are two Japanese phrases used to express requests or ask for something politely. Although they can both be translated as "please" they have slightly different nuances, "kudasai" is more casual and commonly used in daily interactions, while "onegaishimasu" is more formal and appropriate for professional or respectful situations.

Kudasai: （下さい）is a more casual and straightforward way of making a request. It is commonly used in daily conversations and informal settings. "Kudasai" can be attached to the stem of a verb or used independently to ask for something.

Examples:

- 聞いて下さい （kiite kudasai ） "Please listen."
- 座ってください。 （suwatte kudasai） "Please have a seat."

Onegaishimasu: （お願いします）is a more formal and polite expression used to make a request. It is often employed in professional settings, on formal occasions, or when speaking to someone on the phone or of higher status. "Onegaishimasu" is considered more respectful and carries a sense of humility.

Examples:

- よやくをお願いします。（yoyaku wo onegaishimasu） "Please make a reservation"

- 田中さんお願いします。（Tanaka-san onegaishimasu） "May I speak to Mr. Tanaka?"

Unit 1 **How to Use "Kudasai" in a Sentence 1-2**

LESSON 3

"てください"(te kudasai). Meaning: Please do it is used when requesting, instructing, or ordering. The te-form in Japanese, also known as the present progressive, serves several functions. It is called the te-form because it involves modifying the verb to end with "te" (て) in Japanese. The te-form is utilized to transform a verb from its infinitive or dictionary form into the "-ing" form, as illustrated by the following example: 食べる (taberu) becomes 食べて (tabete), which translates from "I eat" or "I will eat" to "I'm eating". (Please refer to Unit 19).

■ LESSON 3 🔊

Japanese Verb Conjugation for Te-form

Japanese conjugation for te-form depends on the type of verb you're using. In Japanese, there are two types of Japanese verbs: "る"-verbs and "う"-verbs.

Conjugating "る"-verbs "る"-verbs are super easy to conjugate. You simply drop the "る"(ru) at the end of the word and add "て"(te).

- 食べる taberu → 食べて tabete → "to eat → eating"

- 見る miru→ 見て mite → "to see → seeing"

- 止める yameru→ 止めて yamete → "to stop → stopping"

The Verbs Can Be Categorized Like This:

- "く"(ku) : Change "く" to "いて".
- "す"(su): Change "す" to "して".
- "ぶ"(bu), む (mu), ぬ (nu): Change "ぶ", "む", or "ぬ" to "んで".
- "ぐ"(gu): Change "ぐ" to "いで".
- "う"(u), つ (tsu), る (ru): Change "う", "つ", or "る" to "って".

❖ Examples of verb conjugations for "write".
  → "く"(ku): "書く"(kaku) → "書いて"(kaite) → "to write" → "writing"

Here are some examples of conjugating these verbs. 🔊

No.	HIRAGANA	RŌMAJI	ENGLISH
1.	ちょっと まってください。	chotto matte kudasai.	Please wait a moment.
2.	やめてください！	yamete kudasai!	Please stop!
3.	もっと ゆっくり いってください。	motto yukkuri itte kudasai.	Please speak more slowly.
4.	にほんごを おしえてください。	nihongo wo oshiete kudasai.	Please teach me Japanese.
5.	やってみてください。	yatte mite kudasai.	Give it a try.

■ **LESSON 4**

When you use the phrase "おねがいします" (o-negaishimasu), it carries a more profound cultural significance and implies a higher level of passivity compared to "kudasai." Using this phrase is like humbling yourself before someone, akin to bowing in respect. These terms are often used together, especially in practices like martial arts. It's customary to say "o-negaishimasu" while bowing before a fight. However, even when used independently, "o-negaishimasu" sets a tone of great respect in various situations. For instance, when meeting someone for the first time, greeting them with "hajimemashite" is common. "o-negaishimasu."

> とうきょうえき　　　ねが
> 東京駅までお願いします。(Toukyou eki made, o-negaishimasu.) To Tokyo Station, please.

東京駅まで(Toukyou eki made): This part means "to Tokyo Station". 東京(Toukyou) refers to Tokyo, and 駅(eki) means "station". まで(made) indicates the direction or destination "to".

お願いします(o-negaishimasu): This phrase is a polite expression that can be translated as "please" or "I kindly request." It is derived from the verb 願う (negau), meaning "to request" or "to wish" The honorific prefix お-(o-) and the respectful suffix -ます（-masu) are added to make it more polite and formal.

So, putting it all together, "東京駅までお願いします。"(Toukyou eki made, onegaishimasu.) can be translated as "To Tokyo Station, please." It's a polite way to request someone's assistance or guidance in getting to Tokyo Station.

> その鞄をお願いします。(sono kaban wo o-negaishimasu.) Can I have that bag, please?

There are specific situations where "おねがいします" is the appropriate phrase to use:

- When accepting an offer or finalizing an order at a restaurant.
- When requesting assistance for something beyond your capability.
- When asking for someone on the phone.

However, it's important to note that "o-negaishimasu" cannot be used for requests involving direct actions, such as "Please listen to this" or "Please write using a pencil."

In such cases, there is a simple formula to follow. First, convert the verb into its て-form and add ください (kudasai). For example:

"Please listen to this" becomes "これをきいてください" (Kore wo kiite kudasai).

"Please write using a pencil" becomes "えんぴつでかいてください" (Enpitsu de kaite kudasai).

UNIT 2

じょ　し
助詞
Particles

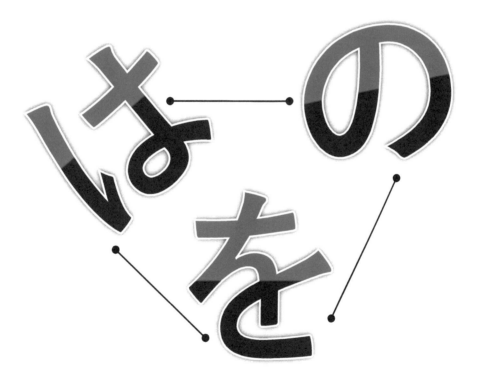

❑ This book contains 15 particles for beginners' level.

Explanation

What is the particle?

In the Japanese language, particles, known as "joshi" (助詞), are small words that establish relationships between words within a sentence.

These particles follow nouns, verbs, and adjectives in a sentence. With a total of 188 particles, they serve a crucial grammatical function by indicating the connections between words and linking the entire sentence together. Understanding how to properly use these various particles is of utmost importance in Japanese, as they provide essential information about the meaning of a sentence.

Incorrect usage of particles can result in a significant alteration or incompleteness in the sentence's overall meaning. Moreover, particles in Japanese play a vital role in indicating the subject of discussion and can function similarly to conjunctions and prepositions in other languages, such as "in," "and," "with," or "to." It is worth noting that Japanese particles are represented by Hiragana characters, and many of them possess multiple meanings depending on their usage.

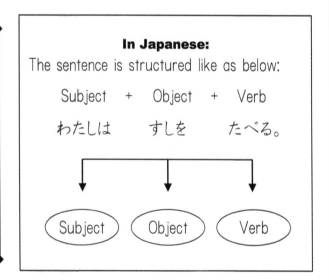

In English:
The sentence is structured like as below:

Subject + Verb + Object

I (S)   eat (V)   sushi (O).

Subject   Verb   Object

In Japanese:
The sentence is structured like as below:

Subject + Object + Verb

わたしは   すしを   たべる。

Subject   Object   Verb

There are No Spaces in Japanese Sentences

In Japanese sentences, spaces are not used, so particles play a crucial role. They indicate the boundaries of words within a sentence, making it easier to read and understand.

Particles are always written in Hiragana unlike nouns and verbs, particles are always written in Hiragana. This makes them stand out visually in a sentence and helps to identify them quickly.

Explanation

Grammatical

Grammatical particles tell us how words in a sentence are related, and these relations are important. A grammatical particle immediately follows the word (or even sentence) it modifies, and as I mentioned earlier, there are lots of them. In this book, we will focus on 15 of the most commonly used particles: は, が, を, へ, に, で, の, と, か, も, から, まで, や, ね, and よ.

Particles have No Conjugation

Particles in Japanese do not undergo any type of conjugation. Unlike verbs, adjectives, and some nouns, particles do not change form depending on the tense, mood, or other grammatical aspects of the sentence.

This means that the same particle can be used in different sentences, regardless of the context or the time frame of the action being described. For example, the particle "を" (wo) is used to indicate the direct object of a sentence, and it is used in the same form regardless of whether the action being described is in the past, present, or future tense.

However, particles do work together with other words in the sentence to convey meaning and grammatical relationships. It is important to understand the functions of different particles in Japanese, and how they work with other parts of speech to form a complete sentence.

Despite not having conjugation, particles in Japanese are a crucial component of the language and play an important role in its syntax and grammar

Particles are Adjuncts

Particles are words such as "が"(ga) and "の"(no) that do not make sense by themselves. They are called adjunct words because they are always attached to other words and follow them to form clauses.

Types of Particles

1. Case particles
2. Conjunctive particles
3. Collective particles (adverbial particles)
4. Final particles
5. Composite particles = Particle equivalents)

❖　Adverbs are sometimes used repeatedly.

は **wa**	が **ga**	を **wo**	へ **e**	に **ni**
で **de**	の **no**	と **to**	か **ka**	も **mo**
から **kara**	まで **made**	や **ya**	ね **ne**	よ **yo**

LESSON 1

	**Pronunciation**	(wa)
	Main use case	Indicates the topic of a sentence
	Formation	[A] wa [B] desu. = [A] is [B]

Explanation

There is always a lot of confusion surrounding the Japanese particle "は"(wa). This particle has multiple usages, and if the wrong particle is used, the whole meaning of the sentence could change, so let's explain it clearly and thoroughly.

"は"(wa) usually indicates the main topic of a sentence.
"は"(wa) formation [topic of the sentence] + [は/wa] + rest of the sentence.
"は"(wa) is often called a topic-marking particle, since it emphasizes what comes after it.

❖ .　　**The Essential Guide to Understanding This Particle**

- Particle "は"(wa) has multiple uses.
- It can be an object, location, or any other grammatical element.
- It is sometimes compared to the English expressions "As for" and "Speaking of".
- Practical "は" is used when a question word (who, where, etc.) Comes after the topic.
- It may also follow some other particles, and the meanings of "は"(wa) can be: am, are.
- This particle is written as the "は"(ha) but, when used as a particle it is pronounced, "wa".

1　　**Using the Particle "Wa" for Asking Questions**

Examples: 🔊

がくせい
1. 学生はだれですか。　　　(gakusei wa dare desu ka?)　　Who is a student?

きょう　　は
2. 今日は晴れですか。　　　(kyou wa hare desu ka?)　　Is it sunny today?

3. トイレはどこですか。　　　(toire wa doko desu ka?)　　Where is the bathroom?

Examples: 🔊

わたし いしゃ　　わたし　　はたら
1. 私は医者です。私はここで働いています。

   (watashi **wa** isha desu. watashi **wa** koko de hataraite imasu.)

   Which means "I am a doctor. I am working here."

Explanation

わたし　　　　　　　　　　　　　　　いしゃ　　　　　　　　はたら
In this example, "私"(watashi) is the topic, and "医者"(isha) and "ここで働いています。"
(koko de hataraite imasu.) are the explanations of the topic.

にほんご むずか　　　　　　　おもしろ
2. 日本語は難しいです。でも、面白いです。

  (Nihongo **wa** muzukashii desu. demo, omoshiroi desu.)

  Which means "Japanese is difficult. But, it is interesting."

Explanation

むずか　　　　　　　　おもしろ
In this example, "日本語"(Nihongo) is the topic, and "難しい"(muzukashii) and "面白い"
(omoshiroi) are the explanations of the topic.

いぬ　　なまえ
3. 私のペットは犬です。名前はポチです。

  (watashi no petto **wa** inu desu. namae **wa** Pochi desu.)

  Which means My pet is a dog. Its name is "Pochi".

Explanation

いぬ　　　　なまえ
In this example, "私のペット"(watashi no petto) is the topic, and "犬"(inu) and "名前はチ"
(namae wa Pochi) are the explanations of the topic.

けさ　　でんしゃ　おく
4. 今朝は電車が遅れていました。(kesa **wa** densha ga okurete imashita.)
This morning, the train was running late.

Explanation

In this sentence, the topic is "今朝"(kesa), which means "this morning" in English.
The particle "は"(wa) is used to mark the topic, and then the speaker explains that the train was
running late.

Examples: 🔊

ぶたにく　た　　　　　　　　とりにく　た
1. 豚肉は食べませんが、鶏肉は食べます。
  (butaniku **wa** tabemasen ga, toriniku **wa** tabemasu.)
   I don't eat pork, but I do eat chicken.

さかな　た　　　　　　　　ぶたにく　た
2. 魚は食べます。　　　　豚肉は食べません。
  (sakana **wa** tabemasu.   butaniku **wa** tabemasen.)
   I eat fish,   I don't eat pork.

Here's another example showing the original sentences, Let's see how it functions.

さかな　た
3. 魚を食べます。(sakana **wo** tabemasu.)   I eat fish.

The object, which in this case is what I eat, is ″魚″(sakana). So ″魚″(sakana) is marked by
the particle ″を″(wo).

た
The negative form of ″食べます″ (tabe**masu**) is ″食べません″ (tabe**masen**).

わたし　ぶたにく　た
So.. 私は豚肉を食べません。(watashi **wa** butaniku **wo** tabemasen.) I don't eat pork.

わたし　ぶたにく　た
If I add the topic, it will be. ″私は豚肉を食べません。″
So now to contrast these two sentences, we replace the particle ″を″(wo) with ″は″(wa).

さかな　た　　　　　　ぶたにく　た
So that gives us. 魚は食べます。· 豚肉は食べません。 (I eat fish, I don't eat pork.)

いぬ　す　　　　　　　ねこ　きら
4. 犬は好きです。でも、猫は嫌いです。(inu **wa** suki desu. demo, neko **wa** kirai desu.)

I like dogs, but I don't like cats. ″でも″(demo) means "but". So, by using ″は″(wa) in this
sentence, we are putting a lot of contrast between the two things or items.

■ The particle ″が″(ga) can also be replaced with ″は″(wa) to show contrast.

Emphasis Marker:

"は"(wa) can be used to add emphasis to a word or phrase, similar to the use of "this" or "that" in English.

Examples: 🔊

1.	これは、本です。	(kore **wa**, hon desu.)	This is a book.
2.	私は、日本人です。	(watashi **wa**, Nihonjin desu.)	I am Japanese
3.	この映画は、すごいです。	(kono eiga **wa**, sugoi desu.)	This movie is amazing.
4.	この本は面白い。	(kono hon **wa** omoshiroi)	This book is interesting.
5.	あの人は、先生です。	(ano hito **wa**, sensei desu.)	That person is a teacher.
6.	明日は、雨です。	(ashita **wa**, ame desu.)	It's going to rain tomorrow.

Quotation Marker:

"は"(wa) is used to indicate that a direct quotation is about to follow.

Examples: 🔊

1. 私は「いい日です。」と言った。   (watashi **wa** "ii hi desu." to itta.)
   I said, Today is a good day.

In this sentence, "は"(wa) is used to introduce a direct quote. The speaker is indicating that they said the words within the quotation marks.

2. 彼は「まだ食べたい」と言っています。(kare **wa** "mada tabetai" to itte imasu.)
   He says, "I still want to eat".

In this sentence, "は"(wa) is also used to introduce a direct quote. The speaker is indicating that the person being referred to "彼"(kare) says the words within the quotation marks.

In both examples, the particle "は"(wa) is used to introduce a direct quote and indicate that the speaker is quoting the exact words that were said by someone else.

Exclusive Particle:

"は" (wa) is used to indicate that one thing is being selected from a group of things and the others are excluded.

Examples: 🔊

わたし がくせい
1. 私は学生です。(watashi **wa** gakusei desu.)
   I am a student (and not a teacher, or something else).

       わたし   き い
2. このレストランは私のお気に入りです。(kono resutoran **wa** watashi no okiniiri desu.)
   This restaurant is my favourite (among all others).

    ほん わたし か
3. この本は私が買ったものです。(kono hon **wa** watashi ga katta mono desu.)
   This book is what I bought (not something someone else bought).

わたし きょう やす
4. 私は今日休みです。(watashi **wa** kyou yasumi desu.)
   I am off today (and not working).

      へや   かのじょ
5. この部屋は彼女のものです。(kono heya **wa** kanojo no mono desu.)
   This room is hers (and not mine or someone else's).

わたし   た
6. 私はやさいだけ食べます。(watashi **wa** yasai dake tabemasu.)
   I only eat vegetables.

      す
7. 私はりんごが好きです。(watashi **wa** ringo ga suki desu.)
   I like apples (implies that there are other fruits that the speaker may or may not like).

    みせ
8. この店はラーメンがおいしいです。(kono mise **wa** rāmen ga oishii desu.)
   This restaurant's ramen is delicious.

In this sentence, the particle "は" (wa) is used to indicate that among all the dishes that the restaurant serves, the speaker is selecting and emphasizing the deliciousness of the ramen, while excluding the other dishes.

Explanation Marker:

"は"(wa) is used to provide additional information or clarification about something.

Examples: 🔊

かのじょ にほんじん　　とうきょう かのじょ しゅっしんち
1. 彼女は日本人です。東京は彼女の出身地です。
   (kanojo wa Nihonjin desu. Toukyou wa kanojo no shusshinchi desu.)
   She is Japanese. Tokyo is her place of origin.

　　　　　　　ゆうめい　　　すし　　　おい　　ひょうばん
2. このレストランは有名です。寿司はとくに美味しいと評判です。
   (kono resutoran wa yuumei desu. sushi wa tokuni oishii to hyouban desu.)
   This restaurant is famous. Sushi has a reputation for being particularly delicious.

　　　　　ともだち　えいが　　　　いっしょ み しゅみ
3. 私たちは友達です。映画は私たちが一緒に見る趣味です。
   (watashitachi wa tomodachi desu. eiga wa watashitachi ga issho ni miru shumi desu.)
   We are friends. Movies are our hobby to watch together.

Event Particle:

Particle "は"(wa) can function as an event particle, which is used to mark the topic of a sentence and indicate the event or action being described.

Examples: 🔊

きょう てん き い
1. 今日は天気が良いです。(kyou wa tenki ga ii desu.) The weather is good today.

かのじょ うた うた
2. 彼女は歌を歌っています。(kanojo wa uta wo utatte imasu.) She is singing a song.

いま ほん よ
3. 私は今本を読んでいます。(watashi wa ima hon wo yonde imasu.) I am reading a book now.

かれ いま
4. 彼は今ジョギングをしています。(kare wa ima jogingu wo shiteimasu.) He jogs now.

LESSON 2

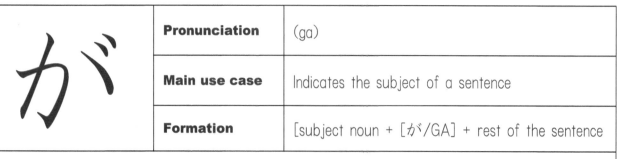

	Pronunciation	(ga)
	Main use case	Indicates the subject of a sentence
	Formation	[subject noun + [が/GA] + rest of the sentence

Explanation

The particle "が"(ga) indicates the subject of a sentence when it is new information for the listener or when the subject is emphasized.

The particle "が"(ga) can also be used to express a question, or to mark the object for certain verbs and adjectives, this particle is often used with "あります"(arimasu) and "います"(imasu), meaning "to have" or "to exist".

1 Using the Particle 'ga' to Indicate a New Subject

Example 1: 🔊

はな　さ
A. 花が咲いています。　　(hana **ga** saite imasu.)　　Flowers are blooming.

B. 花はきれいです。　　(hana **wa** kirei desu.)　　The flowers are beautiful.

Example 2: 🔊

たてもの
建物があります。　　(tatemono **ga** arimasu.)　　There is a building.

Example 3: 🔊

わたしべんきょう
私が勉強します。　　(watashi **ga** benkyou shimasu.)　I will study.

Explanation

■ In the first sentence, "が"(ga) is used because the flower is a newly introduced subject, in the second sentence, "は"(wa) is used because the subject is no longer new information. Thus, there is a particle indicating the subject and the verb "あります"(arimasu). In the third example, "ga" indicates that the subject is "I" and that I am the one studying.

The particle 〝が〟(ga) can be used to emphasize the subject of a sentence, making it clear what the speaker is trying to emphasize.

Examples: 🔊

かれ
1. 彼がかばんをなくした。   (kare **ga** kaban wo nakushita.)
   He lost his bag.

   ともだち   い
2. あなたが友達とあそびに行った。(anata **ga** tomodachi to asobi ni itta.)
   You went to play with your friends.

   わたし くるま がっこう い
3. 私が車で学校に行きました。   (watashi **ga** kuruma de gakkou ni ikimashita.)
   I went to school by car.

---

3   **Contrast the Subject of a Sentence with Other Elements**

The particle 〝ga〟 used to contrast the subject of a sentence with other elements in the sentence:

Examples: 🔊

           わたし か   たか
1. あなたのほうが、私が買ったものよりも高いです。
   (anata no hou **ga**, watashi **ga** katta mono yori mo takai desu.)
   Yours is more expensive than the one I bought.

   わたし か   かのじょ か   ちい
2. 私が買ったジャケットは、彼女が買ったジャケットよりも小さかった。
   (watashi **ga** katta jaketto wa, kanojo **ga** katta jaketto yori mo chiisakatta.)
   The jacket I bought was smaller than the one she bought.

   わたし た   ともだち た   あま
3. 私が食べたキャンディーは、友達が食べたキャンディーよりも甘かった。
   (watashi **ga** tabeta kyandī wa, tomodachi **ga** tabeta kyandī yori mo amakatta.)
   The candy I ate was sweeter than the one my friend ate.

■ In each of these examples, the particle 〝が〟(ga) is used to mark the subject of the sentence, but the sentence structure and use of other particles such as 〝は〟(wa) are used to provide contrast between the subject and other elements in the sentence.

Particle "が"(ga) can be used to express "but" In each of the below examples, the particle "が"(ga) is used to introduce a contrasting idea that qualifies or contradicts the preceding statement.

Examples: 🔊

かれ ゆうめい　　　　　　うま
1. 彼は有名だが、あまり上手くない。
　 (kare wa yuumei da **ga**, amari umakunai.)
　 He is famous but not very good.

い　　　　　　　　かね
2. 行きたいですが、お金がないです。
　 (ikitai desu **ga**, o-kane **ga** nai desu.)
　 I want to go but I don't have money.

りょうり　おい　　　　しおから
3. この料理は美味しいが、塩辛すぎる。
　 (kono ryouri wa oishii **ga**, shiokara sugiru.)
　 This dish is delicious, but too salty.

きょう いそが　　　　あした　　じかん
4. 今日は忙しいが、明日なら時間がある。
　 (kyou wa isogashii **ga**, ashita nara jikan **ga** aru.)
　 I'm busy today, but I have time tomorrow.

たか　　た もの おい
5. このレストランは高いが、食べ物は美味しい。
　 (kono resutoran wa takai **ga**, tabemono wa oishii.)
　 This restaurant is expensive but the food is delicious.

あした てんき よ　　かぜ つよ
6. 明日は天気が良いが、風が強いよほうです。
　 (ashita wa tenki **ga** yoi **ga**, kaze **ga** tsuyoi yohou desu.)
　 Tomorrow will be sunny, but the forecast calls for strong winds.

■ The particle "が"(ga) is used to connect two sentences as "but".

Noun + "ga suru" (する): This construction means "to do" or "to become" something.

Examples: 🔊

わたし　　　　　　　　　　の
1. 私は、コーヒーが飲みたい。(watashi wa kōhī **ga** nomitai.)　I want to drink coffee.

Explanation

The particle "が"(ga) is used to mark the subject of the sentence, which is "コーヒー"(kōhī) meaning "coffee". The verb "飲みたい"(nomitai) means "want to drink", and is a combination of the verb "飲む"(nomu) meaning "to drink" and the auxiliary verb "たい"(tai) indicating desire.

えいご
2. 英語ができる。(Eigo **ga** dekiru.)　to be able to speak English.

Explanation

V-stem + ga dekiru (ができる): This construction is used to express ability or capability to do something.

べんきょう
3. すぐに勉強するがよい。(sugu ni benkyou suru **ga** yoi.) You may study soon.

Explanation

V-stem + ga yoi (がよい): This construction is used to give a suggestion or recommendation, similar to "ga ii" (がいい).

きら
4. 私はマンゴーが嫌いです。(watashi wa mango **ga** kirai desu.) I don't like mangoes.

Explanation

V-stem + ga kirai (が嫌い): This construction is used to express dislike or hate.

■ Also V-stem + ga iru (がいる) / inai (がいない): This construction is used to express presence or absence of a certain person.

For example:

- Kanojo ga iru (彼女がいる。) - She is here. Or He has a girlfriend.
- O-tusan ga inai (お父さんがいない。) - Father is not here. Or Father is gone.

In Japanese, the particle "が"(ga) is used to mark the subject of a sentence, but it can also be used in special circumstances to mark the object of adjectives of desire.

Examples: 🔊

ねこ　す
1. 猫が好きです。

   (neko **ga** suki desu.) I like cats.

   あかいろ　くるま　ほ
2. 私は赤色の車が欲しいです。

   (watashi wa aka-iro no kuruma **ga** hoshii desu.) I want a red car.

   じかん　ほ
3. 私は時間が欲しいです。

   (watashi wa jikan **ga** hoshii desu.) I would like to have time.

Explanation

- ■ In the first and second sentences, the particle marks an object of desire, (like/dislike).
- ■ In the second sentence 私は"I" is the topic of this sentence, so it's marked by the particle は
- ■ "時間が"(jikan ga) as you see that the particle marking the object is "が"(ga).
- ■ 欲しいです (hoshii desu) this is an adjective and means "(I) want".

❖ The structure is [object] "が"(ga) [desire verb or adjective].

---

7   **To Express a Question**

When a question word like "who", "what" or "which" is the subject of a sentence, these words are always followed by "が"(ga), Some verbs and adjectives (expressing like/dislike, desire, potential, necessity, fear, envy etc.) take ga "が"(ga) instead of "を"(wo).

Examples: 🔊

1. どれがいいですか。

   (dore **ga** iidesu ka?) Which one would you like?

 なに　す
2. 何が好きですか。

   (nani **ga** suki desu ka?) What do you like?

 だれ　いちばん　はや　き
3. 誰が一番、早く来ましたか。

   (dare **ga** ichiban, hayaku kimashita ka?) Who came fast?

- ■ The particle "が"(ga) in Japanese is not typically used to form questions.

You might have questioned it, maybe even scrutinized different sentences in an attempt to grasp it, but without arriving at a satisfying conclusion.

It is important to note that "が"(ga) and "は"(wa) serve different grammatical functions. "が"(ga) is a subject marker while "は"(wa) is a topic marker.

は： **Topic marker**

が： **Subject marker**

Distinguishing between subject and topic can be tricky, and many students find this confusing due to the absence of a direct equivalent "topic marker" in English. The grammatical distinction between the Japanese particles "wa" and "ga" lies in "ga" being a case particle and "wa" an adverbial particle. In practical situations, you might notice that "wa" and "ga" can sometimes be used interchangeably in sentences, potentially blurring any differences. However, these particles do carry distinct nuances. While "wa" imparts information already known to everyone, "ga" suggests new information that hasn't been previously known.

In the following example, "Fujisan wa kirei desu." (Mt. Fuji is beautiful.) is used when saying that Mt. Fuji is beautiful in general. In a situation where Mt. Fuji is not in front of us, we are conveying information that everyone knows: the conceptual Mt. Fuji that everyone knows about is beautiful.

On the other hand, "Fujisan ga kirei desu." (Mt. Fuji is beautiful.) has a nuance that conveys new information to the listener in a situation where Mt. Fuji is in front of you.

Examples: 🔊

ふじさん
1. 富士山はきれいです。(Fuji-san **wa** kirei desu.) Mount Fuji is beautiful.
   When the speaker wants to say, Mount Fuji is beautiful in general terms.
   (Provide information that everyone knows.)

ふじさん
2. 富士山がきれいです。(Fuji-san **ga** kirei desu.) Mount Fuji is beautiful.
   In the second sentence "が"(ga) conveying new information to the listener in a situation where the mountain is right in front of you.

LESSON 3

Pronunciation	(wo/o)
Main use case	The Object-Marking Particle
Formation	Noun + wo (を) + verb

Explanation

This particle "を"(wo) is used to express the accusative case. "wo/o"(を) marks the direct object of a Japanese sentence, which is linked to the action of the verb.

The pronunciation of "wo" is close to "o", but with a narrower mouth opening than that of "o". Often referred to as the object particle or object marker, because it usually comes after the direct object of an action.

1   Indicates the Direct Object of an Action

The particle "を"(wo) is used to mark the direct object of a sentence in Japanese. It shows the thing that is directly affected by the action of the verb. The direct object is the noun or noun phrase that receives the action of the verb.

Examples: 🔊

わたし にほんご べんきょう
1. 私は日本語を勉強します。(watashi wa Nihongo **wo** benkyou shimasu.) I study Japanese.

Explanation

In the sentence above, the action of studying is focused on "Nihongo" (Japanese-Direct object) the particle "を" (wo) is used to connect the **noun** "Nihongo" with the **verb** (benkyou shimasu).

かのじょ えいが み
2. 彼女は映画を観ます。(kanojo wa eiga **wo** mimasu.) She watches movies.

Explanation

The particle "を"(wo) marks the direct object of an action. The structure of the sentence is [object] "を"(wo) [verb].

2   Indicates the Place of Movement

The particle "を"(wo) marks where the movement takes place.

Examples: 🔊

はし わた
1. 橋を渡ります。(hashi **wo** watari masu.) I will cross the bridge.

かえ とき こうえん とお
2. 帰る時に公園を通ります。(kaeru toki ni kouen **wo** toori masu.)
    When I go home, I pass through the park.

■ The particle "を"(wo) is typically used to indicate the direct object of a verb in Japanese, rather than the place of movement. However, it can also be used with certain verbs to indicate the destination or direction of movement.

3   Indicates The Object

The particle "を"(wo) is commonly used to indicate the direct object of a verb in Japanese.

Examples: 🔊

ちゅうもん
1. ピザを注文する。   (piza **wo** chuumon suru.)   I order a pizza.

わたし すし た
2. 私は寿司を食べました。   (watshi wa sushi **wo** tabemashita.)   I ate sushi.

かのじょ ほん か
3. 彼女は本を買いました。   (kanojo wa hon **wo** kaimashita.)   She bought a book.

ほん わす
4. 本を忘れました。   (hon **wo** wasure mashita.)   I forgot the book.

おもしろ えいが み
5. 面白い映画を観ました。   (omoshiroi eiga **wo** mimashita.)   I watched an interesting movie.

Conclusion

The particle "を"(wo) marks the direct object in a sentence. The direct object is the noun before "を"(wo) which receives the action of the verb. The particle "を"(wo) also marks the place of movement. [place of movement] "を"(wo) [motion verb].

LESSON 4

	Pronunciation	(e/he)
	Main use case	Indicates a location / direction
	Formation	Location/direction + e (へ)

Explanation

The particle "へ" (e/he) works similarly to "に" (ni), but it emphasizes the direction you're going instead of just arriving.

Both these particles show a direction. "に" (ni) points to a specific spot, while "へ" (e/he) is more about a general area. Both can mean "to" in English, but they have different uses. "へ" (e/he) isn't used for "from," "by," or "at." When written in hiragana, it's "he," but as a particle, it's pronounced as "e." It can also show who receives an action.

Examples: 🔊

えき　い
1. 駅へ行きます。　　　(eki **e** iki masu.)　　　I am going to the station.

ぎんこう　い
2. 銀行へ行きます。　(ginkou **e** iki masu.)　　I am going to the bank.

　　　　　　い
3. アメリカへ行きます。(Amerika **e** iki masu.)　I am going to America.

こうえん　さんぽ
4. 公園へ散歩に行きます。(kouen **e** sanpo ni iki masu.)　I go for a walk in the park.

ともだち　でんわ
5. 友達へ電話をかけました。(tomodachi **e** denwa wo kakemashita.)　I called my friend.

In each of these examples, the particle "へ"(e/he) indicates the destination or direction of the speaker's movement. In example 4 the particle "へ" marks the recipient of an action.

The particle "へ"(e/he) is also commonly used in combination with the verb "行く"(iku) which means "to go". However, it can be used with other verbs as well, such as "送る"(okuru) which means "to send" or "来る"(kuru) which means "to come".

LESSON 5

に	Pronunciation	(ni)
	Main use case	The Location or Time-Marking
	Formation	Place + ni (に)

Explanation

The particle "に" (ni) has a lot of different uses. People often call it the location or time particle, since it's mainly used to show where, when, how long, or movement. It might just be the busiest particle in Japanese, having so many uses. It also shows that something exists, and you use it with "あります" (arimasu) and "います" (imasu) to mean "have" or "exist."

In general, "に"(ni) focuses on the arrival point itself, whereas "へ"(he/e) focuses on a broader scope, including not only the arrival point but also the route or direction to it.

1   Indicates Existence

Examples: 🔊

きのう　がっこう　い
1. 昨日は学校に行きました。(kinou wa gakkou **ni** iki mashita.) Yesterday, I went to school.

らいしゅう　にほん　い
2. 来週、日本に行きます。(raishuu, Nihon **ni** iki masu.) Next week, I will go to Japan.

えき　　　　ひと
3. 駅にたくさん人がいます。(eki **ni** takusan hito ga imasu.) There are many people at the station.

わたし　あたら　いえ　す
4. 私は新しい家に住んでいます。(watashi wa atarashii ie **ni** sunde imasu.) I live in a new house.

かのじょ　ひとり　くうこう　い
5. 彼女は一人で空港に行きました。(kanojo wa hitori de kuukou **ni** iki mashita.)
   She went to the airport alone.

まち　むかし　じんじゃ
6. この町には昔から神社があります。(kono machi **ni** wa mukashi kara jinja ga arimasu.)
   There has been a shrine in this town since ancient times.

The particle "に"(ni) is typically used with verbs such as "いる"(iru) -"to exist [for living things]", "ある"(aru) -"to exist [for non-living things]" & "住む"(sumu) -"to live [somewhere]". It translates into "at" or "in". "行く"(iku) -"to go", "来る"(kuru) -"to come", "会う"(au) -"to meet", "送る"(okuru) -"to send".

■ These are just a few examples of how "に"(ni) can be used with certain verbs in Japanese, and there are many more verbs that can take this particle.

Examples: 🔊

せんせい でんわ
1. 先生に電話をしました。(sensei **ni** denwa wo shimashita.) I called the teacher.

かのじょ あ い
2. 彼女に会いに行きます。(kanojo ni ai **ni** iki masu.) I'm going to meet her.

わたし とうきょう す
3. 私は、東京に住んでいます。(watashi wa, Toukyou **ni** sunde imasu.) I live in Tokyo.

つくえ うえ ほん
4. 机の上に本があります。(tsukue no ue **ni** hon ga arimasu.) There is a book on the desk.

The particle "に" (ni) is like a time guide in Japanese. It teams up with words related to years, months, days, and clock times to point out a specific moment. It's like saying "at," "on," or "in." Just keep in mind, that it doesn't match up with words like "today" or "tomorrow." In English, we use "at" for time, "on" for days of the week, and "in" for months. But in Japanese, "に" (ni) covers all of that.

Examples: 🔊

しちじ お
1. 七時に起きます。(shichiji **ni** oki masu.) I wake up at 7:00.

ごがつ にほん い
2. 五月に日本へ行きます。(gogatsu **ni** Nihon e iki masu.) I will go to Japan in May.

にちようび ともだち べんきょう
3. 日曜日に友達と勉強しました。(nichiyoubi **ni** tomodachi to benkyou shimashita.)
   I studied with a friend on Sunday.

84

4   Indicates the Purpose or Intention of an Action

The particle "に"(ni) can be used to indicate the purpose or intention of an action.

Examples: 🔊

か もの い
1. 買い物に行きます。(kaimono **ni** iki masu.) I will go shopping. (The purpose is to buy things.)

あした はや お　　　はや　ね
2. 明日、早く起きるには、早めに寝なければなりません。
   (ashita, hayaku okiru **ni** wa, hayame ni nenakereba narimasen.)
    In order to wake up early tomorrow, we must go to bed early.
   (The purpose is to wake up early.)

にほんご べんきょう　　　まいにちれんしゅう　　　たいせつ
3. 日本語を勉強するには、毎日練習することが大切です。
   (Nihongo wo benkyou suru **ni** wa, mainichi renshuu suru koto ga taisetsu desu.)
   To study Japanese, it is important to practice every day.

5   Verbal Expression

Indicates purpose. In this case, it translates as "to" or "in order to".

Examples: 🔊

　　　　　い
1.レストランに行く。(resutoran **ni** iku.)　To go to a restaurant.

あさ お
2. 朝に起きる。(asa **ni** okiru.)　To wake up in the morning.

あした でんわ
3. 明日に電話する。(ashita **ni** denwa suru.)　To make a phone call tomorrow.

えいが み い
4. 映画を観に行きました。(eiga wo mi **ni** iki mashita.)　I went to see a movie.

わたし　　　しがつ けっこん
5. 私たちは四月に結婚します。(watashitachi wa shigatsu **ni** kekkon shimasu.)
   We are getting married in April.

■ So the particle "に"(ni) is used to indicate a specific point in time, which can be a year, month, day, or clock time, and it can be translated as "at", "on", or "in" depending on the context.

85

The particle "に"(ni) is used when a motion or action is directed at or on to an object or place.

Examples: 🔊

1. 財布をかばんに入れました。 (saifu wo kaban **ni** ire mashita.)　　I put my wallet in my bag.

2. ここに名前を書いて下さい。 (koko **ni** namae wo kaite kudasai.)　Please write your name here.

3. 田中さんが公園に行った。(Tanaka-san ga kouen **ni** itta.)　Mr. Tanaka went to the park.

The particle "に"(ni) marks the indirect object in the sentence. The indirect object is the person or thing that receives the direct object in the sentence. Let's see how it works exactly.

Examples: 🔊

1. 父は私に本をくれました。 (chichi wa watashi **ni** hon wo kure mashita.)
   My father gave me a book.

Let's break it down

▪私 (watashi) Me/I is the indirect object (receiver) the direct object.

▪本 (hon) the book is the direct object, The Indirect object usually comes before the direct object in a sentence.

2. 先生は生徒にしゅくだいを出した。 (sensei wa seito **ni** shukudai wo dashita.)
   The teacher assigned homework to the students.

3. 彼は友人に日本の文化を紹介した。 (kare wa yuujin **ni** Nihon no bunka wo shoukai shita.)
   He introduced Japanese culture to his friend.

8   Indicates the Purpose or Intention of an Action

"に" indicates the source or agent in passive or causative verbs. It translates as "by" in English.

Examples: 🔊

1. その問題は先生によって説明された。(sono mondai wa sensei **ni** yotte setsumei sareta.)
   The problem was explained by the teacher.

2. その車は父によってしゅうりされた。(sono kuruma wa chichi **ni** yotte shuuri sareta.)
   The car was repaired by my father.

3. この写真は娘によって撮られました。(kono shashin wa musume **ni** yotte toraremashita.)
   This photo was taken by my daughter.

4. 泥棒にお金を盗まれました。(dorobou **ni** o-kane wo nusumaremashita.)
   Money was stolen by a thief.

9   Indicates the Result of a Transformation

The particle "に"(ni) used to indicate the result of a transformation.

Examples: 🔊

1. クリスは先生になった。(Kurisu wa sensei **ni** natta.)
   Chris became a teacher.

2. 茶色の髪の毛が金髪に染まりました。(chairo no kaminoke ga kinpatsu **ni** somarimashita.)
   The brown hair has transformed into blonde hair.

3. 私はダイエットをしたことによって痩せました。(watashi wa daietto wo shita koto **ni** yotte yasemashita.) I lost weight by dieting.

4. 雨に濡れると、服が重くなります。(ame **ni** nureru to, fuku ga omoku narimasu.)
   When you get wet in the rain, your clothes become heavy.

The particle ″に″(ni) is used with frequency expressions such as per day, per week, etc.

Examples: 🔊

まいにち   い
1. 毎日、ジョギングに行きます。(mainichi, jogingu **ni** ikimasu.)
   I go jogging every day.

   いちじかん　いっぽん　でんしゃ　く
2. 一時間に一本の電車が来る。(ichijikan **ni** ippon no densha ga kuru.)
   A train comes every hour.

   いっしゅうかん　いちど　かぞく　がいしょく
3. 一週間に一度、家族で外食する。(isshuukan **ni** ichido, kazoku de gaishoku suru.)
   We eat out as a family once a week.

   いっかげつ　いちど　びよういん　い　　かみ　き
4. 一ヶ月に一度、美容院に行って髪を切る。(ikkagetsu **ni** ichido, biyouin ni itte kami wo kiru.)
   I go to the hair salon once a month to get a haircut.

Conclusion

The particle ″に″ (ni) guides movement and time, indicating where things are going when used with action verbs. It also points out destinations and places where things exist, often accompanied by ″いる″ (iru) or ″ある″ (aru). It can translate as "to," "in/at," or "for."

Note:

The particle ″に″(ni) is used to indicate the exact location or destination of a movement or action. It can also indicate the time or frequency of an action, the indirect object of a verb, or the result of a transformation. The particle ″へ″(e) is used to indicate a general direction or goal of a movement or action. It is often used when the speaker is not familiar with the exact destination or when the destination is not the main focus of the sentence.

In general, particle ″に″(ni) is more specific in indicating the destination or goal of an action, while particle ″へ″(e) is more general and less specific. However, there are many cases where the two particles can be used interchangeably, and the choice of a particle can also depend on the context and nuance of the sentence.

LESSON 6

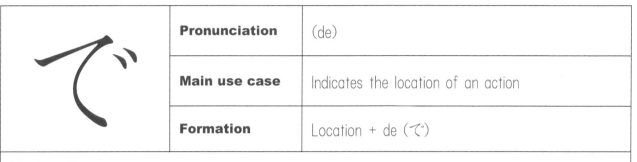

Pronunciation	(de)
Main use case	Indicates the location of an action
Formation	Location + de (で)

Explanation

The particle "で"(de) can show how and where an action or event takes place. It can be used to indicate means or instruments and mark the material from which something is made, similar to how "by", "from", "with", "by means of" or "out of" are used in English. It can also be used like "at" or "in", but can't be used with the verbs "いる"(iru) or "ある"(aru). "で"(de) is also used to mark a means of transportation. "Place"+"ni/de"+"thing/things", When "place" indicates the location or destination of a thing or thing, use "に"(ni). When "place" is used for "thing/thing", "で"(de) is used.

1	**Indicates Place or Location of Action**

Examples: 🔊

　　がっこう　べんきょう
1. 学校で勉強する。(gakkou **de** benkyou suru.) I study at school.

　　じんじゃ　まい
2. 神社でお参りする。(jinja **de** o-mairi suru.) I pray at the shrine.

　　　　　　しょくじ
3. レストランで食事をする。(resutoran **de** shokuji wo suru.) I have a meal at a restaurant.

　　えいがかん　えいが　み
4. 映画館で映画を観る。(eigakan **de** eiga wo miru.) I watch a movie at the movie theatre.

　　　　　　いっぱく
5. ホテルで一泊しました。(hoteru **de** ippaku shimashita.) I stayed for a night at the hotel.

　　ときどき　がっこう　べんきょう
6. 時々、学校で勉強しています。(tokidoki, gakkou **de** benkyou shite imasu.)
　　　　　　　　　　　　I'm studying at the school.

■ Notice that the location is followed by the particle "で"(de) to express the location.

2   Indicates Means

The particle "で"(de) can be used to indicate means, method, or instruments. It translates into "by", "with", "in", and "by means of".

Examples: 🔊

でんしゃ がっこう い
1. 電車で学校に行く。   (densha **de** gakkou ni iku.)   I go to school by train.

くるま   い
2. 車でドライブに行く。   (kuruma **de** doraibu ni iku.)   I go for a drive by car.

じてんしゃ か もの い
3. 自転車で買い物に行く。 (jitensha **de** kaimono ni iku.)   I go shopping by bike.

おんがく べんきょう
4. 音楽で勉強する。   (ongaku **de** benkyou suru.)   I study with music.

でんわ よやく
5. 電話で予約する。   (denwa **de** yoyaku suru.)   I make a reservation by phone.

くるま りょこう い
6. 車で旅行に行きます。   (kuruma **de** ryokou ni iki masu.)   We're going on a trip by car.

かれ   おく
7. 彼はスマートフォンでメールを送った。(kare wa sumaatofon **de** meeru wo okutta.)
                                He sent the email with his smartphone.

3   Indicates Material

The particle "で"(de) can be used to indicate the material or substance that something is made of or composed of. It's equivalent to "with", "from", or "out of" in English.

Examples: 🔊

まど
1. ガラスでできた窓。   (garasu **de** dekita mado.)   A window made of glass.

かわつく
2. 革で作られたバッグ。   (kawa **de** tsukurareta baggu.) A bag made of leather.

つくえ き
3. この机は木でできています。 (kono tsukue wa ki **de** dekite imasu.) This desk is made of wood.

The particle "で"(de) is used to indicate the scope or extent of the total amount, which is "全部"(zenbu), meaning "all" or "entirely".

Examples: 🔊

ぜんぶ　　にせんえん
1. 全部で二千円です。

(zenbu **de** ni-sen en desu.) The total is 2,000 Yen. /Altogether.

かいぎ　に　じかん　お
2. 会議は二時間で終わりました。

(kaigi wa ni-jikan **de** owari mashita.) The meeting ended in two hours.

かれ いちじかん しゅくだい お
3. 彼は一時間で宿題を終えた。

(kare wa ichi-jikan **de** shukudai wo oeta.) He finished his homework in one hour.

わたし いっしゅうかん　　　ほん　よ
4. 私は一週間でその本を読みました。

(watashi wa isshuukan **de** sono hon wo yomi mashita.) I read that book in one week.

5	**Indicates Time**

As an indication of time spent on something, it translates to "in", "within". "for" or "during" is used to indicate a specific point in time.

Examples: 🔊

いちじかん　お
1. 一時間で終わります。(ichi-jikan **de** owari masu.)
I will finish (in total) in one hour.

こんげつ　にほん　き　いちねん
2. 今月で日本に来て一年になります。(kongetsu de Nihon ni kite ichi-nen ni narimasu.)
It will be one year since I came to Japan this month.

なつやす　　いっしゅうかん　　　　　りょこう
3. 夏休みで一週間イタリアに旅行した。(natsuyasumi **de** isshuukan Itaria ni ryokou shita.)
I traveled to Italy for a week during summer vacation.

6　Indicates Cost

The particle ″で″(de) can also indicate the cost of something.

Examples: 🔊

　　　ほん　せんえん　か
1. この本は千円で買えます。(kono hon wa sen-en **de** kaemasu.)
　　You can buy this book for 1,000 yen.

2. このカメラはセールで20％オフでした。
　　(kono kamera wa sēru **de** nijuu-paasento ofu deshita.)
　　　This camera was 20% off on sale.

　　　くるま　しんしゃ　　にひゃくまんえん
3. この車は新車で二百万円です。(kono kuruma wa shinsha **de** ni-hyaku-man-en desu.)
　　This car is a new car and costs 2 million yen.

7　Indicates Cause

This particle is used to show a casual reason or motive behind an action or event. It's like saying "because of" or "due to" in English.

Examples: 🔊

　　た　す　　　なか　いた
1. 食べ過ぎでお腹が痛い。(tabesugi **de** onaka ga itai.)
　　My stomach hurts because I ate too much.

　　かぜ　せき　と
2. 風邪で咳が止まらない。(kaze **de** seki ga tomaranai.)
　　I can't stop coughing because of my cold.

　　ゆき　でんしゃ　と
3. 雪で電車が止まりました。(yuki **de** densha ga tomarimashita.)
　　The train stopped because of the snow.

　　じ　こ　　みち　じゅうたい
4. 事故で道が渋滞しています。(jiko **de** michi ga juutai shite imasu.)
　　The road is congested due to an accident.

◼️　　When using ″で″ (de) to indicate a causal reason, remember that ″が″ (you) can also be used depending on the context, but ″で″ is usually the more common option.

The particle "で" (de) can also define groups of people. It sets a boundary around the number of individuals engaged in an activity or event.

Example 1: 🔊

Question: 何人で海に行きますか。(nannin **de** umi ni ikimasu ka?)
     How many people will go to the sea?

Answer: 三人で行きます。(san'nin **de** ikimasu.)
     Three people will go.

Explanation

In this case, "で"(de) is used to ask about the number of people who will go to the sea, as in "How many people will go to the sea?" or "In how many people will you go to the sea?". The answer to this question might include a number, such as "三人で行きます"(san nin **de** ikimasu), which means "We will go with three people".

■ When used to indicate a group of people, it is typically used in combination with a counter word for people such as "人"(nin).

Example 2: 🔊

四人でレストランに行きました。(yonin **de** resutoran ni ikimashita.)
We went to the restaurant with four people.

Example 3: 🔊

五人で公園でピクニックをしました。(gonin **de** kouen **de** pikunikku wo shimashita.)
We had a picnic in the park with five people.

■ The Particle "で"(de) is used to indicate the means or method by which the action was carried out, and the counter word for people specifies the number of individuals in the group.

LESSON 7

	**Pronunciation**	(no)
	Main use case	Indicates possession
	Formation	Object1 + の + Object2

Explanation

The particle "の" (pronounced as "no") helps express possession or a connection between two nouns, even for multiple relationships. It functions as a possessive particle, showcasing ownership and turning nouns into modifiers.

"の" (no) is often used to indicate possession, like "私の" (watashi no) for "my" or "山田さんの" (Yamada-san no) for "Yamada's." There are diverse uses for "の" (no) in Japanese, its meaning is shaped by the context and accompanying words.

1　Indicates Possession

The particle 「の」 (no) is used to indicate possession. It is similar to the English possessive apostrophe ('s). To form a possessive phrase, simply put the subject followed by 「の」 and then the object. Just like in English, "my dad," "my friend," "my sister" or "my bag", etc.

Examples: 🔊

かいしゃ　でんわ
1. 会社の電話。(kaisha **no** denwa.)　　Company's phone.　　　　　　　　　(Possession)

にほん　くるま
2. 日本の車。(Nihon **no** kuruma.)　　A Japanese car.　　　　　　　　　　(Possession)

わたし　かばん
3. これは私の鞄です。(kore wa watashi **no** kaban desu.)　This is my bag.　　(Possession)

かあ　　　げんき
4. あなたのお母さんは元気ですか。(anata **no** okaasan wa genki desu ka?)　　(Possession)
　　How is your mother doing?

■ In each of these sentences, the particle "の"(no) is used to indicate that the following noun is in the possession of the person or thing that comes before it.

2   Indicates Modification

The particle "の"(no) can also be used to indicate modification.

Examples: 🔊

あたら いえ かぎ
1. 新しい家の鍵。   (atarashii ie **no** kagi.)   The key to the new house.

あか   ほ
2. あの赤いのが欲しい。   (ano akai **no** ga hoshii.)   I want the red one.

わたし あま   す
3. 私は甘いのが好きです。(watashi wa amai **no** ga suki desu.) I like sweet things.

たか   か
4. あの高いのは買えません。(ano takai **no** wa kaemasen.)   I can't afford that expensive one.

ふる
5. この古いのはいくらですか。(kono furui **no** wa ikura desu ka?) How much is this old one?

3   Indicates Explanation

The particle "の"(no) can be used to indicate explanation.

Examples: 🔊

ひと いしゃ
1. あの人は医者のようです。
   (ano hito wa isha **no** you desu.)
   That person seems to be a doctor.

い   ほんとう
2. あなたが言ったのは本当ですか。
   (anata ga itta **no** wa hontou desu ka?)
   Is it true what you said?

> **Note:**
>
> In each of these sentences, the particle "の"(no) is used to provide a reason or explanation for the preceding statement.
>
> The modified noun is often a verb or adjective, and it's used to describe the reason or circumstance behind the situation.

みせ こ   べつ みせ い
3. この店は混んでいるので、別の店に行きましょう。
   (kono mise wa konde iru no de, betsu **no** mise ni ikimashou.)
   This store is crowded, so let's go to another store.

In each of these sentences, the particle "の"(no) is used to indicate the relative position or location of a noun. The modified noun is often a location, such as "desk", "house", "window", "conference room", or "restaurant".

Examples: 🔊

1. テーブルの下の猫。   (tēburu **no** shita **no** neko.)
   The cat under the table.

2. ソファの後ろに置いてください。 (sofa **no** ushiro ni oite kudasai.)
   Please put it behind the sofa.

3. レストランの外で待っていてください。 (resutoran **no** soto de matte ite kudasai.)
   Please wait outside of the restaurant.

4. 私の机の上に本があります。 (watashi **no** tsukue **no** ue ni hon ga arimasu.)
   There is a book on top of my desk.

5. あなたの家の近くに公園はありますか。 (anata **no** ie **no** chikaku ni kouen wa arimasu ka?)
   Is there a park near your house?

6. 田中さんは会議室の中で話をしていた。
   (Tanaka-san wa kaigishitsu **no** naka de hanashi wo shite ita.)
   Tanaka-san was talking inside the conference room.

7. 駅の前のビルの後ろにコンビニがあります。
   (eki **no** mae **no** biru **no** ushiro ni konbini ga arimasu.)
   There is a convenience store behind the building in front of the station.

8. 窓の外にはきれいな景色が広がっている。
   (mado **no** soto ni wa kirei na keshiki ga hirogatte iru.)
   There is a beautiful scenery outside the window.

The particle ″の″(no) can be used to link two nouns that have the same referent, similar to using "that is" in English.

Example 1: 🔊

わたし　ともだち　やまだ　　　　いしゃ
1. 私の友達の山田さんは医者です。

    (watashi **no** tomodachi **no** Yamada-san wa isha desu.)

     My friend Yamada-san is a doctor.

Explanation

In this sentence, ″私の友達″(watashi no tomodachi) means my friend, and ″山田さん″(Yamada-san) is in apposition to it, meaning they are the same person.The comma is often used to indicate apposition in Japanese.

Example 2: 🔊

わたし　がっこう　　たなかせんせい まいにち はやお
2. 私の学校の田中先生は毎日、早起きします。

    (watashi **no** gakkou no Tanaka-sensei wa mainichi hayaoki shimasu.)

     Mr. Tanaka at my school gets up early every day.

Explanation
In this sentence, ″私の学校″(watashi no gakkou) means my school and ″田中先生″(Tanaka-sensei) is in apposition to it, indicating that Tanaka-teacher is the specific person being referred to as the speaker's teacher.

Example 3: 🔊

かのじょ いもうと　　こ　　　しょうがくせい
3. 彼女の妹のあの子はまだ小学生です。

    (kanojo **no** imouto no ano ko wa mada shougakusei desu.)

     Her younger sister, that one, is still in elementary school.

Explanation

In this sentence, ″彼女の妹″(kanojo no imouto) means her younger sister, and ″あの子″ (ano ko) is in apposition to it, indicating that ″あの子″ and ″彼女の妹″ refer to the same person.

6   The Same as the English Word "of"

Sometimes it can be helpful to think of the particle "の"(no) as the English word "of".

Examples: 🔊

えいご　せんせい
1. 英語の先生。 (eigo **no** sensei.) Teacher of English. (English teacher)

にほんご　ほん
2. 日本語の本。　 (Nihongo **no** hon.) Book of Japanese. (Japanese book)

7   Another Use

Here the particle 「の」 function is to show a relationship between the two nouns.

Examples: 🔊

ともだち　たなか
1. 友達の田中さんです。 (tomodachi **no** Tanaka-san desu.)
　 This is my friend Tanaka-san.

わたし　ともだち　なまえ　やまだ
2. 私の友達の名前は山田です。(watashi **no** tomodachi **no** namae wa Yamada desu.)
　 My friend's name is Yamada.

わたし　　　　いえ　やま　ちゅうふく
3. 私たちの家は山の中腹にあります。(watashitachi **no** ie wa yama **no** chuufuku ni arimasu.)
　 Our house is located on the mountainside.

Conclusion

The Japanese particle "の"(no) indicates possession or relationships between nouns, tells the location of something, or is used to modify or describe other nouns.

Tips and Advice

Nihon hon (Japanese book) or eigo sensei (English teacher) cannot be said without the particle "の" (no).
To say them correctly, the particle must be included, as in "日本の本"(Nihon **no** hon) Japanese book and "英語の先生"(eigo **no** sensei) English teacher.

LESSON 8

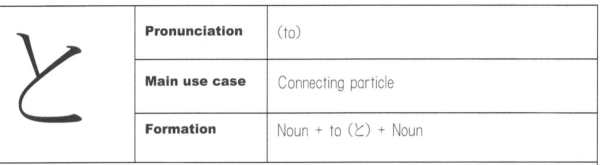

	Pronunciation	(to)
と	Main use case	Connecting particle
	Formation	Noun + to (と) + Noun

Explanation

The particle "と"(to) is used to connect two or more nouns in a sentence. It is translated as "and" or "with" in English. Here are the main usages:

1. Comparison: To compare two things or actions, indicating a standard or basis of comparison.
2. Quotation Marker: "と" is often used to mark direct quotations or reported speech.
3. Conditional "If": "と" can be used to express conditions or hypothetical situations.
4. Accompaniment: Indicate the company of someone or something else.
5. Onomatopoeic words: Indicate the manner or state in which an action is performed.

1   Particle (to) as "And"

In the examples below, "と"(to) means "and". It connects the two nouns.

Examples: 🔊

1. リンゴとバナナを買いました。(ringo **to** banana wo kaimashita.)   I bought apples and bananas.

2. 日本語と英語を話します。(Nihongo **to** eigo wo hanashimasu.)   I speak Japanese and English.

3. 彼女は美しくて優しいと思います。    To connect adjectives
   (kanojo wa utsukushikute yasashii **to** omoimasu.)
   I think she is beautiful and kind.

4. 毎日、勉強をして成績を上げたいと思います。   To connect verbs
   (mainichi, benkyou wo shite seiseki wo agetai **to** omoimasu.)
   I want to study every day and improve my grades.)

The particle ″と″(to) can be used to indicates a comparison or a contrast.

Examples: 🔊

1. ジュースとコーヒー、どちらが好^すきですか。

   (jūsu **to** kōhī, dochira ga suki desu ka?)

   Which do you like, juice or coffee?

2. ピザとパスタのどちらが好^すきですか。

   (piza **to** pasuta no dochira ga suki desu ka?)

   Do you prefer pizza or pasta?

3. 彼女^{かのじょ}は私^{わたし}と同^{おな}じくらい背^せが高^{たか}いです。

   (kanojo wa watashi **to** onaji kurai se ga takai desu.)

   She is as tall as me.

4. 彼女^{かのじょ}は美^{うつく}しいとともに、賢^{かしこ}いという評判^{ひょうばん}がある。

   (kanojo wa utsukushii to tomoni, kashikoi **to** iu hyouban ga aru.)

   She has a reputation for being both beautiful and intelligent.

5.日本^{にほん}の降雪量^{こうせつりょう}は世界一^{せかいいち}多^{おお}いと言^いわれています。

   (Nihon no kousetsuryou wa sekaiichi ooi **to** iwarete imasu.)

   It is said that the amount of snowfall in Japan is the highest in the world.

6.この本^{ほん}は長^{なが}いけど、面白^{おもしろ}いと言^いわれています。

   (kono hon wa nagai kedo, omoshiroi **to** iwarete imasu.)

   This book is long, but it's said to be interesting.

7. 日本^{にほん}とアメリカの文化^{ぶんか}には大^{おお}きな違^{ちが}いがあると思^{おも}います。

   (Nihon **to** Amerika no bunka ni wa ookina chigai ga aru **to** omoimasu.)

   I think there are big differences between Japanese and American culture.

The particle ″と″(to) can also be used to mark the end of a thought or quotation that is being reported, and it is often preceded by the plain form of a verb and followed by verbs like ″言う″(iu) –"to say", ″思う″(omou) –"to think", and ″聞く″(kiku) –"to listen/hear".

Examples: 🔊

にほんご むずか　　おも
1. 日本語は難しいと思います。
   (Nihongo wa muzukashii **to** omoimasu.)
   I think Japanese is difficult.

　　　あやこ　　　　　　　　おも
2. これは綾子さんのバッグだと思います。
   (kore wa Ayako-san no baggu da **to** omoimasu.)
   I think this is Ayako's bag.

はは　　なか　　　　い　　　　ゆうしょく　したく　はじ
3. 母が「お腹がすいた」と言ったので、夕食の支度を始めた。
   (haha ga "onaka ga suita" **to** itta node, yuushoku no shitaku wo hajimeta.)
   When my mother said, "I'm hungry", I started preparing dinner.

Explanation

⬛ In this sentence, the particle ″と″(to) marks the end of the quotation, which reports what the mother said using the verb ″言う″(iu).

かれ　なんど　　　　　あやま　　き
4. 彼は何度も「すみません」と謝ったと聞きました。
   (kare wa nando mo "sumimasen" **to** ayamatta to kiki mashita.)
   I heard that he apologized many times, saying "I'm sorry".

Explanation

⬛ In this sentence, the particle ″と″(to) is not used, but the verb ″聞く″(kiku) is used to indicate what the speaker heard from someone else, and the reported speech is marked by the verb ″言う″(iu).

When you want to express a conditional situation in Japanese, you use the conditional particle "と" (to). You can also add it after a verb or an adjective to create a conditional context. This helps convey meanings like "as soon as," "when," or "if."

Examples: 🔊

いえ かえ　　だれ
1. 家に帰ると、誰もいませんでした。　　　(ie ni kaeru **to**, daremo imasen deshita.)
   When I got home, nobody was there.

　　　　　　お　　　　　あ
2. このボタンを押すと、ドアが開きます。　　(kono botan wo osu **to**, doa ga hirakimasu.)
   If you push this button, the door will open.

しごと お　　　　　　　いえ かえ
3. 仕事が終わると、すぐに家に帰りました。　(shigoto ga owaru **to**, sugu ni ie ni kaerimashita.)
   As soon as work was over, I went home.

　　みち　　　　　い　うみ み
4. この道をまっすぐ行くと、海が見えます。　(kono michi wo massugu iku **to**, umi ga miemasu.)
   If you go straight on this road, you can see the sea.

よる　　　　　　の　ねむ
5. 夜にコーヒーを飲むと眠れなくなります。　(yoru ni kōhī wo nomu **to** nemurenaku narimasu.)
   If I drink coffee at night, I can't sleep.

In Japanese, the particle "と"(to) is sometimes used with onomatopoeia. However, here are some examples of onomatopoeia.

Examples: 🔊

とり　　　　　　　　　な
1. 鳥がちゅんちゅんと鳴いています。(tori ga chunchun **to** naite imasu.) Birds are chirping.

ねこ　　　　　　　　な
2. 猫がにゃあにゃあと鳴いています。(neko ga nyaanyaa **to** naite imasu.) The cat is meowing.

あめ　　　　　ふ
3. 雨がざあざあと降っています。(ame ga zaazaa **to** futte imasu.) Rain is pouring down in torrents.

◼ The particle "と"(to) can be used after onomatopoetic adverbs.

LESSON 9

か	Pronunciation	(ka)
	Main use case	At the end of a sentence indicating a question
	Formation	[sentence] か (ka)

Explanation

The particle "か"(ka) is usually used at the end of a sentence to turn it into a question. However, this particle has other uses as well.

Here we will introduce its four main usages:

1. か (ka) as a question marker with "です"(desu), "ます"(masu) etc.
2. か (ka) as a connection of two questions.
3. か (どうか) (ka) (douka)-I don't know if.
4. か (ka) as "or".

1   Indicates Question

The particle "か"(ka) is used to form questions in Japanese, whether it is a yes-or-no question or a question that requires more detailed information.

Examples: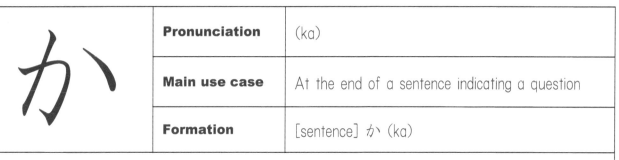

なに
1. 何をしていますか。   (nani wo shite imasu **ka**?)   What are you doing?

なに　た
2. 何を食べましたか。   (nani wo tabemashita **ka**?)   What did you eat?

せんせい
3. あなたは先生ですか。   (anata wa sensei desu **ka**?)   Are you a teacher?

なんさい
4. あなたは何歳ですか。   (anata wa nan saidesu **ka**?)   How old are you?

きょう　きんようび
5. 今日は金曜日ですか。   (kyou wa kin-youbi desu **ka**?)   Is it Friday today?

The particle ″か″(ka) can be used in several ways as a connection in Japanese.

Examples: 🔊

1. ピザか パスタを注文してください。(piza **ka** pasuta wo chuumon shite kudasai.)
   Please order either pizza or pasta.

2. どちらかと言うと、甘いものが好きかしら。(dochira **ka** to iu to, amaimono ga suki kashira?)
   What do you prefer, sweet or savoury food?

The particle ″か″(ka) can be used to express uncertainty or doubt.

Examples: 🔊

1. 明日は雨かどうか分からない。
   (ashita wa ame **ka** dou **ka** wakaranai.)
   I'm not sure if it will rain or not tomorrow.

2. 明日会議があるかどうか知りません。
   (ashita kaigi ga aru **ka** dou **ka** shirimasen.)
   I don't know if there is a meeting tomorrow.

3. 彼女は今日来るかどうかわからない。
   (kanojo wa kyou kuru **ka** dou **ka** wakaranai.)
   I'm not sure if she will come today.

4. 私もその話が本当かどうか分かりません。
   (watashi mo sono hanashi ga hontou **ka** dou **ka** wakarimasen.)
   I'm not sure if that story is true either.

5. このレストランは美味しいかどうかわからない。
   (kono resutoran wa oishii **ka** dou **ka** wakaranai.)
   I don't know if this restaurant is good or not.

Here are some examples of how the particle "か"(ka) can be used as "or".

Examples: 🔊

た
1. ラーメン**か**パスタが食べたいです。

   (rāmen **ka** pasuta ga tabetai desu.)

    I want to eat ramen or pasta.

あした こうえん うみ　い　よてい
2. 明日は公園**か**海に行く予定です。

   (ashita wa kouen **ka** umi ni iku yotei desu.)

    I'm planning to go to the park or the beach tomorrow.

らいしゅう きんようび　　どようび　とうきょう　い
3. 来週の金曜日**か**土曜日に東京に行きます。

   (raishuu no kinyoubi **ka** do-youbi ni Toukyou ni ikimasu.)

    I will go to Tokyo next Friday or Saturday.

Conclusion

The particle "か"(ka) has several different uses and meanings in the language. It can be used to form yes/no questions, to express doubt or uncertainty, to indicate a choice or alternatives, and to indicate a question or request.

It is a versatile particle that can be used in a variety of situations, and is an important component of Japanese grammar. Learning how to use "か"(ka) correctly can help learners of Japanese to communicate more effectively and accurately in the language.

Tips and Advice

Pay attention to intonation: In Japanese, intonation plays an important role in conveying meaning. When using "か"(ka) to form a question, it's important to raise your intonation at the end of the sentence to indicate that it's a question.

Practice using "か"(ka) in context: As with any aspect of language learning, practice is key to mastering the use of "か"(ka). Try using "か"(ka) in context by speaking with native speakers, or by practicing writing sentences that include "か"(ka).

■ **LESSON 10**

	**Pronunciation**	(mo)
	Main use case	Means "too", "either", "also"
	Formation	[Object] も [property1/action1] です.

Explanation

The particle "も"(mo) is similar to the English words "too" or "also." It is always related to the preceding noun. If the noun would otherwise be followed by the particles "が"(ga) or "は"(wa), these are replaced by "も"(mo).

In cases where the preceding noun would be followed by the particles "に"(ni) or "で"(de), the particle "も"(mo) is attached to the preceding particle.

1   Indicates as "Too" or "Also"

The particle "も"(mo) indicates "also" or "too".

Examples: 🔊

わたし い
1. 私も行きます。(watashi **mo** ikimasu.)   I am going too.

きょう あつ
2. 今日も暑いですね。(kyou **mo** atsui desu ne.) It's hot today too, isn't it?

かれ す
3. 彼もコーヒーが好きです。(kare **mo** kōhī ga suki desu.) He also likes coffee.

わたし にほんご す
4. 私も日本語が好きです。(watashi **mo** Nihongo ga suki desu.) I also like Japanese.

わたし てつだ
5. 私たちも手伝いたいです。(watashitachi **mo** tetsudaitai desu.) We also want to help.

わたし す
6. 私もこのゲームが好きです。(watashi **mo** kono gēmu ga sukidesu) I like this game too.

2   Indicates "Equally" or "Both"

The particle "も"(mo) can also indicate "equally". In each of below examples, the particle "も"(mo) is used to indicate that something is equally true or important as something else.

Examples: 🔊

あに うみ やま おな　　す
1. 兄は海も山も同じくらい好きです。(ani wa umi **mo** yama **mo** onaji kurai sukidesu.)
   My brother likes the sea and the mountains equally.

くだもの やさい す
2. 果物も野菜も好き。(kudamono mo yasai **mo** suki.) I like both fruits and vegetables.

わたし いぬ ねこ す
3. 私は犬も猫も好きです。(watashi wa inu mo neko **mo** sukidesu.) I like both dogs and cats.

3   Indicates "Neither"

The particle "も"(mo) plays a slightly different role in the sentence, so it's important to pay attention to the context to understand how it is being used.

Examples: 🔊

わたし　　　　す
1. 私もタバコは吸いません。(watashi **mo** tabako wa suimasen.) I don't smoke either.

かれ えいが　　　　　み
2. 彼は映画もスポーツも見ません。(kare wa eiga **mo** supootsu **mo** mimasen.)
   He doesn't watch either movies or sports.

みせ ようしょく わしょく だ
3. あの店は洋食も和食も出さない。(ano mise wa youshoku **mo** washoku **mo** dasanai.)
   That restaurant doesn't serve either Western food or Japanese food.

わたし あね　　　　　ちゃ の
4. 私の姉はコーヒーもお茶も飲みません。(watashi no ane wa ko hi **mo** ocha **mo** nomimasen.)
   My sister doesn't drink either coffee or tea.

■ This usage of "も"(mo) is particularly helpful for creating negative sentences that express what someone doesn't do or doesn't have.

An emphasis is placed on the amount or quantity that comes before the particle "も"(mo), and it expressesthe feeling that something is a lot/long/too much/too long/big.

Examples: 🔊

さんじゅうまんえん
1. 三十万円も、もらった。(san-juu-man-en **mo,** moratta.)
   I received 300,000 yen.

　　　ほん　ごかい よ
2. その本は五回も読みました。(sono hon wa go-kai **mo** yomimashita.)
   I read that book five times.

わたし いちにち　に じかんうんどう
3. 私は一日に二時間も運動する。(watashi wa ichinichi ni ni-jikan **mo** undou suru.)
   I exercise as much as two hours a day.

■ In each of these examples, the particle "も"(mo) is used to emphasize the amount or extent of something. This usage of "も"(mo) is often used to indicate that the quantity is more than expected or significant in some way.

CONCLUSION

The particle "も"(mo) is a versatile particle in the Japanese language that can be used in several ways, depending on the context. Here's a quick summary of the main uses of the particle "も"(mo):

To indicate "also" or "too" in a sentence.

To indicate "even" or "as much as" in a sentence.

To indicate "neither" in a sentence.

To emphasize the amount or extent of something in a sentence.

When using the particle "も"(mo), it is important to pay attention to the context of the sentence, as it can have different nuances and meanings depending on how it is used.

With practice and exposure to different examples, you can become more comfortable with using this particle in your own Japanese communication.

LESSON 11

	Pronunciation	(kara)
から	**Main use case**	Indicates a starting point in time or place
	Formation	Noun + kara (から)

Explanation

This particle indicates the starting point of something, and it's used for both temporary and geographical situations. It's often referred to as the "starting point" particle because it shows when or where something begins. When you place it after a noun or a time phrase, it's typically translated as "from" or "because" in English.

1 Indicates the Starting Point as "From"

The particle "から" (kara) is a Japanese particle that indicates the starting point of an action, a cause, a reason, or a source.

Examples: 🔊

1. どこから来たんですか。   (doko **kara** kita n desu ka?)
   Where are you from?

2. 東京から京都へ行きます。   (Toukyou **kara** Kyouto e ikimasu.)
   I'm going from Tokyo to Kyoto.

3. 私は学校から帰ります。   (watashi wa gakkou **kara** kaerimasu.)
   I'm going home from school.

4. ここから駅は近いです。   (koko **kara** eki wa chikai desu.)
   From here, the train station is close.

5. 駅から学校まで歩いて行きます。   (eki **kara** gakkou made aruite ikimasu.)
   I'm going to walk from the station to school.

6. 日本からアメリカに来ました。   (Nihon **kara** Amerika ni kimashita.)
   I came from Japan to America.

The particle "から"(kara) expresses the point at which a period of time starts.

Examples: 🔊

<ruby>八時<rt>はちじ</rt></ruby> <ruby>始<rt>はじ</rt></ruby>
1. 八時から始まります。(hachi-ji **kara** hajimarimasu.) It starts from 8 o'clock.

<ruby>会議<rt>かいぎ</rt></ruby> <ruby>十時<rt>じゅうじ</rt></ruby>
2. 会議は十時からです。(kaigi wa juu-ji **kara** desu.) The meeting starts from ten o'clock.

<ruby>今<rt>いま</rt></ruby> <ruby>部屋<rt>へや</rt></ruby> <ruby>掃除<rt>そうじ</rt></ruby>
3. 今から部屋を掃除します。(ima **kara** heya wo souji shimasu.) I will clean my room now.

<ruby>朝<rt>あさ</rt></ruby> <ruby>雨<rt>あめ</rt></ruby> <ruby>降<rt>ふ</rt></ruby>
4. 朝から雨が降っています。(asa **kara** ame ga futteimasu.) It has been raining since morning.

<ruby>九時<rt>くじ</rt></ruby> <ruby>授業<rt>じゅぎょう</rt></ruby> <ruby>始<rt>はじ</rt></ruby>
5. 九時から授業が始まります。(ku-ji **kara** jugyou ga hajimarimasu.) Class starts at nine O'clock.

In the below sentences, "から"(kara) is used to indicate the reason or cause for the main clause that follows it.

Examples: 🔊

<ruby>私<rt>わたし</rt></ruby> <ruby>眠<rt>ねむ</rt></ruby>
1. 私は眠いからあそべない。
   (watashi wa nemui **kara** asobenai.)
   I can't play because I'm tired.

<ruby>場所<rt>ばしょ</rt></ruby> <ruby>昔<rt>むかし</rt></ruby> <ruby>人気<rt>にんき</rt></ruby>
2. この場所は昔から、人気がある。
   (kono basho wa mukashi **kara**, ninki ga aru.)
   This place has been popular since a long time ago.

<ruby>天気<rt>てんき</rt></ruby> <ruby>悪<rt>わる</rt></ruby> <ruby>運動会<rt>うんどうかい</rt></ruby> <ruby>中止<rt>ちゅうし</rt></ruby>
3. 天気が悪かったから、運動会は中止になった。
   (tenki ga warukatta **kara**, undoukai wa chuushi ni natta.)
   The sports day was cancelled because the weather was bad.

> ■ It's important to pay attention to the context of the sentence in order to determine whether "から"(kara) is being used to indicate "because" or "since". The use of other particles, such as "ので"(node) or "のである"(node aru), may also indicate a reason or cause, while "以来"(irai) or "以後"(igo) may indicate a starting point in time.
>
> ■ The book doesn't cover these particles since they aren't for beginners.

The particle "から"(kara) can be used as a conjunction that indicates "that's why" or "because of that". It is often used to explain the reason or cause behind a particular situation or action.

Examples: 🔊

わたし　　　　　　　　　　　ともだち
1. 私はひまだった。**だから**友達とあそんだ。
　　(watashi wa hima datta. **dakara** tomodachi to asonda.)
　　I was bored, so I played with my friends.

　　　　　　おそ　ね　　　　　　　　　め　あか
2. あなたは遅くに寝ました。**だから**あなたの目が赤いのです。
　　(anata wa osoku ni nemashita, **dakara** anata no me ga akai no desu.)
　　You slept late. That is why your eyes are red.

　　きのう　　いそが　　　　　きょう　　　やす
3. 昨日はとても忙しかった**から**、今日はゆっくり休みたい。
　　(kinou wa totemo isogashikatta **kara**, kyou wa yukkuri yasumitai.)
　　I want to take it easy today because I was very busy yesterday.

　　きのう　おそ　はたら　　　きょう　はや　ね
4. 昨日は遅くまで働いた**から**、今日は早く寝たい。
　　(kinou wa osoku made hataraita **kara**, kyou wa hayaku netai.)
　　I worked late yesterday, so I want to go to bed early today.

　わたし　いもうと　かぜ　　　　きょう　やす
5. 私の妹が風邪をひいた**から**、今日は休みます。
　　(watashi no imouto ga kaze wo hiita **kara**, kyou wa yasumimasu.)
　　My (little) sister caught a cold, so she will be absent today.

　あした　　　　　　　　　　　きょう　べんきょう
6. 明日はテストがあります。**だから**、今日は勉強しなくてはいけません。
　　(ashita wa tesuto ga arimasu. **dakara**, kyou wa benkyou shinakutewa ikemasen.)
　　Tomorrow I have a test. So I have to study today.

■ When you combine "から" with "だ" (the short form of "です"), you can place it at the start of a sentence to express something like "And that's why." For a slightly more polite tone, you can use "だから" (dakara) or interchange it with "ですから" (desukara).

The particle "から" (kara) can also indicate "raw materials," the substances used to create something. This is because raw materials are the basis or origin (like the starting point).

Examples: 🔊

き　つく　　かみ
1. 木から作られた紙。(ki **kara** tsukurareta kami.) Paper made from wood.

つく
2. ぶどうからワインを作る。(budou **kara** wain wo tsukuru.) Make wine from grapes.

こむぎ　つく
3. パンは小麦から作られています。(pan wa komugi **kara** tsukurarete imasu.)
   Bread is made from wheat.

ふく　こうきゅう めん
4. この服は高級な綿からできています。(kono fuku wa koukyuu na men **kara** dekiteimasu.)
   This clothing is made from high-quality cotton.

たまご こむぎこ　さとう　つく
5. このケーキは卵と小麦粉と砂糖から作られています。
   (kono kēki wa tamago to komugiko to satou **kara** tsukurareteimasu.)
   This cake is made from eggs, flour, and sugar.

Difference Between
（から）and（で）

The particle "で" (de) serves a similar purpose. It also tells us what something is made of.

But how are they different?

When the material's nature is clear, go with "で" (de).

If the material comes from a complex process, you can choose between "で" or "から" (kara) for marking the material.

■ When the particle "から"(kara) marks the materials, something is made of or from the sentence structure is [materials] "から"(kara) [product] "を 作ります"(wo tsukurimasu). However, the choice between "で"(de) and "から"(kara) may also depend on the speaker's intention or the context of the sentence.

LESSON 12

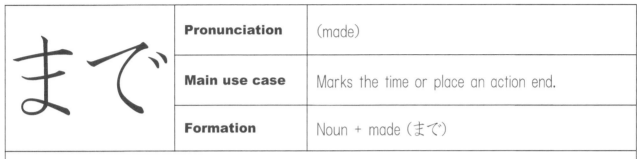

Pronunciation	(made)
Main use case	Marks the time or place an action end.
Formation	Noun + made (まで)

Explanation

This particle has three main uses and can be combined with other particles like "から" (kara) and "に" (ni). In English, it translates to "until" or "to." It's also known as the "limitation" particle. Let's differentiate "へ", "に", and "まで." "へ" originally indicates direction, while "に" points to an arrival spot. "に" clarifies the destination point.

Both "に" and "まで" emphasize the arrival point, but sometimes "まで" implies that the point isn't the final destination, but rather a transitional stop (like in Example 3).

1   Indicates a Point in Time as "Until" or "To"

The particle "まで" indicates the point in time until which an action is performed or a state exists.

Examples: 🔊

1. 今夜のパーティーは十一時までです。(konya no pātī wa juuichi-ji **made** desu.)
   Tonight's party goes until 11 o'clock.

2. ここから駅までどのくらいかかりますか。(koko kara eki **made** dono kurai kakarimasu ka?
   How long does it take from here to the station?

3. この道をまっすぐ進んで、駅に着くまで三十分くらいです。
   (kono michi wo massugu susunde, eki ni tsuku **made** sanju-ppun kurai desu.)
   Continue straight down this road and it takes about 30 minutes to reach the station.

The particle "まで"(made) to indicate an endpoint in time.

Examples: 🔊

あさって　　　　　へんじ
1. 明後日までに返事をください。
    (asatte **made** ni henji wo kudasai.)
    Please reply by the day after tomorrow.

> The particle "まで"(made) is used to indicate a specific endpoint in time, so it's important to use it in the context of a specific time frame or deadline.

かいぎ　じゅうじ　　　　お
2. 会議は十時までに終わります。
    (kaigi wa juu-ji **made** ni owarimasu.)
    The meeting ends at 10 o'clock.

らいしゅう　きんようび　　　　ていしゅつ
3. このレポートは来週の金曜日までに提出してください。
    (kono repooto wa raishuu no kin-youbi **made** ni teishutsu shite kudasai.)
    Please submit this report by next Friday.

しごと　あした　　　お
4. この仕事は明日までに終わらせなければなりません。
    (kono shigoto wa ashita **made** ni owarase nakereba narimasen.)
    This job must be finished by tomorrow.

こんげつ　きゅうりょう　げつまつ　　　しはら
5. 今月の給料は月末までに支払われます。
    (kongetsu no kyuuryou wa getsumatsu **made** ni shiharawaremasu.)
    This month's salary will be paid by the end of the month.

ひこうき　にほん　い　　　じゅうにじかん
6. 飛行機で日本に行くまで、十二時間かかります。
    (hikouki de Nihon ni iku **made**, juuni-jikan kakarimasu.)
    It takes 12 hours to go to Japan by plane.

らいしゅう　かようび　　　　　　　　　　　お
7. 来週の火曜日までには、このプロジェクトを終えなければなりません。
    (raishuu no ka-youbi **made** ni wa, kono purojekuto wo oe nakereba narimasen.)
    I have to finish this project by next Tuesday.

The particle "まで"(made) can also be used emphatically and adds the nuance of "even" while emphasizing something surprising, extreme or unexpected.

Examples: 🔊

むずか かんじ　　よ
1. 難しい漢字まで読める。
   (muzukashii kanji **made** yomeru.)
   I can even read difficult kanji.

Explanation

The particle "まで"(made) is used to indicate the extent of the reader's ability to read kanji, specifically that they can read even difficult ones.

The sentence "難しい漢字まで読める"(muzukashii kanji made yomeru) simply means "can read even difficult Kanji." The word "まで" (made) emphasizes that the reader can comprehend not only simple or intermediate kanji but also complex ones.

さかな す　　　　　ほね　た
2. 魚が好きです。骨まで食べます。
   (sakana ga sukidesu. hone **made** tabemasu.)
   I like fish. I even eat the bones.

Explanation

The particle "まで"(made) is used to indicate the extent of what the speaker likes to eat. The phrase "骨まで食べます" (hone made tabemasu) means "I even eat the bones" and shows that the speaker enjoys eating fish to the point of consuming everything, including the bones.
The particle "まで"(made) emphasizes the speaker's willingness to eat even something that is usually not consumed, in this case, the bones.

かのじょ うた うま　　　たか おんいき　こえ とど
3. 彼女は歌が上手い！高い音域まで声が届くんだ。
   (Kanojo wa uta ga umai! takai on'iki **made** koe ga todokun da.)
   She sings so well! Her voice reaches all the way to the high register.

■ When the particle "まで"(made) is used to indicate an unexpected object, it often means "even" or "also". This usage of "まで"(made) suggests that the object is unexpected or unusual, and is often used to express surprise or disbelief.

The particle "まで" (made) is used to indicate the time or period related to a particular location.

Examples: 🔊

1. 東京から名古屋まではどのぐらい掛かりますか。
   (Tokyo kara Nagoya **made** wa dono gurai kakarimasuka.)
   How long does it take from Tokyo to Nagoya?

2. 今から出発して、東京まで三時間かかります。
   (ima kara shuppatsu shite, Toukyou **made** san-jikan kakarimasu.)
   We'll depart now and it will take three hours to get to Tokyo.

3. 学校から駅まで五分。(gakkou kara eki **made** go-fun.) 5 minutes from school to station.

5 **Indicates a Certain Category, Age, Group of People, Species**

The particle "まで" (made) indicates the age and group of people.

Examples: 🔊

1. 三歳から五歳までのクラス。
   (san-sai kara go-sai **made** no kurasu.)
   The class is from three to five years old.

2. このゲームは子供から大人まで楽しめます。
   (kono gēmu wa kodomo kara otona **made** tanoshimemasu.)
   This game is enjoyable for people of all ages, spanning from children to adults.

3. お年寄りまでが使いやすい携帯電話が欲しいです。
   (O-toshiyori **made** ga tsukai yasui keitai denwa ga hoshii desu.)
   I want a mobile phone that is easy to use, even for elderly people.

■ While "まで" (made) does not specifically indicate age or group, it can be used in a sentence to indirectly convey such information depending on the context.

LESSON 13

Pronunciation	(ya)	
Main use case	To list multiple items	
Formation	Noun + や + Noun / Quantity + や + Quantity	

Explanation

The particle "や" (ya) is used to create a list of multiple items while suggesting that there might be additional things to include. It's quite similar to the particle "と" (to), but there's a subtle difference between them. When you use "や" (ya), it implies the possibility of other items not mentioned in the list, and that not all listed items necessarily apply. In English, you could compare it to saying "and/or, etc." The particle "と" (pronounced "to") can also list items in Japanese, but with a slight difference in meaning. "と" (to) indicate a complete and exhaustive list, leaving no room for additional items. "春と夏と秋と冬" (haru to natsu to aki to fuyu), it would mean "spring, summer, fall, and winter," with no other seasons that could be added to the list.

1 Listing Items 1–2

Listing items: When used in a list, "や"(ya) is similar to the English word "and" and indicates that more items on the list are not being mentioned.

Examples: 🔊

でんしゃ　　　　　たび　す
1. 電車やバスでの旅は好きです。(densha **ya** basu de no tabi wa suki desu.)
    I like traveling by train and bus, (car etc, items in the list that are not being mentioned.)

　　　　　　ほん
2. デスクには、ペンや本やハサミがある。(desuku ni wa, pen **ya** hon **ya** hasami ga aru.)
    There are pens, books and scissors on the desk.

まいあさたまご　　　　　　た
3. 毎朝、卵やパンなどを食べています。(maiasa, tamago **ya** pan nado wo tabete imasu.)
    Every morning I eat egg and bread (and so on.)

117

The Particle "や"(ya) connects two nouns.

Example: 🔊

とうきょう おおさか い
4. 東京や大阪に行きました。(Toukyou **ya** Ousaka ni ikimashita.)
   I went to Tokyo and Osaka.

Explanation

"や"(ya) connects two nouns, implying that examples are being offered and that you are not citing the full list. (As per example 4 you may have visited other places as well).

3   **Indicates Quantity (Approximate)**

The particle "や" (ya) in indicating quantity.

Examples: 🔊

あか   みどり   みせ か
1. 赤いりんごや緑のりんごをあの店で買いました。
   (akai ringo **ya** midori no ringo wo ano mise de kaimashita.)
   I bought red apples and green apples at that store.

わたし いちにち   にわ さんわ ものがたり よ
2. 私は一日で、二話や三話の物語を読みました。
   (watashi wa ichinichi de, ni-wa **ya** san-wa no monogatari wo yomimashita.)
   I read two or three stories in one day.

きのう さんじかん よじかん   ね   おも
3. 昨日は三時間や四時間ぐらい寝たと思います。
   (kinou wa san-jikan **ya** yo-jikan gurai neta to omoimasu.)
   Yesterday, I slept for about 3 or 4 hours, I think.

■ You can use "や"(ya) to list examples of (small) quantities, often accompanied by counters, to indicate an approximate amount.

■ "や"(ya) cannot be used after verb phrases. This is done with "たり"(tari), or "とか"(toka), "や"(ya) is used for nouns. "たり"(tari) is used for verbs or adjectives.

LESSON 14

Pronunciation	(ne)
Main use case	Seeking the listener's agreement, and confirming
Formation	Sentence + Ending Particle ね

Explanation

The particle "ね" (ne) is used at the end of a sentence. It's a bit like saying, "Isn't it?" or "You agree, right?" It's a way to check if the person you're speaking to shares your thoughts. It's a friendly and relaxed way to show you're on the same page. But remember, it's not the best option for serious conversations.

❖　To Seek for Agreement or Confirmation

Examples: 🔊

きょう　あつ
1. 今日は暑いですね。 (kyou wa atsui desu **ne**.)　It's hot today. (don't you agree?)
❖ This is a very common comment in Japanese, and a response would be:
そうですね。 (sou desu **ne**.)　　It is, that's right.

きょう　　　てんき
2. 今日はいい天気ですね。 (kyou wa ii tenki desu **ne**.)　Nice weather today, isn't it?

おい
3. これはとても美味しいですね。 (kore wa totemo oishii desu **ne**.)　It's so delicious, isn't it?

かいだん なが　たいへん
4. この階段は長くて大変ですね。 (kono kaidan wa nagakute taihen desu **ne**.)
These stairs are long and difficult, aren't they?

ふね　　　　　　　　おお
5. あの船のエンジンはとても大きいですね。 (ano fune no enjin wa totemo ookii desu **ne**.)
The engines on that boat are very big, aren't they?

■ This phrase is really helpful when you want to show that you agree with what someone has said.

LESSON 15

よ	**Pronunciation**	(wa)
	Main use case	Indicates the topic of a sentence
	Formation	[A] wa [B] desu. = [A] is [B]

Explanation

The particle ″よ″(yo) indicates the speaker's assumption that the listener doesn't share the speaker's opinion or information, or when the speaker wishes to emphasize new information. It is mostly used in spoken Japanese and can be translated into English as "you know" or "I tell you." Also used for acceptance, agreement or permission. You can use ″よ″(yo) and ″ね″(ne) together as the sentence ending particle ″よね″(yone). In Japanese, the particle ″よ″(yo) is often used to emphasize a statement or to add emphasis to a sentence. It is similar in function to the English exclamation mark or the phrase "you know" or "just so you know".

1   New Information – Using the Particle (yo) to Emphasize

Examples: 🔊

わたし　さけ　の
1. 私はお酒が飲めないよ。(watashi wa o-sake ga nomenai **yo**.)
   I can't drink alcohol, you know.

えいが　　　　おもしろ
2. あの映画はすごく面白かったよ。(ano eiga wa sugoku omoshirokatta **yo**.)
   That movie was really interesting.

おとどい あたま いた　ね
3. 一昨日は頭が痛くて寝ていたよ。(ototoi wa atama ga itakute nete ita **yo**.)
   The day before yesterday I was in bed with a headache.

ひ い いそが
4. すいません。その日は忙しいんですよ。(suimasen. sono hi wa isogashii ndesu **yo**.)
   Excuse me. I'm busy that day.

■ Telling someone new information, using the particle ″よ″(yo) to emphasize this.

This particle can be used when you want to agree on something. This is because if someone asks you a question, your response will be new information to them.

Examples: 🔊

■ You can use ″よ″ when someone is asking something of you.

^{つか}
1. あなたのパソコンを使ってもいいですか。(anata no pasokon wo tsukatte mo iidesu ka?)

Can I use your laptop?

Response: いいですよ。(ii desu **yo.**) Okay.

■ You can use ″よ″ when agreeing to do someone a favor.

^{つか かた おし}
2. 使い方を教えてくれませんか。(tsukaikata wo oshiete kuremasen ka?)

Can you tell me how to use it?

Response: いいですよ。(ii desu **yo.**) Okay.

The combination of the particles ″よ″(yo) and ″ね″(ne) is a common phrase in Japanese and is often used in casual conversation. It can be used to seek agreement or confirmation from the listener, or to express agreement or confirmation.

Examples: 🔊

^{すし おい}
1. この寿司、美味しいよね。(kono sushi, oishii **yone**?) This restaurant is delicious, isn't it?

^{けしき}
2. この景色、きれいだよね。 (kono keshiki, kirei da **yone**?) This view is beautiful, isn't it?

^{きょう てんき}
3. 今日はいい天気だよね。 (kyou wa ii tenki da **yone**?) The weather is nice today, isn't it?

■ In those examples, the speaker thinks that the listener probably agrees with them, and is asking for confirmation.

Complete the sentences below, using either "は" or "が"

1.	きょう　　　あめ 今日【　　】雨です。 Today is rain.	kyou【　　】ame desu.
2.	かのじょ　　　せんせい 彼女【　　】先生です。 She is a teacher.	kanojo【　　】sensei desu.
3.	あなた【　　】どこから来ましたか。 　　　　　　　　　　　　き Where are you from?	anata【　　】doko kara kimashita ka?
4.	あね　　　つく　　　　　　おい 姉【　　】作るケーキは美味しいです。 The cakes that (my) older sister makes are delicious.	ane【　　】tsukuru kēki wa oishii desu.
5.	の　もの なに 飲み物は何【　　】いいですか。 What would you like to drink?	nomimono wa nani【　　】ii desu ka?
6.	いぬ　　　きら あなた【　　】犬【　　】嫌いです。 You don't like dogs.	anata【　　】inu【　　】kirai desu.
7.	わたし　　　ほん　　　す 私【　　】本【　　】好きです。 I like books.	watashi【　　】hon【　　】suki desu.
8.	にほんご　　　わ 日本語【　　】分かりません。 I don't understand Japanese.	Nihongo【　　】wakarimasen.
9.	かぜ　　　つよ 風【　　】強いですね。 The wind is strong, isn't it?	kaze【　　】tsuyoi desu ne?
10.	やま　　　み あなた【　　】あの山【　　】見えませんか。 Can't you see that mountain?	anata【　　】ano yama【　　】 miemasen ka?
11.	にほん　けしき　　　　うつく 日本の景色【　　】美しいです。 Japanese landscapes are beautiful.	Nihon no keshiki【　　】utsukushii desu.

■ Review □Awesome! □Excellent! □Good! □Average! □Poor!

Complete the sentences, using either "は", "が" or "を"

1.	鶏肉【　】美味しいです。 The chicken is delicious.	toriniku 【　】 oishii desu.
2.	私【　】新しい車【　】買いました。 I bought a new car.	watashi 【　】 atarashii kuruma 【　】 kaimashita.
3.	昨日【　】雪【　】降りました。 It snowed yesterday.	kinou 【　】 yuki 【　】 furimashita.
4.	私のバッグ【　】探しています。 I'm looking for my bag.	watashi no baggu 【　】 sagashite imasu.
5.	どこの学校【　】卒業しましたか。 which school did you graduate from?	doko no gakkou 【　】 sotsugyou shimashita ka?
6.	誰【　】これ【　】書いたのですか。 Who wrote this?	dare 【　】 kore 【　】 kaita no desu ka?
7.	そのシャツ【　】見せてください。 Please show me that shirt.	sono shatsu 【　】 misete kudasai.
8.	私【　】日本語【　】勉強します。 I study Japanese.	watashi 【　】 Nihongo 【　】 benkyou shimasu.
9.	倉庫の鍵【　】忘れました。 I forgot my warehouse key.	souko no kagi 【　】 wasuremashita.
10.	あの店の角【　】右に曲がってください。 Please turn right at the corner of that store.	ano mise no kado 【　】 migi ni magatte kudasai.
11.	映画【　】一緒に観ませんか。 Would you like to watch a movie together?	eiga 【　】 issho ni mimasen ka?

■ Review ☐Awesome! ☐Excellent! ☐Good! ☐Average! ☐Poor!

Complete the sentences below, using either "へ" or "に"

1.	わたしたち 私達【　】のプレゼントは何ですか。 What is your present for us?	watashitachi 【　】 no purezento wa nan desu ka?
2.	ともだち　　　でんわ 友達【　】電話をかけました。 I called my friend.	tomodachi 【　】 denwa wo kakemashita.
3.	あした　うみ　　　い 明日は海【　】行くつもりです。 I plan to go to the sea tomorrow.	ashita wa umi 【　】 iku tsumori desu.
4.	わたし はは　ちち　　　てがみ あず 私は母から父【　】の手紙を預かりました。 I received a letter from my mother to my father.	watashi wa haha kara chichi 【　】 no tegami azukarimashita.
5.	おおさか　　　い 大阪【　】行ってみました。 I went to Osaka.	Oosaka 【　】 itte mimashita.
6.	わたし こうえん　　　　い　かた　し 私は公園【　】の行き方は知りません。 I don't know how to get to the park.	watashi wa kouen 【　】 no ikikata wa shirimasen.
7.	こうえん　いす　　　ねこ 公園の椅子【　】猫がいました。 There was a cat on a chair in the park.	kouen no isu 【　】 neko ga imashita.
8.	わたし こうべ　　　　す 私は神戸【　】住んでいます。 I live in Kobe. (City)	watashi wa Koube 【　】 sundeimasu.
9.	あさ ろくじ　　お　うみ　い 朝、六時【　】起きて海【　】行きました。 I woke up at 6 in the morning and went to the beach.	asa, rokuji 【　】 okite umi 【　】 ikimashita.
10.	らいげつ　　　ひろしま　　　い 来月【　】広島【　】行きませんか。 Would you like to go to Hiroshima next month?	raigetsu 【　】 Hiroshima 【　】 ikimasen ka?
11.	ミルク【　】バナナを入れて混ぜましょう。 Add the banana to the milk and mix.	miruku 【　】 banana wo irete mazemashou.

■ Review □Awesome! □Excellent! □Good! □Average! □Poor!

1.	にほんご べんきょう カフェ【 　 】日本語を勉強しています。 I study Japanese at a cafe.	kafe【 　 】Nihongo wo benkyou shiteimasu.
2.	くるま ほっかいどう い 車【 　 】北海道に行きます。 I will go to Hokkaidou by car.	kuruma【 　 】Hokkaidou ni ikimasu.
3.	きもの きぬ でき この着物は絹【 　 】出来ています。 This kimono is made of silk.	kono kimono wa kinu【 　 】dekiteimasu.
4.	よ じかん かえ き 四時間【 　 】帰って来ます。 I will be back in four hours.	yojikan【 　 】kaette kimasu.
5.	ひゃくえん う はな み 百円【 　 】売っている花を見ました。 I saw a flower that sells for 100 yen.	hyakuen【 　 】utteiru hana wo mimashita.
6.	なんにん と 何人【 　 】泊まりますか。 How many people will you be staying with?	nan-nin【 　 】tomarimasu ka?
7.	かさ か どこ【 　 】傘を買ったのですか。 Where did you buy your umbrella?	doko【 　 】kasa wo kattanodesu ka?
8.	としょかん べんきょう 図書館【 　 】勉強しました。 I studied at the library.	toshokan【 　 】benkyou shimashita.
9.	じてんしゃ がっこう い 自転車【 　 】学校に行きます。 I go to school by bike.	jitensha【 　 】gakkou ni ikimasu.
10.	にほんご はな くだ 日本語【 　 】話して下さい。 Please speak in Japanese.	nihongo【 　 】hanashite kudasai.
11.	たいふう いえ こわ 台風【 　 】家が壊れました。 The house was destroyed due to typhoon.	taifuu【 　 】ie ga kowaremashita.

Exercise 4 — Complete the sentences below, using "で"

■ Review □Awesome! □Excellent! □Good! □Average! □Poor!

125

Complete the sentences below, using either "の" or "と"

1.	これはあなた【　　】鉛筆ですか。 （えんぴつ） Is this your pencil?	kore wa anata 【　　】 enpitsu desu ka?
2.	猫【　　】犬を飼っています。 （ねこ　いぬ　か） I have a cat and a dog.	neko 【　　】 inu wo katteimasu.
3.	妻【　　】映画を楽しみました。 （つま　えいが　たの） I enjoyed watching movies with my wife.	tsuma 【　　】 eiga wo tanoshimi mashita
4.	日本【　　】写真はありますか。 （にほん　しゃしん） Do you have any photos of Japan?	Nihon 【　　】 shashin wa arimasu ka?
5.	卵【　　】牛乳を買いました。 （たまご　ぎゅうにゅう　か） I bought eggs and milk.	tamago 【　　】 gyunyu wo kaimashita.
6.	水族館【　　】後ろに海が見えます。 （すいぞくかん　うし　うみ　み） You can see the sea behind the aquarium.	suizokukan 【　　】 ushiro ni umi ga miemasu.
7.	もし、これを食べる【　　】太りますか。 （た　ふと） If I eat this, will I gain weight?	moshi, kore wo taberu 【　　】 futori masu ka?
8.	難しい質問だ【　　】思います。 （むずか　しつもん　おも） I think that it's a difficult question.	muzukashii shitsumon da 【　　】 omoimasu.
9.	明日は彼【　　】誕生日ですか。 （あした　かれ　たんじょうび） Is it his birthday tomorrow?	ashita wa kare 【　　】 tanjyoubi desu ka?
10.	白【　　】黒のどちらの色が好きですか。 （しろ　くろ　いろ　す） Which color do you prefer, white or black?	shiro 【　　】 kuro no dochira no iro ga suki desu ka?
11.	机【　　】下や鞄の中を探しました。 （つくえ　した　かばんなか　さが） I searched under my desk and in my bag.	tsukue 【　　】 shita ya kaban no naka wo sagashimashiita.

■ Review □Awesome! □Excellent! □Good! □Average! □Poor!

126

Complete the sentences below, using "か"

1.	なんさい あなたは何歳です【　　】。 How old are you?	anata wa nan-sai desu 【　　】?
2.	あした　きんようび 明日は金曜日です【　　】。 Is it Friday tomorrow?	ashita wa kin'youbi desu 【　　】?
3.	いっしょ　た 一緒に食べましょう【　　】。 Shall we eat together?	issho ni tabemashou 【　　】?
4.	しごと　なん あなたの仕事は何です【　　】。 What is your job?	anata no shigoto wa nan desu 【　　】?
5.	なんじ　はじ　　　　　し 何時に始まる【　　】知っていますか。 Do you know what time it will start?	nanji ni hajimaru 【　　】 shitteimasu ka?
6.	さる　　　　　　　み あれが猿【　　】どうかよく見えません。 I can't quite see if that is a monkey or not.	are ga saru 【　　】 dou ka yoku miemasen.
7.	おど　おど　　　　　　き 踊るか踊らない【　　】決めていない。 I haven't decided whether to dance or not.	odoru ka odoranai 【　　】 kimeteinai.
8.	や　とり　　　　すし　た 焼き鳥【　　】寿司が食べたいです。 I would like to eat yakitori or sushi.	yakitori 【　　】 sushi ga tabetaidesu.
9.	た　　ふと もし、これを食べると太ります【　　】。 If I eat this, will I gain weight?	moshi, kore wo taberu to futorimasu 【　　】?
10.	こんしゅう　　　らいしゅう　にもつ　おく 今週【　　】来週には荷物を送れます。 I can send a package this week or next.	konshuu 【　　】 raishuu niwa nimotsu wo okuremasu.
11.	あした　あめ　　　　　　わ 明日は雨【　　】どう【　　】分からない。 I'm not sure if it will rain or not tomorrow.	ashita wa ame 【　　】 dou 【　　】 wakaranai.

■　Review　☐Awesome!　☐Excellent!　☐Good!　☐Average!　☐Poor!

Complete the sentences below, using either "も" or "や"

1.	あなた【　】行きませんか。 Why don't you go too?	anata 【　】 iki masen ka?
2.	母は花【　】果物【　】買いました。 My mother bought both flowers and fruit.	haha wa hana 【　】 kudamon 【　】 kaimashita.
3.	一匹【　】二匹の魚だけでは足りません。 One or two fish is not enough.	ippiki 【　】 nihiki no sakana dake dewa tarimasen.
4.	彼【　】来なかった。 He didn't come either.	kare 【　】 konakatta.
5.	電車【　】バスで来てください。 Please come by train or bus.	densha 【　】 basu de kitekudasai.
6.	秋には葉が赤【　】黄色に変わる。 The leaves turn red and yellow in fall.	aki niwa ha ga aka 【　】 kiiro ni kawaru.
7.	百個【　】それを作りました。 I made a hundred of those.	hyakko 【　】 sore wo tukurimashita.
8.	七台【　】八台の車が行くのを見ました。 I saw seven or eight cars going.	nana-dai 【　】 hachi-dai no kuruma ga iku nowo mimashita.
9.	海【　】川に行くのが好きです。 I like to go to the sea or river.	umi 【　】 kawa ni iku noga suki desu.
10.	何度【　】これを確認しました。 I have confirmed this many times.	nando 【　】 kore wo kakunin shimashita.
11.	サラダにトマト【　】胡瓜も入れました。 I added both tomatoes and cucumbers to the salad.	sarada ni tomato 【　】 kyuuri mo iremashita.

■ Review　☐Awesome!　☐Excellent!　☐Good!　☐Average!　☐Poor!

Complete the sentences below using either "から" or "まで"

1.	山【　　】一羽の鷹が飛んで来ました。 A hawk flew in from the mountains.	yama 【　　】 ichi-wa no taka ga tondekimashita.
2.	あの仕事をするのは明日【　　】です。 I have until tomorrow to do that job.	ano shigoto wo suru nowa ashita 【　　】 desu.
3.	九月【　　】ハワイに住む予定です。 I will be living in Hawaii from September.	kugatsu 【　　】 Hawaii ni sumu yotei desu.
4.	ここ【　　】駅【　　】は近いですか。 Is it close to the station from here?	koko 【　　】 eki 【　　】 wa chikai desu ka?
5.	最後【　　】頑張りましょう。 Let's do our best till the end.	saigo 【　　】 ganbarimashou.
6.	十時【　　】出掛けます。 I will go out at ten o'clock.	jyuu-ji 【　　】 dekakemasu.
7.	家から公園【　　】歩いて六分です。 Six-minute walk from the house to the park.	ie kara kouen 【　　】 aruite ro-ppun desu.
8.	寒い【　　】その戸を閉めてください。 Close that door because it's cold.	samui 【　　】 sono to wo shimetekudasai.
9.	彼は優しい【　　】好きです。 He is kind, that's why I like him.	kare wa yasashii 【　　】 suki desu.
10.	ここ【　　】そこ【　　】は遠いですよ。 That's really far from here!	koko 【　　】 soko 【　　】 wa tooi desu yo!
11.	それは熱い【　　】、気をつけてください。 That is hot, so be careful.	sore wa atsui 【　　】 ki wo tsuketekudasai.

■ Review □Awesome! □Excellent! □Good! □Average! □Poor!

1.	きょう てんき 今日の天気はいいです 【　　】。 Today's weather is nice, isn't it?	kyou no tenki wa ii desu 【　　】.
2.	あした　　　　あつ 明日はもっと暑いでしょう 【　　】。 It will be hotter tomorrow, won't it?	ashita wa motto atsui deshou 【　　】?
3.	わたし　　　　きら 私はミルクが嫌いなんです 【　　】。 I don't really like milk, you know?	watashi wa miruku ga kirai nan desu 【　　】.
4.	たいへん それは大変です 【　　】。 That's too bad.	sore wa taihen desu 【　　】.
5.	ま ちょっと、待って 【　　】。 Wait a moment!	chotto, matte 【　　】!
6.	あと また後で 【　　】。 See you later!	mata ato de 【　　】!
7.	みち あなたはこっちの道です 【　　】【　　】。 You go this way, right?	anata wa kocchi no michi desu 【　　】【　　】?
8.	がんば 頑張ってください 【　　】。 Please try your best, alright?	ganbatte kudasai 【　　】!
9.	こと そんな事しないで 【　　】。 Don't do something like that.	sonna koto shinai de 【　　】.
10.	あぶ それは危ない 【　　】。 It's dangerous!	sore wa abunai 【　　】.
11.	あつ それは熱くなかったです 【　　】。 It wasn't that hot, you know?	sore wa atsuku nakatta desu 【　　】?

■ Review □Awesome! □Excellent! □Good! □Average! □Poor!

Try to identify the following particles function.

1. Which particle indicates the topic of a sentence?

が	で	は	の

2. Which particle indicates the subject of a sentence?

は	に	も	が

3. Which particle indicates a direct object?

を	の	よ	は

4. Which particle indicates to a location or time particle?

まで	から	に	へ

5. Which particle is used to connect two or more nouns It is translated as "and" or "with"?

も	と	や	を

6. Which particle indicates that a statement is generally a question and is found at the end of a phrase?

が	も	と	か

7. Which particle indicates possession?

の	か	と	ね

■ Review ☐Awesome! ☐Excellent! ☐Good! ☐Average! ☐Poor!

Try to identify the following particle's function.

1. Which particle indicates the object of a sentence and can follow nouns and noun phrases?

は	で	を	に

2. Which particle indicates the direction in which someone or something moves, with focus on arrival rather than on direction?

と	に	を	で

3. Which particle conjoins two or more nouns to show that they exist together, but are used in a listed manner?

や	へ	から	と

4. Which particle indicates the location of an action and follows the subject phrase in a sentence?

で	か	も	まで

5. Particle is similar to the English words "too" or "also". It always is related to the precedent noun?

から	よ	で	も

6. Which particle indicates an endpoint in time?

に	から	まで	で

7. Which particle is used for confirmation and seeking the listener's agreement?

へ	ね	よ	か

■ Review ☐Awesome! ☐Excellent! ☐Good! ☐Average! ☐Poor!

Exercise 1		Exercise 2		Exercise 3		Exercise 4		Exercise 5		Exercise 6	
1	は	1	は	1	へ	1	で	1	の	1	か
2	は	2	は-を	2	に	2	で	2	と	2	か
3	は	3	は-が	3	に&へ	3	で	3	と	3	か
4	が	4	を	4	へ	4	で	4	の	4	か
5	が	5	を	5	に&へ	5	で	5	と	5	か
6	は-が	6	が-を	6	へ	6	で	6	の	6	か
7	は-が	7	を	7	に	7	で	7	と	7	か
8	は	8	は-を	8	に	8	で	8	と	8	か
9	が	9	を	9	に-に	9	で	9	の	9	か
10	は-が	10	を	10	に&へ	10	で	10	と	10	か
11	は	11	を	11	に	11	で	11	の	11	か

Exercise 7			
1	も	7	も
2	や-も	8	や
3	や	9	や
4	も	10	も
5	や	11	や
6	や		

Exercise 8			
1	から	7	まで
2	まで	8	から
3	から	9	から
4	から-まで	10	から-まで
5	まで	11	から
6	から		

Exercise 10		Exercise 11	
1	は	1	を
2	が	2	に
3	を	3	と
4	に	4	で
5	と	5	も
6	か	6	まで
7	の	7	ね

Exercise 9	1	2	3	4	5	6	7	8	9	10	11
	ね	ね	よ	ね	よ	ね	よ-ね	ね	よ	よ	よ

Note:

QUIZ 3: In sentences 3, 5, and 10, either へ or に can be used. Both へ and に are used to determine a location or direction and can sometimes be used interchangeably.

However, they do express slightly different things. へ ("e") was originally the particle that describes a direction, while に ("ni") was used to indicate a place and a destination.

は Indicates the topic

あしたは土曜日です。
ashita wa doyoubi desu.
As for tomorrow, it's Saturday.

Marks the topic

肉は食べませんが、鶏肉は食べます。
niku wa tabemasen ga, toriniku wa tabemasu.
I don't eat meat, but I do eat chicken.

Marks a contrast

が Indicates the subject

あそこに、コンビニがあります。
asoko ni konbini ga arimasu.
There's a convenience store over there.

Marks the subject

猫が好きです。
neko ga suki desu.
I like cats.

Marks an object of desire

を Indicates the direct object

私は、日本語を勉強します。
watashi wa Nihongo wo benkyou shimasu.
I study Japanese.

Marks the object

橋を渡ります。
hashi wo watari masu.
I will cross the bridge.

Marks the place of motion

へ Indicates direction/destination

これは空港へ行きますか。
kore wa kuukou e ikimasu ka?
Does this go to the airport?

Marks a direction or destination

友達へ電話をかけました。
tomodachi e denwa wo kakemashita.
I called my friend.

Marks the recipient of an action

に Indicates the location or time

わたしは図書館にいます。
watashi wa toshokan ni imasu.
I'm in the library.

Marks location

六月に日本へ行きます。
roku-gatsu ni Nihon e ikimasu.
I'm going to Japan in June.

Marks time

で Indicates location of an action

東京で会いましょう。
Toukyou de aimashou.
See you in Tokyo.

Mark the location of an action

この机は木でできています。
kono tsukue wa ki de dekiteimasu.
This desk is made of wood.

Marks material

の Indicate possession

これは、私の本です。
kore wa, watashi no hon desu.
This is my book.

Indicate possession

日本の車が好きです。
Nihon no kuruma ga suki desu.
I like Japanese cars.

Indicate a category

と Connecting particle

卵と牛乳を買いました。
tamago to gyuunyuu wo kaimashita.
I bought eggs and milk.

Means "and"

田中さんと食事をしました。
Tanaka-san to shokuji wo shimashita.
I had a meal with Mr.Tanaka.

Means "with"

か Marks a question

あなたは何歳ですか。
anata wa nan-sai desu ka?
How old are you?

Marks a question

行くか行かないか分からない。
iku ka ikanai ka wakaranai.
I don't know if I'll go or not.

As "or".

も Means "also"

くつが欲しい。かばんも欲しい。
kutsu ga hoshii. kaban mo hoshii.
I want shoes. And I also want a bag.

Means "also" or "too"

その本は何度も読みました。
sono hon wa nando mo yomimashita.
I read that book many times.

Mark emphasis

から Indicates a starting point

ここから駅は近いです。
koko kara eki wa chikai desu.
From here, the train station is close.

Means "from"

ぶどうからワインを作る。
budou kara wain wo tsukuru.
I make wine from grapes.

Indicates materials

まで Indicates an endpoint in time

会議は十時までに終わります。
kaigi wa juu-ji made ni owarimasu.
The meeting ends at 10 o'clock.

Marks an endpoint in time

明日まで待ちます。
ashita made machimasu.
I will wait until tomorrow.

Indicates a time limitation

Summary of Basic Particles

や Indicates a list of multiple items

電車やバスでの旅は好きです。
densha ya basu deno tabi wa suki desu.
I like traveling by train and bus .

Marks a list of multiple items

東京や大阪に行きました。
Toukyou ya Osaka ni ikimashita.
I went to Tokyo and Osaka.

Noun + や + noun.

よ Indicates emphasis at the end of a sentence

私はお酒が飲めないよ。
watashi wa o-sake ga nomenai yo.
I can't drink alcohol, you know.

Emphasizes

あの映画はすごく面白かったよ。
ano eiga wa sugoku omoshirokatta yo.
That movie was really interesting.

Emphasizes

ね Indicates a Agreement, and confirmation

今日はいい天気ですね。
kyou wa ii tenki desu ne?
Nice weather today, isn't it?

Seeks agreement or confirmation

美味しいですね。
oishii desu ne?
It's delicious, isn't it?

Seeks agreement or confirmation

136

UNIT 3

<ruby>紹<rt>しょう</rt>介<rt>かい</rt></ruby>する

Self-introduction

- Introducing myself.
- Conversation.
- Bowing.

LESSON 1

> ➤ あみさん

こんにちは、はじめまして。あみです。 （Hello, Nice to meet to you. I'm Ami.）
 konichiwa, hajimemashite. Ami desu.

わたし だいがく がくせい
私は、大学の学生です。 （I am a university student.）
 watashi wa, daigaku no gakusei desu.

だいがく びじゅつまな
大学では、美術を学んでいます。
daigaku de wa, bijutsu wo manande imasu. （I'm studying art at university.）

ねが
どうぞ、よろしくお願いします。
 douzo, yoroshiku o-negaishimasu. （I'm so pleasured to meet you.）

The standard form of saying your name in Japanese uses the following sentence patterns:

"わたしは (name) です。"

"わたしは"(watashi wa) means "I am". "です"(desu) at the end of a sentence signifies politeness.

Formal

When introducing yourself formally in Japanese, you would use the following sentence pattern: (name) と、もうします。 "This expression" (The word) と、もうします (to moushi masu) translates to "I am called." It is considered more polite and appropriate for formal situations.

Informal

To casually introduce yourself, you can say your name and add "です"(desu).
For example, "あみです。" It means "I'm Ami." This informal way is commonly used when meeting someone of the same age or status, like a friend of a friend, or during informal gatherings.

■ **LESSON 2**

The conversation "会話"(かいわ-kaiwa) is between two people who are meeting for the first time. Chris is an American studying the Japanese language and Ami is a Japanese student. (Informal occasion or meeting).

あみ(Ami)：はじめまして、あみです。　　Nice to meet to you, I'm Ami.
　　　　　　(hajimemashite. Ami desu.)

クリス(Chris)：はじめまして、クリスです。Nice to meet to you, I'm Chris.
　　　　　　　(hajimemashite. Chris desu.)

　　　　　　　　　　　　　き
あみ(Ami)：どちらから来ましたか。　　　　Where are you from?
　　　　　　(dochira kara kimashita ka?)

　　　　　わたし　　　　　　き
クリス(Chris)：私はアメリカから来ました。　　I came from America.
　　　　　　　(watashi wa Amerika kara kimashita.)

　　　　　　　　　　き
あみ(Ami)：いつ ここに来ましたか。　　　When did you come here?
　　　　　　(itsu koko ni kimashita ka?)

　　　　　　　ねん　がつ　き
クリス(Chris)：2019年10月に来ました。　　I came at October in 2019.
　　　　　　　(ni-sen juu-kyuu-nen Juu-gatsu ni kimashita.)

　　　　　　　　　　ねが
あみ(Ami)：どうぞ、よろしくお願いします、クリスさん。I'm so pleasured to meet you, Mr.Chris.
　　　　　　(douzo, yoroshiku o-negaishimasu, Kurisu-san.)

❖　The phrase "yoroshiku o-negaisimasu" has various meanings. It is mainly used when you want to ask for something, when you want to show respect or favor to someone, or when you want someone to accept you.

❖　There is no English equivalent to this common phrase that properly summarizes its many meanings when spoken in Japanese, it depends on the situation.

LESSON 3

The politeness system in Japanese is very complex, which is often cited as one of the main reasons for its difficulty. I agree with this completely. You may use different words, or even completely different expressions, based on the relationship between you and the person/people you are speaking with.

1. How Do You Ask Age in Japanese

To ask someone "How old are you?," you can say:

　　　なんさい
1. 何歳ですか。   (nan-sai desu ka?) (Casual)

2. おいくつですか。(o-ikutsu desu ka?) (Polite)

3. おいくつになりますか。(o-ikutsu ni nari masu ka?)
   How old will you be?   (More polite)

> **Note:** Asking someone's age would be rude in Japan, where most people do not want to divulge much about themselves.

> Check out **unit 5 page 165** to learn how to say your age in Japanese.

> **Note:** In some cases, the person who is asked the question may be distrustful, and there is a tendency that it is impolite to ask questions about age, especially to women, so ask this on birthdays, etc.

2. How Do You Ask Someone Name in Japanese

Asking for someone's name is a simple task.

　　なまえ
1. 名前は。   (namae wa?) What is your name?   (Casual).

2. お名前は。(o-namae wa?) What is your name? (Polite).

❑   The honorific "お" adds , you must use it for polite form.

140

LESSON 4 🔊

Many students or learner Japanese know the word "watashi"－私（わたし）, which means "I", however, In Japan, there are many words for talking about oneself. For example, watashi, boku, and ore you may be confused about which is the most appropriate one.

1. watashi（わたし）

"watashi" is a neutral and polite pronoun and can be used in most formal and informal situations. Both men and women can use it without issues. It's the standard pronoun for self-reference and is widely accepted across various contexts.

Example: 私は日本人です。（watashi wa nihonjin desu.）I am Japanese.

2. boku（ぼく）

"boku"（ぼく）is a word men and young boys use in Japanese to refer to themselves. It's like saying "I" or "me" in English. In more formal situations, a man might use "watashi"（わたし）instead. But in everyday conversations, "boku" is the common choice for guys to talk about themselves.

Example: ぼくは学生です。（boku wa gakusei desu.）I am a student.

3. ore（おれ）

"ore" is another word Japanese men often use. However, it's essential to be careful because it can come across as rude, depending on the situation and the person they're talking to. So, Japanese men use these three words "Boku"（ぼく）"Watashi"（わたし）, and "Ore"（おれ）depending on whom they're speaking with and the specific situation they are in.

Example: おれは音楽が好きだ。（ore wa ongaku ga suki da.）I like music.

Notes:

- "Ore" can sound cocky and is often used to show aggressiveness and masculinity.

- When meeting someone for the first time, it's better to use "Watashi" Once you've become somewhat close, you can use "Boku" And if you become very close, you can use "ore."

- For women, "Watashi" is suitable to use in any situation and with anyone.

- Another word for "I" is "Watakushi" "Watakushi" is the more polite version of "Watashi"

■ **LESSON 5** 🔊

Learning the most frequent expressions you use daily and adding them to your Japanese vocabulary is a great way to learn; if you've recently moved to Japan or are planning on it, you'll need to learn all the most useful Japanese phrases.

1. hai (はい)

"hai" means "yes" and is one of the first things you probably learned to say in Japanese. It's a polite way to say "yes" in formal situations. If you're having a casual conversation, you can also use "ee" (ええ) or "un" (うん), depending on the situation and your speaking style. However, "hai" will always work no matter what the context.

Example: はい、分かりました。(hai, wakarimashita.) Yes, I understand.

2. iie (いいえ)

"iie" means "no" in Japanese. It's a formal way to say it. However, in everyday conversations, Japanese people often use various expressions to avoid giving a strong "no." For instance, they might use "iya" (いや) or "uun" (ううん) instead of a direct "no." These softer expressions are commonly used to maintain a more polite and harmonious tone during interactions.

Example: いいえ、それはできません。(iie, sore wa dekimasen.) No, that's not possible.

3. sou desu (そうです)

"sou desu" means "It is so" or "That's right" in Japanese. You can shorten it in a casual speech by omitting "desu" and saying "sou." It's often used together with (はい、そうです。), which means "Yes, that's right."

Example:

せき
Q: ここはあなたの席ですか。(Q: koko wa anata no seki desu ka?)
　　Is this your seat?

せき
A: はい、そうです、わたしの席です。(A: hai sou desu, watashi no seki desu.)
　　Yes, that's right, this is my seat.

■ **LESSON 5** 🔊

Learning the most frequent expressions you use daily and adding them to your Japanese vocabulary is a great way to learn; if you've recently moved to Japan or are planning on it, you'll need to learn all the most useful Japanese phrases.

4. chigaimasu（ちがいます）

"chigaimasu" means "wrong" or "You're wrong" It's used when someone asks a question or makes a statement, and you want to disagree or correct them politely. In a friendly context, it's a way of expressing a different opinion or view on something.

Example:

やまだ　　　ほん
Q: これは山田さんの本ですか。(Q: kore wa Yamada-san no hon desu ka?)

Is this Mr. Yamada's book?

ほん
A: いいえ、ちがいます。これは私の本です。(A: iie, chigaimasu. kore wa watashi no hon desu.)

No, that's not correct. This is my book.

5. maa maa desu（まあまあです）

"maa maa" is a Japanese expression that can be translated as "It's okay" or "So-so" It's used when you want to describe something as being average or just okay, neither good nor bad.

Example1:

ちょうし
Q: 調子はどうですか。(choushi wa dou desu ka?) How is it going?

A: まあまあです。(maa maa desu.) Just okay, neither good nor bad.

Example2:

よ そだ
Q: ぶどうは良く育っていますか。 (Q: budou wa yoku sodatte imasu ka?) Are the grapes growing well?

A: まあまあです。(A: maa maa desu.) It's okay. / So-so.

143

LESSON 5

---

6. genki (げんき)

"genki" is a Japanese word often used to express being energetic, lively, healthy, or full of vitality. It conveys a sense of well-being and good physical and mental health. When someone says they are "genki" it means they feel good and healthy. The Kanji "元"(gen) means "origin" or "source" and the Kanji "気" (ki) means "energy" or "spirit" Together, they form "元気" which still represent being lively, energetic, and healthy. In casual conversation, you might hear friends asking each other, "Genki desu ka?" which translates to "How are you feeling?" or "Are you doing well?" But In more formal settings or when speaking to someone older or of higher status, it is customary to add the honorific "お" (o) at the beginning of "元気" (genki). This addition shows respect and politeness when inquiring about someone's well-being.

Example:

Q: お元気ですか。(O-genki desu ka?) How are you feeling?

A: はい、元気です。 (Hai, genki desu.)

---

7. wakarimasu ka (わかりますか)

Is a polite way of asking "Do you understand?" or "Do you get it?" The verb "わかります" means "to understand," and "か"(ka) is a particle indicating the statement into a question.

8. wakarimasen (わかりません)

Is a negative form of the verb "wakarimasu" It means "(I) don't understand" Depending on the context, "wakarimasen" means I don't know or I don't understand. It is the polite negative form of the verb "wakaru" (わかる), which means to understand.

Example:

きょう　しゅくだい
先生: 今日の宿題はわかりますか。(Sensei: kyou no shukudai wa wakarimasu ka?)
 Teacher: What is today's homework?

生徒: すみません、わかりません。 (Seito: sumimasen, wakarimasen.)
 Student: I'm sorry, I don't know.

Note: You might have heard Japanese speakers say "わからない" (wakaranai). So, what's the difference between "wakarimasen" and "wakaranai"? It's pretty simple! Both mean "I don't understand" or "I don't know," but "wakarimasen" is the polite version. "On the other hand, "wakaranai" is more casual and can be used with friends or people you know well.

LESSON 5 🔊

9. daijoubu (だいじょうぶ)

"Daijoubu" in Japanese can mean "It's okay." or "I'm okay." depending on the situation or context. The meaning of the expression can vary based on the situation and the subject involved.

Affirmative informal	大丈夫。	(daijoubu.)
Affirmative formal	大丈夫です。	(daijoubu desu.)
Informal interrogative	大丈夫。	(daijoubu?)
Formal interrogative	大丈夫ですか。	(daijoubu desu ka?)

- You can also just say 大丈夫？ (daijoubu?) With a rising intonation but this more casual.
- 大丈夫です (daijoubu desu) means I'm okay or it's okay in Japanese.
- 大丈夫ですか？ (daijoubu desu ka?) Means are you okay?

How to you use (daijoubu)

- When you see someone feeling uncomfortable or meet someone who is in trouble, and you want to show your concern or give a hand, you can ask "大丈夫ですか？"

Example 1: あなたは**大丈夫ですか**。
　　　　　anata wa **daijoubu desu ka**?
　　　　　Are you okay?

- If you wish to inquire, paying by credit card is accepted at the store.

Example 2: クレジットカードで**大丈夫ですか**。
　　　　　kurejittokādo de **daijobu desu ka**?
　　　　　Can I pay by credit card?

■ **LESSON 6**

In Japan, people often bow as a way of showing respect or humility in various daily situations. It's called "お辞儀" (o-jigi) and carries significant meanings, making it an essential aspect of Japanese culture.

Bows are a common practice in Japan and have various uses in social interactions:

- When meeting someone for the first time.
- During religious ceremonies, especially in Shinto.
- In workplaces, like training staff and company employees.
- In service-related jobs or when dealing with customers.
- For saying hello, goodbye, showing gratitude, or apologizing.
- In ceremonial events, such as weddings and other religious occasions.
- In sports events, martial arts tournaments, and artistic performances.
- At formal meetings, people exchange business cards as they introduce themselves.

Most Japanese people don't expect foreigners to know all the bowing rules, so a simple nod of the head is usually enough. Regarding bowing, both men and women maintain a straight back and keep their hands at their sides.

There are three main types of bows:

1. Informal Bow: This is a casual bow where you just tilt your head forward about 15 degrees.

2. Formal Bow: A more respectful bow is done at a 30-degree angle, which is deeper than the informal bow.

3. Deep Bow: The most formal bow, where you bend your back about 45 degrees, lower your head, and hold the bow for more than three seconds.

 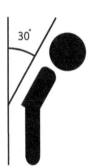 

UNIT 4

<ruby>数<rt>かず</rt></ruby>の<ruby>数<rt>かぞ</rt></ruby>え<ruby>方<rt>かた</rt></ruby>

How to count numbers

1 2 3 4 5
一 二 三 四 五

6 7 8 9 0
六 七 八 九 零

- Numbers up to one Hundred.
- Bigger numbers.

LESSON 1

Counting up to 100 in Japanese becomes surprisingly easy once you understand the first ten numbers. The exciting thing is that there's a consistent pattern to follow! After you reach 10, you can just add the next number to continue counting.

Here's how that looks:

じゅういち
11 is 十一 (juuichi): 10 + 1
and so on up to 19.

じゅうに
12 is 十二 (juuni): 10 + 2

Once you reach twenty, the concept remains the same, but you begin by counting the 10s.

にじゅう
20 is 二十 (nijuu): 2 10's
and so on, up to 99.

にじゅういち
21 is 二十一 (nijuuichi): 2 10's + 1

ひゃく
100 gets a new word: 百 (hyaku).

No.	Hiragana	Kanji	Rōmaji
1	いち	一	ichi
2	に	二	ni
3	さん	三	san
4	よん/し	四	yon/shi
5	ご	五	go
6	ろく/む	六	roku
7	なな/しち	七	nana/shichi
8	はち	八	hachi
9	きゅう/く	九	kyuu/ku
10	じゅう	十	juu

■ **LESSON 2** 🔊

In Japanese, we express 20 as '2 of 10,' 30 as '3 of 10,' and so on. For instance, 20 is said as 'ni juu' (two ten). This pattern continues for numbers from 30 to 90. However, there's a little twist with 40, 70, and 90 because there are two ways to say the numbers 4, 7, and 9 in Japanese, 40 can be pronounced as 'yonjuu' or 'shijuu,' while 70 can be 'nanajuu' or 'shichijuu.'

No.	Hiragana	Kanji	Rōmaji
11	じゅういち	十一	juuichi
12	じゅうに	十二	juuni
13	じゅうさん	十三	juusan
14	じゅうよん/じゅうし	十四	juuyon/juushi
15	じゅうご	十五	juugo
16	じゅうろく	十六	juuroku
17	じゅうなな/じゅうしち	十七	juunana/jyuushichi
18	じゅうはち	十八	juuhachi
19	じゅうく/じゅうきゅう	十九	juukyu/juukyuu
20	に ni　じゅう juu　にじゅう nijuu 2　X　10　=　20	二十	nijuu

No.	Hiragana	Kanji	Rōmaji
30	さんじゅう	三十	sanjuu
40	よんじゅう	四十	yonjuu
50	ごじゅう	五十	gojuu
60	ろくじゅう	六十	rokujuu
70	ななじゅう/しちじゅう	七十	nanajuu/shitijyuu
80	はちじゅう	八十	hachijuu
90	きゅうじゅう	九十	kyuujuu
100	ひゃく	百	hyaku

LESSON 3 🔊

The primary unit in the English number system is one thousand (1,000), and one million is one thousand thousand.

However, in the Japanese number system, the primary unit is ten thousand (10,000), and ten thousand (万 – man) forms the next unit, "hundred million" (億 – oku). Translating large numbers between English and Japanese can be challenging for language learners.

Numbers	Kanji	Kana + Romaji
1	一	いち (ichi)
2	二	に (ni)
3	三	さん (san)
4	四	よん (yon)
5	五	ご (go)
6	六	ろく (roku)
7	七	なな (nana)
8	八	はち (hachi)
9	九	きゅう (kyuu)
10	十	じゅう (juu)
100	百	ひゃく (hyaku)
1,000	千	せん (sen)
10,000	万	まん (man)
100,000	十万	じゅうまん (juuman)
1,000,000	百万	ひゃくまん (hyakuman)
10,000,000	千万	せんまん (senman)
100,000,000	一億	いちおく (ichioku)
1,000,000,000	十億	じゅうおく (juuoku)
1,000,000,000,000	一兆	いっちょう (icchou)

UNIT 5

ひ　つき　ねん　しゅう
日、月、年、週

Days, Months,
Years, Weeks

- Days of the week.
- Counting weeks.
- Useful words related to the week.
- Days of the month.
- Months.
- Counting months.
- Useful words related to the month.
- Date in Japanese.
- Years.
- Counting years / Vocabulary.
- Year Age.
- The actual words talk about age in Japanese.
- Weather.
- Seasons.

LESSON 1

The Week 週 (しゅう-shuu)

In Japanese, the days of the week are represented by specific kanji characters, each connected to one of the five elements (wood, fire, earth, metal, and water) and the sun and moon.

Remember that each day ends with the kanji "曜日-よう び" (youbi), and they are associated with different elements of nature. "youbi" means "day of the week" and is pronounced like "yoh" in yo-yo and "bee," with emphasis on "yoh." The varying part in the names of the days is what comes first.

The good news is that the first part of each day's name has a straightforward meaning and corresponding kanji, making them easy to remember.

Hiragana	Kanji	Rōmaji	English	Radical
げつようび	月曜日	getsu you bi	Monday	Moon
かようび	火曜日	ka you bi	Tuesday	Fire
すいようび	水曜日	sui you bi	Wednesday	Water
もくようび	木曜日	moku you bi	Thursday	Tree
きんようび	金曜日	kin you bi	Friday	Gold
どようび	土曜日	do you bi	Saturday	Earth
にちようび	日曜日	nichi you bi	Sunday	Sun

LESSON 2 🔊

週間 (shuukan)

After learning about the days of the week, let's move on to counting weeks in Japanese.

Below is a table showing how to count the weeks:

Hiragana	Kanji	Rōmaji	English
いっしゅうかん	1週間	i sshuu kan	One week
にしゅうかん	2週間	ni shuu kan	Two weeks
さんしゅうかん	3週間	san shuu kan	Three weeks
よんしゅうかん	4週間	yon shuu kan	Four weeks
ごしゅうかん	5週間	go shuu kan	Five weeks

■ You can use the same pattern as other counters to count more than five weeks in Japanese.

Here are the numbers for counting weeks:

6週間　　　　　roku shuu kan　　　　6 weeks

7週間　　　　　nana shuu kan　　　　7 weeks

8週間　　　　　ha sshuu kan　　　　8 weeks

9週間　　　　　kyuu shuu kan　　　　9 weeks

10週間　　　　　ju sshuu kan　　　　10 weeks

11週間　　　　　juu i sshuu kan　　　　11 weeks

12週間　　　　　juu ni shuu kan　　　　12 weeks

LESSON 3 🔊

Here are some useful words related to the week in Japanese:

1. konshuu（こんしゅう）

"This week" is pronounced, "konshuu"（今週）. The first kanji is ″今″ just like with ″今日″ and the second kanji is ″週″(shuu), meaning "week."

こんしゅうとうきょう　い
Example 1:　今週は東京に行きます。
　　　　　　　　（konshuu wa toukyou ni ikimasu.)
　　　　　　　　I'm going to Tokyo this week.

こんしゅうてんき
Example 2:　今週は天気がいい。
　　　　　　　　（konshuu wa tenki ga ii.)
　　　　　　　　The weather is nice this week.

こんしゅう　にほんご
Example 3:　今週は日本語のテストがあります。
　　　　　　　　（konshuu wa Nihongo no tesuto ga arimasu.)
　　　　　　　　I have a Japanese test this week.

2024年3月

日	月	火	水	木	金	土
			1	2	3	4
5	6	7	8	9	10	11
12	13	14	15	16	17	18
19	20	21	22	23	24	25
26	27	28	29	30	31	

2. senshuu（せんしゅう）

"Last week" is pronounced, "senshuu"（先週）. The first kanji is ″先″(sen) and means "previous".

せんしゅう　　　　　い
Example 1:　先週、東京に行きました。
　　　　　　　　（senshuu, toukyou ni ikimashita.)
　　　　　　　　I went to Tokyo last week.

せんしゅう　しごと　やす
Example 2:　先週は仕事を休みました。
　　　　　　　　（senshuu wa shigoto wo yasumimashita.)
　　　　　　　　I was off work last week.

▌ **LESSON 3** 🔊

Here are some useful words related to the week in Japanese

3. raishuu (らいしゅう)

"Next week" is pronounced, "raishuu"(来週). The first kanji is 〝来〞(rai), and it means "next."

らいしゅう　　　　　　　い
Example 1: 来週はアメリカに行きます。
　　　　　　　(raishuu wa amerika ni ikimasu.)
　　　　　　　　I'm going to America next week.

らいしゅうれんらく
Example 2: 来週、連絡いたします。
　　　　　　　(raishuu, renraku itashimasu.)
　　　　　　　　I will contact you next week.

　　　　　　　　　　　　　らいしゅう
Example 3: ぼくのたんじょうびは来週です。
　　　　　　　(boku no tanjoubi wa raishuu desu.)
　　　　　　　　My birthday's next week.

4. saraishuu (さらいしゅう)

"The week after next" is pronounced, "saraishuu"（再来週）. The first kanji is 再 (sai), and it means again; twice.

さらいしゅう　もくようび
Example 1: 再来週の木曜日はどうですか。
　　　　　　　(saraishuu no mokuyoubi wa dou desu ka?)
　　　　　　　How about Thursday 2 weeks from now?

　　　　　さらいしゅう
Example 2: また、再来週。
　　　　　　　(mata, saraishuu.)
　　　　　　　See you the week after next week.

LESSON 4 🔊

1st	ついたち tsuitachi 一日	11th	じゅういちにち juuichi-nichi 十一日	21st	にじゅういちにち nijuuichi-nichi 二十一日
2nd	ふつか futsuka 二日	12th	じゅうににち juuni-nichi 十二日	22nd	にじゅうににち nijuuni-nichi 二十二日
3rd	みっか mikka 三日	13th	じゅうさんにち juusan-nichi 十三日	23rd	にじゅうさんにち nijuusan-nichi 二十三日
4th	よっか yokka 四日	14th	じゅうよっか juuyokka 十四日	24th	にじゅうよっか nijuuyokka 二十四日
5th	いつか itsuka 五日	15th	じゅうごにち juugo-nichi 十五日	25th	にじゅうごにち nijuugo-nichi 二十五日
6th	むいか muika 六日	16th	じゅうろくにち juuroku-nichi 十六日	26th	にじゅうろくにち nijuuroku-nichi 二十六日
7th	なのか nanoka 七日	17th	じゅうしちにち juushichi-nichi 十七日	27th	にじゅうしちにち nijuushichi-nichi 二十七日
8th	ようか youka 八日	18th	じゅうはちにち juuhachi-nichi 十八日	28th	にじゅうはちにち nijuuhachi-nichi 二十八日
9th	ここのか kokonoka 九日	19th	じゅうくにち juuku-nichi 十九日	29th	にじゅうくにち nijuuku-nichi 二十九日
10th	とおか tooka 十日	20th	はつか hatsuka 二十日	30th	さんじゅうにち sanjuu-nichi 三十日
				31st	さんじゅういちにち sanjuu-ichinichi 三十一日

LESSON 5 🔊

As opposed to English where every month has its name, the months in Japanese are named with numbers "いち"(ichi), "に"(ni), "さん"(san), "し"(shi).

- When it comes to months in Japanese, things can get a bit confusing. There are three ways to talk about months: "がつ" (gatsu), "つき" (tsuki), and "かげつ" (ka-getsu).

Let's break down the differences:

1. "がつ"(月in Kanji) "gatsu" → for the name of each month (January, February, etc.).

2. "つき"(月in Kanji) "tsuki" → for counting months with traditional Japanese numbers.

3. "かげつ"(か月orケ月using Kanji) "ka-getsu" → for counting months with Kanji numbers.

Hiragana	Kanji	Rōmaji	English
いち がつ	一月	ichi-gatsu	January
に がつ	二月	ni-gatsu	February
さん がつ	三月	san-gatsu	March
し がつ	四月	shi-gatsu	April
ご がつ	五月	go-gatsu	May
ろく がつ	六月	roku-gatsu	June
しち/なな がつ	七月	shichi/nana-gatsu	July
はち がつ	八月	hachi-gatsu	August
く がつ	九月	ku-gatsu	September
じゅう がつ	十月	juu-gatsu	October
じゅういち がつ	十一月	juuichi-gatsu	November
じゅうに がつ	十二月	juuni-gatsu	December

❖ Pay attention when mentioning April, July, and September in Japanese because there are two ways to say the numbers four, seven, and nine.

❖ (Not "yon" gatsu) , (Not "nana" gatsu) , (Not "kyuu" gatsu).

LESSON 6

The Japanese counter for months very simple, all you have to do is add "ヶ月"(kagetsu).

Hiragana	Kanji	Rōmaji	English
いっかげつ	一ヶ月	i kka getsu	One month
にかげつ	二ヶ月	ni ka getsu	Two months
さんかげつ	三ヶ月	san ka getsu	Three months
よんかげつ	四ヶ月	yon ka getsu	Four months
ごかげつ	五ヶ月	go ka getsu	Five months
ろっかげつ	六ヶ月	ro kka getsu	Six months
ななかげつ	七ヶ月	nana ka getsu	Seven months
はちかげつ	八ヶ月	hachi ka getsu	Eight months
きゅうかげつ	九ヶ月	kyuu ka gatsu	Nine months
じゅっかげつ	十ヶ月	ju kka getsu	Ten months
じゅういっかげつ	十一ヶ月	juu i kka getsu	Eleven months
じゅうにかげつ	十二ヶ月	juu ni ka getsu	Twelve months

■ Take note that the "月" kanji is pronounced as "gatsu" (がつ) when referring to "January" is a calendar month. However, it is pronounced as "getsu" (げつ) when expressing "one month" or counting lengths of time. Depending on the usage context, these are two distinct readings of the same kanji.

■ Some numbers in Japanese have multiple readings:

➤ The number four (四) can be pronounced as "shi" (し) or "yon" (よん).

➤ The number seven (七) can be pronounced as "shichi" (しち) or "nana" (なな).

➤ The number nine (九) can be pronounced as "ku" (く) or "kyuu" (きゅう).

■ There are multiple ways to write "か月" (kagetsu) in Japanese"か月"(kagetsu) months: "ヵ月", "ヶ月", "箇月" etc.

■ **LESSON 7**

1. kongetsu（こんげつ）

"This Month" kongetsu – 今月（こんげつ）: a noun meaning 'this month' in Japanese.

Example 1:
こんげつ　　　　あつ
今月は、とても暑い。
(**kongetsu** wa, totemo atsui.)
It is very hot this month.

Example 2:
こんげつ　　まいにちべんきょう
今月は、毎日勉強します。
(**kongetsu** wa, mainichi benkyou shimasu.)
I will study every day this month.

Example 3:
こんげつ　　　　いそが
今月は、とても忙しい。
(**kongetsu** wa, totemo isogashii.)
I'm very busy this month.

2. sengetsu（せんげつ）

"Last month" is pronounced "sengetsu."

Example 1:
わたしたち　せんげつ　いそが
私達は、先月から忙しい。
(watashitachi wa **sengetsu** kara isogashii.)
We have been busy since last month.

Example 2:
はは　せんげつ　　びょうき
母は、先月から病気だ。
(haha wa, **sengetsu** kara byouki da.)
My mother has been ill since last month.

Example 3:
わたし　せんげつかぜ　　ひ
私は、先月風邪を引いた。
(watashi wa **sengetsu** kaze wo hiita.)
I caught a cold last month.

■ **LESSON 7** 🔊

Useful Words Related to the Month in Japanese

3. raigetsu (らいげつ)

"Next month" is pronounced, "raigetsu" （来月）.

わたし　らいげつ　　　　　　くるま　か
Example 1: 私は、来月あたらしい車を買います。
(watashi wa, **raigetsu** atarashii kuruma wo kaimasu.)
I will buy a new car next month.

かのじょ　らいげつ　とうきょう　はな
Example 2: 彼女は来月、東京を離れます。
(kanojo wa **raigetsu**, Toukyou wo hanare masu.)
She will leave Tokyo next month.

らいげつ　ともだち　いえ　い
Example 3: 来月、友達の家に行きます。
(**raigetsu**, tomodachi no ie ni ikimasu.)
I will go to my friend's house next month.

4. saraigetsu (さらいげつ)

"The month after next" is pronounced, "saraigetsu" （再来月）.

さらいげつ　じゅうにがつ
Example 1: 再来月は、十二月です。
(**saraigetsu** wa, juu-ni-gatsu desu.)
The month after next is December.

さらいげつわたし　　　　　　　　しごと　はじ
Example 2: 再来月、私はあたらしい仕事を始めます。
(**saraigetsu**, watashi wa atarashii shigoto wo hajime masu.)
I will start a new job, the month after next.

> 再 さい sai
> 6 strokes (JLPT 2)
> (It's not required for beginners level.)
>
> Meaning:
> again, twice, second time, repeated
>
> On'yomi: サイ, サ (sai, sa)
>
> Kun'yomi: ふたた.び (futata. bi)

LESSON 8 🔊

In Japanese, saying dates is straightforward. Dates are written with the year first, then the month, and finally the day.

Dates in Japanese are Written as Follows:

- 年 (nen) : Year
- 月 (gatsu) : Month
- 日 (nichi) : Day

❑ Japanese date includes days of the week is written as follows:

2022年4月30日（火曜）or（火）

Reading: ni-sen ni-juu-ni nen/ shi-gatsu/ san-juu-nichi/ ka-you.

Tuesday, April 30th, 2022

▪ In Japanese, the days of the week are often written in a round bracket "( )" after the day's name. The day's name is usually expressed in a short form. For example, Tuesday is 火曜日 (ka-youbi), but in written form, it's commonly simplified to 火曜 (ka-you) or just 火 (ka).

Example 1:   今日は、二千二十二年二月十五日です。
きょう　　にせんにじゅうにねんにがつじゅうごにち
(kyou wa, ni-sen ni-juu-ni-nen ni-gatsu juu-go-nichi desu.)
 Today is February 15th, 2022.

Example 2:   テストは、2022年8月30日です。
(tesuto wa, ni-sen ni-juu-ni-nen hachi-gatsu san-juu-nichi desu.)
 The examination is on August 30th, 2022.

■ **LESSON 9** 🔊

To express the year in Japanese, simply state the year and then add "nen 年" (ねん), which is a year counter.

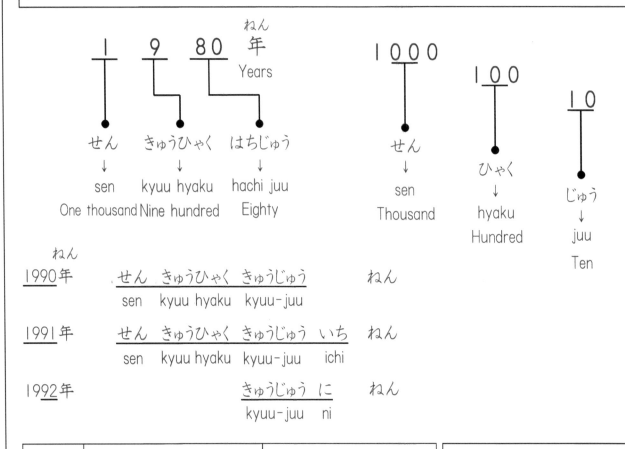

ねん 1990年	せん　きゅうひゃく　きゅうじゅう sen　kyuu hyaku　kyuu-juu	ねん
1991年	せん　きゅうひゃく　きゅうじゅう　いち sen　kyuu hyaku　kyuu-juu　ichi	ねん
1992年	きゅうじゅう　に kyuu-juu　ni	ねん

				Japanese Era Calendar
1993年	きゅうじゅうさん ねん	kyuu-juu-san nen		The Japanese-era calendar, known as 和暦 (wareki) this calendar system is established according to the rule of Japanese emperors.
1994年	きゅうじゅうよ ねん	kyuu-juu-yo nen		
1995年	きゅうじゅうご ねん	kyuu-juu-go nen		
1996年	きゅうじゅうろく ねん	kyuu-juu-roku nen		
1997年	きゅうじゅうなな/しち ねん	kyuu-juu-nana/shichi nen		The current era is called 令和 (reiwa), beginning on May 1, 2019.
1998年	きゅうじゅうはち ねん	kyuu-juu-hachi nen		
1999年	きゅうじゅうく/きゅう ねん	kyuu-juu-ku/kyuu nen		This traditional Japanese era calendar is commonly used for official occasions and in written records, like those used in government services at city offices.
2000年	にせん ねん	ni sen nen		
2001年	にせんいち ねん	ni sen ichi nen		
2010年	にせんじゅう ねん	ni sen juu nen		

LESSON 10 🔊

In Japanese, "年" (ねん or nen) is the character used for counting years.
It represents the concept of "year" and is commonly used in various time-related expressions.

Hiragana	Kanji	Rōmaji	English
いちねん	一年	ichi nen	One year
にねん	二年	ni-nen	Two years
さんねん	三年	san-nen	Three years
じゅうねん	十年	juu nen	Ten years
ひゃくねん	百年	hyaku nen	100 years

❑   Now that you've familiarized yourself with the time units for days, months, and years, you can confidently talk about and understand specific dates.

Useful Words for Describing Relative Years

- 今年 ことし (kotoshi) : This year
- 去年 きょねん (kyonen) : Last year
- 一昨年 おととし (ototoshi) : The year before last
- 来年 らいねん (rainen) : Next year
- 再来年 さらいねん (sarainen) : The year after next
- 閏年 うるうどし (uruudoshi) : Leap year
- 毎年 まいとし (maitoshi) : Every year

Example 1:

きょねん　　　ねん
去年は2022年です。
(kyonen wa ni-sen ni-juu-ni-nen desu.)
 Last year was 2022.

Example 2:

わたし らいねんだいがくせい
　私は来年、大学生になります。
(watashi wa rainen, daigakusei ni nari masu.)
 I will become a university student next year.

LESSON 11 🔊

In Japanese, expressing age is done by adding 〝歳／才〞(さい or sai) after each number, similar to saying "years old" in English.

Hiragana	Kanji	Rōmaji	English
いっさい	一歳／才	i ssai	1 year old
にさい	二歳／才	ni sai	2 years old
さんさい	三歳／才	san sai	3 years old
よんさい	四歳／才	yon sai	4 years old
ごさい	五歳／才	go sai	5 years old
ろくさい	六歳／才	roku sai	6 years old
ななさい	七歳／才	nana sai	7 years old
はち/はっさい	八歳／才	hachi sai/ha ssai	8 years old
きゅうさい	九歳／才	kyuu sai	9 years old
じゅっさい	十歳／才	jussai	10 years old

❑ However, there are some pronunciation adjustments for specific numbers. For instance, when referring to 1-year-old, 8 years old, and 10 years old, adjustments occur as below:

```
1 year old    1才/歳：いっさい      → "i ssai"        → ✕ いちさい 'Not ichi sai'
4 years old    4才/歳：よんさい      → "yon sai"       → ✕ しさい 'Not shi sai'
7 years old    7才/歳：ななさい      → "nana sai"      → ✕ しちさい 'No shichi sai'
8 years old    8才/歳：はっさい      → "ha ssai"       → ✕ はちさい 'Not hachi sai'
9 years old    9才/歳：きゅうさい    → "kyuu sai"      → ✕ くさい 'Not ku sai'
10 years old   10才/歳：じゅっさい   → "ju ssai"       → ✕ じゅうさい 'Not juu sai'
20 years old   20才/歳：はたち/にじゅっさい → "hatachi/ni ju ssai" → ✕ にじゅうさい 'Not ni juu sai'
```

❖ Note that writing the kanji character 〝歳〞(sai) can be challenging. As a result, there are instances where it is substituted with another kanji, 〝才〞(sai), which is more straightforward and more commonly used.

LESSON 11 🔊

In Japanese, you use the counter "才" (sai) when indicating your age. To express your age, you start by saying "私は" (watashi wa), which means "I am." Then, add your age and the counter "才" (sai). This structure allows you to tell others how old you are in Japanese.

Telling your age in Japanese is straightforward. If someone asks how old you are, you can simply state the number followed by "才-さい" (sai) and then "です" (desu). Here are some examples:

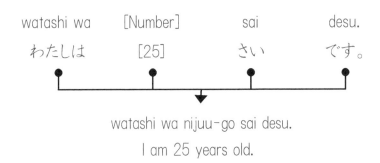

watashi wa nijuu-go sai desu.

I am 25 years old.

Examples: 20 years old – はたち (hatachi) です。

31 years old – さんじゅういっ さい (san juu i ssai) です。

44 years old – よんじゅうよん さい (yon juu yon sai) です。

57 years old – ごじゅうなな さい (go juu nana sai) です。

68 years old – ろくじゅうはっ さい (roku juu ha ssai) です。

79 years old – ななじゅうきゅう さい (nana juu kyuu sai) です。

なんさい
Questions: 何歳ですか。　(nan sai desu ka?)　**(Casual).**

おいくつですか。(o-ikutsu desu ka?) **(Polite).**

Note: There are more polite ways to ask someone's age, like:

- o-toshi wa, o-ikutsu desu ka? おとしは、おいくつですか。
- o-ikutsu de rasshai masu ka? おいくつでらしゃいますか。

LESSON 12

nenrei (ねんれい) is the Japanese word for 'age'

IIn Japanese, "年齢" (ねんれい or nenrei) is the word for 'age.' It's a noun used to refer to someone's age or how old they are. Native speakers commonly use "nenrei" when discussing age in Japanese society.

It's essential to note that "nenrei" refers to the age in general and does not specify a particular age, such as "30 years of age," for example. It is a more general term used to discuss age without being specific about the exact number of years.

かのじょ　ぼく　ねんれい　し
Example 1: 彼女は僕の年齢を知らないです。
　　　　　　(kanojo wa boku no nenrei wo shira nai desu.)
　　　　　　She doesn't know my age.

かのじょ　ねんれい　　　　　わか
Example 2: 彼女は年齢よりずっと若いです。
　　　　　　(kanojo wa nenrei yori zutto wakai desu.)
　　　　　　She looks younger than her age.

The Japanese word "nenrei" is composed of two kanji characters:

1. 年 (ねん or nen): This kanji is commonly used for 'age' or 'year' in Japanese.

2. 齢 (れい or rei): This kanji specifically means 'age.'

Note that the word "toshi" (年) can refer to "year" in a general sense, like any year.
For example, "今年" (kotoshi) means "this (current) year." However, when combined with the character 齢, it forms "年齢" (nenrei), which specifically denotes a person's 'age.'

Aging and Getting Old

When talking about age and aging, the word "年" (toshi) is used in various other terms. For instance, to express someone being older or younger than another person, the word "toshi" is combined with directional words in Japanese to create "年上" (toshiue) and "年下" (toshishita). These phrases literally mean "year above" (elder) and "year below" (junior), respectively.

LESSON 13 🔊

In Japan, every season showcases its own charm and distinct weather. It's a topic that naturally comes up in daily conversations. Mastering how to talk about the weather in Japanese will enhance your language skills and add a personal touch to your interactions. Let's start by exploring essential vocabulary to describe the ever-changing Japanese weather.

1. Japanese Weather Vocabulary: The Basics.

- Weather: 天気（てんき）　tenki-The Japanese word for weather.

- The Sun: 太陽（たいよう）taiyou

- Sunny:　晴れ（はれ）　hare

- The Rain: 雨（あめ）　　ame

- Cloudy:　曇り（くもり）　kumori

- Windy:　風（かぜ）　　kaze

- Snow:　雪（ゆき）　　yuki

週間天気   2022年8月14日 20時00分発表

日付	8月16日(火)	8月17日(水)	8月18日(木)	8月19日(金)	8月20日(土)	8月21日(日)
天気	曇一時雨	曇一時雨	曇時々晴	曇時々晴	曇一時雨	曇時々晴
気温(℃)	34 26	30 23	30 23	32 23	30 23	31 23
降水 確率(%)	70	80	40	20	50	30

　　　　　きょう　てんき　　なん
Example 1: 今日の**天気**は、何ですか。
　　　　　　（kyou no **tenki** wa, nan desu ka?)
　　　　　　What's the weather like today?

　　　　　きょう　　てんき
Example 2: 今日の**天気**は、どうですか。
　　　　　　（kyou no tenki wa, doudesu ka?)
　　　　　　 How's the weather today?

Note: In example 2, if you're having a casual chat with your friends, there's no need to include the "ですか" at the end; it can be left out to maintain a more relaxed and informal tone.

Mastering how to express temperatures and weather phrases can be incredibly helpful in daily conversations and when following weather news.

2. Weather Words – Temperature

- Temperature: 気温（きおん）　　kion – Temperature

- Hot: 暑い（あつい）　　atsui

- Cold: 寒い（さむい）　　samui

- Cool: 涼しい（すずしい）　suzushii

- Mist/Fog: 霧（きり）　　kiri

- Humidity: 湿度（しつど）　　shitsudo

3. Weather Adjectives in Japanese (Weather Phrases)

1.	そよかぜ	soyokaze	そよ風	Breeze
2.	たいふう	taifuu	台風	Typhoon
3.	ごうう	gouu	豪雨	Downpour
4.	はるさめ	harusame	春雨	Spring rain
5.	かんき	kanki	寒気	Cold air
6.	きょうふう	kyoufuu	強風	Strong wind
7.	かみなり	kaminari	雷	Thunder / lightning
8.	こさめ	kosame	小雨	Light rain / drizzle
9.	らいう	raiu	雷雨	Thunder-rainstorm
10.	つゆ	tsuyu	梅雨	Rainy season (Especially in Japan)

LESSON 14 🔊

The Japanese term for seasons is "季節-きせつ" (kisetsu). In Japanese, the word for "four seasons" can be expressed in a couple of ways:

1. 四季 (shiki) - which literally means "four seasons".

2. 春夏秋冬 (haru-natsu-aki-fuyu) - literally, "spring, summer, fall, winter."

- Most kanji characters have multiple readings, and "季節" (kisetsu) is no exception, having two different ways to read it.

Hiragana	Kanji	Rōmaji	English
しき	四季	shiki	Four seasons
はる	春	haru	Spring
なつ	夏	natsu	Summer
あき	秋	aki	Fall
ふゆ	冬	fuyu	Winter

UNIT 6

<ruby>不<rt>ふ</rt>可<rt>か</rt>欠<rt>けつ</rt></ruby>な<ruby>日<rt>に</rt>本<rt>ほん</rt>語<rt>ご</rt></ruby>
Japanese Essentials

- Question words.
- Basic questions and answers.

█ LESSON 1 🔊

You can ask a question in Japanese by adding the particle ″か″ at the end of a declarative sentence. A Japanese particle called "ka" can transform almost any phrase into a question.
As you progress through the lesson, you will learn how to ask questions and the fundamentals of what to look for, as well as how to use these words correctly.

❑ Question Words

1. nani/nan（なに／なん）

"What" in Japanese ″何″ has two readings:　″なに″（nani）and nan. ″なん″（nan）is always used before ″です″（desu）, ″でも″（demo）, ″で″（de）, and ″の″（no）, while nani is for all other cases.

Example 1: それは**何**ですか。(sore wa **nan** desu ka?) What is that?

Example 2: **何**が好きですか。(**nani** ga suki desu ka?) What do you like?

Example 3: 今、**何**時ですか。(ima, **nan**ji desu ka?) What time is it now?

Example 4: 今日は**何**を食べましたか。(kyou wa **nani** wo tabemashita ka?)
　　　　　　　What did you eat today?

❖　**Note:** The final particle ″か″ indicates that the sentence is a question, so that can be seen as the **question mark** in Japanese.

2. dare（だれ）

"Who" in Japanese ″だれ″（dare）It is used much the same way as in English.

Example 1: あの人は**誰**ですか。(ano hito wa **dare** desu ka?) Who is that person?

Example 2: これは**誰**のかさですか。(kore wa **dare** no kasa desu ka?) Whose umbrella is this?

Example 3: それは**誰**のかばんですか。(sore wa **dare** no kaban desu ka?) Whose bag is this?

■ LESSON 1

❑ **Question Words**

3. doko（どこ）

"Doko" means "where" in Japanese. It's used to ask about the location or place of something. For example, you might use it to ask where someone is going or where an object is located.

Example 1: トイレはどこですか。(toire wa **doko** desu ka?) Where is the restroom?

Example 2: 駅はどこですか。(eki wa **doko** desu ka?) Where is the train station?

4.itsu（いつ）

"Itsu" means "when" in Japanese. You use it to ask about the time or date of an event or action. You could ask when someone is planning to do something or when an event will take place.

Example 1: いつ日本に来ましたか。(**itsu** Nihon ni kimashita ka?) When did you come to Japan?

Example 2: 私たちはいつ会えますか。(watashi tachi wa **itsu** ae masu ka?) When can we meet?

5. naze/doushite（なぜ/どうして）

"Naze" and "Doushite" both mean "why" in Japanese. They are used to inquire about the reason or cause behind something. For example, you might ask why someone made a certain decision or why a particular situation occurred.

This is the polite and formal version of why. You can use "なぜ" in formal writing and speech.

❖ There are different ways to ask "why" in Japanese, ranging from formal to informal.

■ "どうして"(doushite): Can be used in everyday conversation with anyone.

Example 1: どうして泣くの。(**doushite** naku no?) Why are you crying?

■ 何で（なんで）: You use this phrase in casual settings with your close friends or family.

Example 2: 何で怒るの。(**nande** okoru no?) Why are you angry?

■ LESSON 1 🔊

❑ Question Words

6. dou(どう)

"How" As seen previously, some question words will have various instantiations or different endings added onto the same root.

```
どう - How
どうですか - How is it?
どうやって - How do you do it?
```

Example 1: これはどうですか。(kore wa **dou** desu ka?)
　　　　　　How is this?

Example 2: 明日の夜はどうですか。(ashita no yoru wa **dou desu ka**?)
　　　　　　How about tomorrow night?

Example 3: 新しい仕事はどうですか。(atarashii shigoto wa **dou desu ka**?)
　　　　　　How is your new job?

Example 4: これはどうやって使いますか。(kore wa **dou yatte** tsukaimasu ka?)
　　　　　　How do you use this?

7. ikutsu (いくつ)

Just like English 'how many', "いくつ"(ikutsu) is a question word for asking the number of countable things.

Example: 　いくつありますか。(**ikutsu** arimasu ka?) How many are there?

❖ "いくつ"(ikutsu) can be used to ask the age of people as well.

■ **LESSON 1** 🔊

❏ Question Words

8. ikura（いくら）

This question can use a couple of different words in Japanese depending on what you're asking about. If you're asking about how much time it will take, that will use one word or something else, such as "to what degree" a thing will go, and then that will be a different word. "ikura" means "how much? How many?" in English, asking about the cost (price) of something. It can also, in some cases, mean how many.

■ To ask how much just use this phrase: いくらですか。(ikura desu ka?) How much is it?

Example 1: この車はいくらですか。(kono kuruma wa **ikura** desu ka?)
How much is this car?

Example 2: この花はいくらですか。(kono hana wa **ikura** desu ka?)
How much is this flower?

Example 3: あなたはいくらもらいましたか。(anata wa **ikura** moraimashita ka?)
How many have you received?

9. dono kurai（どのくらい）

"Dono kurai" translates to "how much" or "how long" in English. It's used to ask about the extent, amount, duration, or degree of something. For instance, you might use it to ask how much time a task will take or how long it will take.

Example 1: ここからどのくらいかかりますか。(koko kara **dono kurai** kakarimasu ka?)
How long does it take from here? How much time does it take to get there?

Example 2: どのくらい時間がかかりますか。(**dono kurai** jikan ga kakarimasu ka?)
How long does it take?

174

LESSON 1 🔊

❑ Question Words

10. dochira（どちら）

There are two options available, you can use "どちら"(dochira) or "どっち"(docchi) to say 'which one' "どちら"(dochira) is formal while "どっち"(docchi) is an informal version.

Example 1: リンゴかバナナ、**どちら**がいいですか。(ringo ka banana, **dochira** ga ii desu ka?)
　　　　　　　Which do you prefer, an apple or a banana?

Example 2: お国は**どちら**ですか。(o-kuni wa **dochira** desu ka?)
　　　　　　　Where are you originally from?

Caution

❖ "どっち"・"どちら" will be used when there are only 2 possible choices.

❖ There are other word that means which どの, you can use it when you have more than three options.

Example 1: どの色が好きですか。(dono-iro ga suki desu ka?) Which colour do you like?

Since the answer could be any color, どの will be used instead.

Example 2: どの皿を使いますか。(dono sara wo tsukaimasu ka?) Which plate will you use?

"どちら" is a more polite way of saying "どの" or "どっち" and "どれ". "どちら" can be used at work, but "どっち", "どの" and "どれ" is a frank expression, and it is appropriate to refrain from using them except in close relationships.

■ LESSON 2

Basic questions and answers in Japanese will be extremely helpful for you while in Japan.

❑ Phrases

Question 1:

なまえ　なん
Japanese: (あなたの)名前は何ですか。

Reading:　(anata no) namae wa nan desu ka?

English:　"What is (your) name?"

> ❖ (noun + possessive particle の)

❑　This is one of the most common phrases that's used when meeting someone new.

Answer:

Japanese: 私の名前は、あみです。

Reading:　watashi no namae wa, Ami desu.

English:　"My name is Ami."

> ❖ In a casual conversation, you can omit the Subject 私は(watashi wa), meaning "I."
> ❖ In polite 私は(name) です。
> ❖ Super polite (name) と もうします。

Question 2:

しゅっしん
Japanese: (あなたの)出身はどこですか。

Reading:　(anata no) shusshin wa doko desu ka?

English:　"Where are you from?"

Answer:

Japanese: 私はアメリカ出身です。

Reading:　watashi wa Amerika shusshin desu.

English:　"I'm from America."

❑　This is one of the most popular Japanese questions that foreigners may be asked.

Question 3: **This is another common way**

Japanese: お国はどこですか。

Reading:　o-kuni wa doko desu ka?

English:　Which country/Where are you from?

Answer:

Japanese: 私はアメリカから来ました。

Reading:　watashi wa Amerika kara kimashita.

English:　"I'm from America."

Question 4:

Japanese: 日本のりょうりは好きですか。

Reading:　Nihon no ryouri wa suki desu ka?

English:　Do you like Japanese food?

Answer:

Japanese: はい、好きです。

Reading:　hai, suki desu.

English:　"Yes, I like it."

■ LESSON 2 🔊

Basic questions and answers in Japanese will be extremely helpful for you while in Japan.

❏ Phrases

Question 1:

Japanese: どこに住んでいますか。

Reading:　doko ni sunde imasu ka?

English:　"Where do you live?"

Answer:

Japanese: 私は大阪に住んでいます。

Reading:　watashi wa Oosaka ni sunde imasu.

English: "I live in Osaka."

Question 2:

Japanese: お仕事は何ですか。

Reading:　o-shigoto wa nan desu ka?

English:　"What is your job?"

Answer:

Japanese: エンジニアです。

Reading:　enjinia desu.

English:　"(I'm) an engineer."

Question 3:

Japanese: どのくらい日本語を習っていますか。

Reading:　dono kurai Nihongo wo naratte imasu ka?

English:　"How long have you been studying Japanese?"

Answer:

Japanese: 1年5か月です。

Reading:　ichi-nen go-kagetsu desu.

English:　"For a year and five months."

Question 4:

Japanese: 皇居に行ったことがありますか。

Reading:　koukyo ni itta koto ga arimasu ka?

"Have you been to the Imperial Palace?"

Answer:

Japanese: はい、行ったことがあります。

Reading:　hai, itta koto ga arimasu.

English:　"Yes, I've been there."

⇕

❏　This is a negative sentence for answering "no."

Japanese: いいえ、行ったことがありません。

Reading: Iie, itta koto ga arimasen.

English: " "No, I have never been."

■ LESSON 2 🔊

Basic questions and answers in Japanese will be extremely helpful for you while in Japan.

❑ Phrases

Question:

Japanese: あなたは日本語を話しますか。

Reading: anata wa Nihon-go wo hanashimasu ka?

English: "Do you speak Japanese?"

Answer:

Japanese: はい、私は少し日本語を話します。

Reading: hai, watashi wa sukoshi Nihon-go wo hanashimasu.

English: "Yes, I speak Japanese a little."

❑ Below answer is a negative form you can use to say that you can't speak the language.

Japanese: 私はフランス語を話せません。

Reading: watashi wa Furansu-go wo hanasemasen.

English: "I can't speak France."

❑ The name of a language is expressed with the word 語 (-go), meaning "language".

English	Japanese	Reading	English	Japanese	Reading
English	英語	Ei-go	Spanish	スペイン語	Supein-go
Japanese	日本語	Nihon-go	Russian	ロシア語	Roshia-go
French	フランス語	Furansu-go	Chinese	中国語	Chuugoku-go
Italian	イタリア語	Itaria-go	Turkey	トルコ語	Toruko-go
Holland	オランダ語	Oranda-go	Thailand	タイ語	Tai-go

UNIT 7

<ruby>謝<rt>しゃ</rt>罪<rt>ざい</rt></ruby>

Apologizing

- Apologizing.

LESSON 1

In Japan, saying sorry or apologizing (which is called ″謝罪″ or ″しゃざい″) is a really important part of being polite, even when you didn't do anything wrong. Apologizing is a big deal in Japanese culture, and there are lots of different ways to do it depending on the situation.

1. sumimasen (すみません)

The flexible expression ″すみません″ serves as both an apology and a way to excuse oneself. It's incredibly useful for those learning Japanese since it fits many situations. For instance, you can use it if you accidentally bump into someone on the train or need assistance from a waiter at a restaurant or in a shopping mall. When apologizing for something that occurred in the past, you would add "deshita": ″すみませんでした.″

Apology:

Example:
しんぱい
ご心配を おかけして、**すみませんでした。**
g-oshinpai wo o-kake shite **sumimasen deshita.**
I'm sorry for making you worry.

Appreciation:

Example:
めいわく
ご迷惑 を おかけして、どうも**すみません。**
go-meiwaku wo okake shite, doumo **sumimasen.**
Sorry for the inconvenience.

Request:

Example:
すみません、これをしていただいていいですか。
sumimasen, kore wo shite itadaite ii desu ka?
Excuse me, can you do this?

■ **LESSON 2** 🔊

You can apologize in different ways in Japanese. The one you choose depends on the situation, as some are better suited than others.

2. gomen'nasai（ごめんなさい）

A casual way to apologize is with the use of gomen. You can make this phrase more polite by saying gomen nasai. Is used with family, friends, and acquaintances in a lower hierarchy than you. It can be used in any informal situation and can be made even more informal by shortening it to "gomen"（ごめん）.

おそ
Example: 遅くなって、ごめんなさい。
osoku natte, gomen'nasai.
Sorry for being late.

Here are some variations:

1. ごめん。（＊casual）
gomen.

2. ごめんね。（＊casual, a bit childish）
gomen ne.

3. ごめんなさい。
gomen'nasai.

Culture Point

In Japan, people often apologize for many things. It doesn't mean we are always personally in the wrong but rather, it shows awareness of our part in an interaction. Whether you are apologizing for your own mistake or for a general situation, make sure you're using the right phrase for each situation.

❖ (This is the most common way to apologize in Japanese and is a sort of catch-all term)
However, it's considered rude to use this phrase to apologize to superiors, managers, bosses. Remember to use the right polite phrases when apologizing:

- "Shitsurei itashimashita"（"失礼いたしました。"）: Similar to "Excuse me" or "I'm sorry."
- "Gomeiwaku wo kake shimashita"（"ご迷惑をおかけしました。"）: "I caused you trouble."
- "Kokoroyori owabi moushiagemasu"（心よりお詫び申し上げます）: "I sincerely apologize."
- "Moushiwake gozaimasen"（申し訳ございません）: Used in business and with superiors.
- "Gomen nasai"（"ごめんなさい。"）: Not always suitable for every situation.

❖ Learning these expressions will help you a lot in making connections in Japan and getting to know Japanese culture better.

LESSON 3

> If you remember more of these phrases, you'll be better prepared to apologize in any situation. (For More Formal Apologies).

3. moushi wake arimasen（申し訳ありません）

When you need to apologize more properly, you can use "moushi wake arimasen." This is a formal way to say sorry, especially when speaking to clients or people in higher positions in business or society. It's a serious phrase, especially suitable for apologizing to superiors or authority figures. It holds more weight than "sumimasen" and "gomen nasai."

Example: 朝はやくから、電話して**申し訳ありません**。

（asa hayaku kara, denwa shite **moushiwake arimasen.**）

I apologize for calling so early.

4. shitsurei shimasu（失礼します）

When combined with the verb "shimasu," this phrase has various uses. You can use it when you want to interrupt a conversation, enter or leave a room, say goodbye, or even for gentle apologies.

Example: お話し中、**失礼します**。

（o-hanashi-chuu, **shitsurei shimasu.**）

I'm sorry to disturb you while you're talking.

Note: The Japanese language offers a range of apology phrases, and the choice depends on the specific situation.

UNIT 8

<ruby>表現<rt>ひょう げん</rt></ruby>

Expressions

- Expressions starting eating.
- Expressions ending eating.
- Hungry / Stuffed.

■ LESSON 1

In Japan, an important tradition is to put your hands together and say "itadakimasu!" before a meal. This is a way to show respect and express thoughts and feelings. People use the same hand gesture when praying to a deity or an ancestor. But, some folks simply say the greeting without clapping their hands during meals.

itadakimasu（いただきます）

What does "itadakimasu" mean?

The word "itadakimasu" is a polite way of saying "itadaku," which expresses humility when receiving and eating. Its origin lies in the Japanese character "頂," which signifies the top of the head. This refers to the posture of kneeling, bowing the head, and extending the arms upward while accepting something from a higher-ranked person.

Translating "itadakimasu" gives us "I humbly receive." Saying this expresses gratitude for the meal. First, because "itadaku" also implies, "Thank you very much for sacrificing your life for me to live mine." Second, it's a way to show appreciation to the person who prepared the meal.

いただきます！

Example: 美味しそうですね！いただきます！
（oishisou desu ne ! itadakimasu !）
Looks delicious! I am about to start eating.

■ itadakimasu has its origin rooted in Japanese ancient history.

Should Foreigners Say "itadakimasu" Before Eating?

Yes, of course!

The most positive approach for foreigners is to engage with local customs and culture just like the Japanese do. Fully embrace your new environment and make the most of your time during your stay in Japan.

■ LESSON 2 🔊

In Japan, after they're done eating, people usually say ″ご馳走様です″ which is pronounced as "go-chisou sama desu" or ″ごちそうさまでした″ which is pronounced as "go-chisou sama deshita." This is a way to express gratitude for the meal. Similar to "itadakimasu," this phrase is a form of showing thankfulness to everyone who took part in making your meal.

---

gochisou sama desu（ごちそうさまです）

What does ごちそうさまです "gochisosama" mean?

″ごちそうさまです″ (gochisosama desu) is a Japanese phrase often used after a meal to express gratitude and appreciation. It's like saying "Thank you for the meal" or "That was a great feast." It's commonly used to acknowledge the efforts of the cook or the host and to show respect for the food that was prepared and enjoyed.

Example:

料理がとてもおいしかったです。ごちそうさまです。ryouri ga totemo oishikattadesu. gochisou sama desu.

The Japanese characters 御馳走様 (read as "go-chisou sama") has an interesting meaning.
The part "chiso" suggests running, harking back to a time without fridges when ingredients had to be gathered from various places for a meal.

"Go-chisosama" is a way of showing respect and gratitude to those who made the meal. When combined, the term means something like, "Thank you a lot for putting in so much effort to make this wonderful meal."

<u>(Clapping hands together again. ごちそうさまでした。 "go-chisou sama deshita!").</u>

❑ The "go" part adds formality to the word and is used for more respect. "go-chiso" then means a feastful and luxurious meal. "sama" is a respectful suffix that is usually added after a person's name.

oishii（おいしい）

The word "oishii" translates to "The food or drink tastes delicious." People of all ages and genders, including children and the elderly, use it. In kanji, it's written as ″美味しい″ (oishii).

Example: このケーキ、とてもおいしいです。(kono kēki, totemo oishii desu.)
      This cake is very delicious.

LESSON 3

In Japanese, you have two main ways to say "I'm hungry": "o-naka ga suita" and "o-naka ga hetta." Both mean the same thing. Also, the phrase "o-naka ippai" refers to your stomach being full. The "o" in front of words makes them polite, and "naka" means stomach. So, "o-naka ippai" is like saying your stomach is filled with food or drink.

o-naka ga suita (おなかがすいた)

When you want to say "I'm hungry" in Japanese, you can use "o-naka suita." Another option you might hear is "はらがへった" (hara ga hetta), but this can sound a bit informal. For most situations, I suggest using "おなかすいた" (o-naka suita).

Now, let's explore the meaning of this phrase more deeply. The "o" at the start is a way to make the following word polite. "Naka" means 'stomach' in Japanese. So, "o-naka" is a polite way to refer to your stomach. "が" (ga) is a particle that shows the subject of a sentence. It's added after "o-naka" to indicate the subject.

The word "空い（すい）" (sui) is a conjugation of the verb "suku," which means 'to empty' or 'to get empty' in Japanese. The final "た" (ta) is an auxiliary verb used to make the tense past, and it's added after a verb, adjective, auxiliary verb, or phrase.

Question: おなかがすいていますか。(o-naka ga suiteimasu ka?)

Are you hungry?

Example 1: わたしはおなかがすいた。(watashi wa o-naka ga suita.)
I'm hungry.

Example 2: The negative form; おなかがすいていない。(o-naka suite inai.)
I'm not hungry.

o-naka ga hetta (おなかがへった)

"hara ga hetta" is a casual and somewhat masculine way of saying."減っ（へっ）"-hett: one conjugation of the verb, "heru", which means 'to decrease' in Japanese. The negative form is; "腹は減っていない。"(hara wa hette inai.).

■ **LESSON 4** 🔊

> The phrase "おなかいっぱい"(o-naka-ippai) is used to describe the state of being satisfied with a meal or drink. It contains feelings of gratitude and the meaning of "I can't eat any more or I'm full".

o-naka-ippai (おなかいっぱい)

Meaning in English: full, stuffed, my tummy is full!
The word "いっぱい" (ippai) translates to "full," like when something fills up completely.
The difference between "いっぱい" (ippai) and "たくさん" (takusan, meaning "a lot") is about the level of quantity. "いっぱい" (ippai) is used when something is already filled to the point of almost overflowing. On the other hand, "たくさん" (takusan) refers to a large amount, whether it's enough or almost overflowing. "たくさん" (takusan) is often used when speaking respectfully to superiors, while "いっぱい" (ippai) has a more casual tone, often used by children.

Example 1: ごちそうさまでした、**お腹いっぱい**です。(gochisousama deshita, **o-naka-ippai** desu.)

　　　　　　Thanks for the meal. I'm full.

Example 2: **お腹いっぱい**です。もう食べられません。(**o-naka-ippai** desu. mou taberare masen.)

　　　　　　I'm stuffed. I can't eat anymore.

o-kawari (おかわり)

Refers to receiving the same drink or food, or the food given to you. When eating, you may have another bowl of white rice, another cup of coffee or tea, etc.

Example 1: おかわりをください。(**o-kawari** wo kudasai.)

　　　　　　Please give me a refill.

Example 2: ごはんは、**おかわり**できますか。 (gohan wa, **o-kawari** dekimasu ka?)

　　　　　　Can I get some more rice?

Example 3: コーヒーの**おかわり**はいかがですか。(kōhī no **o-kawari** wa ikaga desu ka?)

　　　　　　Would you like another cup of coffee?

umai (うまい)

Using "umai" is like a casual way of saying "おいしい" (oishii), which means "delicious." So it is better to use it in a close relationship. "umai" is also used more by men than women.

UNIT 9

<ruby>家<rt>か</rt>族<rt>ぞく</rt></ruby>

Family

- How to talk about family.
- Basic family vocabularies.
- Introducing my family.
- Family members.

◼ **LESSON 1**   🔊

Conversation skills can be enhanced by knowing how to talk about your family in Japanese, However, Talking about family can be difficult in Japanese, So throughout this lesson, I will teach you how to talk about family and useful phrases.

Talking About Your Own Family

Understanding how to talk about your own family and someone else's family is important in Japanese. These situations require using distinct vocabulary and speech styles. When discussing someone else's family, even if you know them well, it's essential to use a more polite form.

When mentioning your mother, you can use the word "母" (pronounced as "haha").

はは　　　さい
Example: 母は、54才です。(**haha** wa, gojuu yon sai desu.)
My mother is 54 years old.

❖ When talking about your mother to other people in formal speech you should use 母(haha).

Talk About Someone Else's Family

Now let's look at how you'd talk about someone else's family.

とう
Example 1: お父さんはどこですか。(o-tou-**san** wa **doko** desu ka?)
(Casual)   Where is your father?

とうさま
Example 2: お父様はどちらですか。(o-tou-**sama** wa **dochira** desu ka?)
(Polite)   Where is your father?

❖ When talking about someone else mother you should use "お母さん"(o-kaa-san) or "様" (o-kaa-sama). The honorific "さん" adds, you must use it for polite form.

LESSON 1

The Japanese word for father is ″お父さん″(o-tou-san).
When talking about your father to other people in formal speech you should use ″父″(chichi) instead.

---

1. Talking about your own Father

私の父はまじめな人です。
　　ちち

watashi no **chichi** wa majime na hito desu.

My father is a serious person.

2. Talking about someone else's Father

あなたのお父さんの仕事は何ですか。
　　　　　　　とう　　　しごと　なん

anata no **o-tou-san** no shigoto wa nan desu ka?

What is your father's job?

3. Talking about your own older sister

私の姉は高校生です。
　　あね　こうこうせい

watashi no **ane** wa koukousei desu.

My older sister is a high school student

4. Talking about
someone else's older sister

あなたのお姉さんは大学生ですか。
　　　　　　ねえ　　　だいがくせい

anata no **o-nee-san** wa daigakusei desu ka?

Is your older sister a college student?

Conclusion:

Japanese has a culture that they need to pay respect (尊敬-そんけい"son-kei") to other people when mentioning someone's family members, so if they have to mention someone's family members in a conversation, they will address them with words that are more respectful for the Japanese family members.

LESSON 2 🔊

Now, it's time to learn some basic Japanese words for family members.

Your family	Reading	Someone else's family	Reading	English
かぞく 家族	(kazoku)	ごかぞく ご家族	(go-kazoku)	Family
ちち 父	(chichi)	おとうさん お父さん	(o-tou-san)	Father
はは 母	(haha)	おかあさん お母さん	(o-kaa-san)	Mother
あに 兄	(ani)	おにいさん お兄さん	(o-nii-san)	Older brother
あね 姉	(ane)	おねえさん お姉さん	(o-nee-san)	Older sister
おとうと 弟	(otouto)	おとうとさん 弟さん	(otouto-san)	Younger brother
いもうと 妹	(imouto)	いもうとさん 妹さん	(imouto-san)	Younger sister
おっと 夫	(otto)	ごしゅじん ご主人	(go-shujin)	Husband
つま 妻	(tsuma)	おくさん 奥さん	(o-ku-san)	Wife
むすこ 息子	(musuko)	むすこさん 息子さん	(musuko-san)	Son
むすめ 娘	(musume)	おじょうさん お嬢さん	(o-jou-san)	Daughter
おじ 叔父	(oji)	おじさん 叔父さん	(oji-san)	Uncle
おば 叔母	(oba)	おばさん 叔母さん	(oba-san)	Aunt

LESSON 2

Now, it's time to learn some basic Japanese words for family members.

Your family	Reading	Someone else's family	Reading	English
そふ 祖父	(sofu)	おじいさん お爺さん	(o-jii-san)	Grandfather
そぼ 祖母	(sobo)	おばあさん お婆さん	(o-baa-san)	Grandmother
りょうしん 両親	(ryoushin)	ごりょうしん ご両親	(go-ryoushin)	Parents
きょうだい 兄弟	(kyoudai)	ごきょうだい ご兄弟	(go-kyoudai)	Siblings
こども 子供	(kodomo)	おこさん お子さん	(o-ko-san)	Children
おい 甥	(oi)	おいごさん 甥御さん	(oi-go-san)	Nephew
めい 姪	(mei)	めいごさん 姪御さん	(mei-go-san)	Niece
まご 孫	(mago)	おまごさん お孫さん	(o-mago-san)	Grandchild
あかちゃん 赤ちゃん	(aka-chan)	あかちゃん 赤ちゃん	(aka-chan)	Baby

■ **LESSON 3** 🔊

Learning how to describe your family in Japanese is an essential part of expanding your vocabulary and improving your conversational skills. So throughout this lesson, "Ami" will introduce her family.

Introducing My Family 家族の紹介（かぞくのしょうかい）

➢ 私はあみです。　I'm Ami.

❖ kazoku – "Family" in Japanese
Kanji: 家族 / Hiragana: かぞく

わたし かぞく しょうかい
私の家族を 紹介します。

watashi no kazoku wo shoukai shimasu. I'm going to introduce my family.

か ぞく ろくにん
家族は、六人です。kazoku wa, roku-nin desu. The family is 6 People.

はは ごじゅうよんさい
母は、五十四才です。

haha wa, go-juu-yon-sai desu.
My mother is 54 years old.

こうこう えいご せんせい
高校の英語の先生です。

koukou no eigo no sensei desu.
(She's) high school English teacher.

ちち ごじゅうろくさい
父は、五十六才です。

chichi wa, go-juu-roku-sai desu.
My father is 56 years old.

かいけいし
会計士です。

(He's) an accountant.
kaikeishi desu.

ぎんこういん
兄は、銀行員です。

ani wa ginkouin desu.
My brother is a bank clerk.

いもうとおとうと こうこうせい
妹と弟は、高校生です。

imouto to otouto wa koukousei desu.
My sister and brother are high school students.

LESSON 3

Learning how to describe your family in Japanese is an essential part of expanding your vocabulary and improving your conversational skills. So throughout this lesson, "Chris" will introduce his family.

Introducing My Family 家族の紹介（かぞくのしょうかい）

➢ クリスです。I'm Chris.

❖ kazoku – "Family" in Japanese
Kanji: 家族 / Hiragana: かぞく

わたし かぞく しょうかい
私の家族を 紹介します。

watashi no kazoku wo shoukai shimasu. I'm going to introduce my family.

か ぞく ななにん
家族は、七人です。kazoku wa, nana-nin desu. The family is 7 People.

はは ごじゅっさい
母は、五十オです。

haha wa go-jyu-ssai desu.
My mother is 50 years old.

しゅふ
主婦です。

shufu desu.
She's a housewife.

ちち ごじゅうさんさい
父は、五十三オです。

chichi wa, go-juu-san-sai desu.
My father is 53 years old.

じどうしゃ かいしゃ しゃちょう
自動車の会社の社長です。

jidousha no kaisha no shachou desu.
Owner of an automobile company.

あね ふたり ふたご
姉が二人いて、双子です。

ane ga futari ite futago desu.
I have two older sisters and they are twins.

ななじゅうななさい
おじいさんとおばあさんは、77オです。

o-jii-san to o-baa-san wa nana-juu-nana-sai desu.
Grandfather and grandmother are 77 years old.

りこう す
旅行が好きです。

ryokou ga suki desu.
(They) like traveling.

194

LESSON 4 🔊

Throughout this lesson, "Ami" asks "Chris" about his family.

あみ（Ami）： ご家族は 何人ですか。 ─────➤
      go-kazoku wa nan-nin desu ka?
      How many people in your family?

クリス（Chris）： 家族は 七人です。
      kazoku wa nana-nin desu.
      The family is 7 People.

あみ（Ami）： ご家族の、お住まいはどちらですか。
      go-kazoku no, o-sumai wa dochira desu ka?
      Where do your family live?

クリス（Chris） 私の家族は、テキサスに住んでいます。
      watashi no kazoku wa, tekisasu ni sundeimasu.
      My family lives in Texas.

あみ（Ami）： きょうだいは いますか。
      kyoudai wa imasu ka?
      Do you have any brother or sister?

クリス（Chris）： 姉が二人いて、双子です。
      ane ga futari ite futago desu.
      I have two older sisters and they are twins.

あみ（Ami）： 仕事は 何をしていますか。
      shigoto wa nani wo shiteimasu ka?
      What is their job?

クリス（Chris）： 医者と弁護士をしています。
      isha to bengoshi wo shiteimasu.
      My sister is doctor and other sister is lawyer.

Note:

When Ami asked about Chris's family she used go-kazoku, not kazoku.

But when Chris answered he used kazoku without any honorifics.

You must use it for polite form, As I mentioned before It is important to understand the difference between talking about your own family and talking about someone else's.

Here are two key points to remember:

1. Add "desu"（です) and "masu"（ます) to your verbs.

2. Add "san"（さん) after someone's name to show respect (Unless they say otherwise).

Remember !
This doesn't apply to yourself.

UNIT 10

にほん　かず　かぞ　かた
日本の数の数え方
Japanese counters

- Counting people.
- Counting things.
- Flat objects.
- Small animals.
- Large animals.
- Rabbits and birds.
- Vocabulary – Japanese Animal Names.
- Books and magazines.
- Machines computers, televisions, and appliances.
- Number of times something happens, or frequency.
- Floors of a building.
- Counting money.

GUIDE

First Step Guide

In Japanese, various counters depend on what you're counting, so it's crucial to learn them and their usage. However, it's worth noting that Japanese counters encompass a vast range, with hundreds of different counters. A counter is a word that describes the item you're counting, such as people, time, clothes, animals, and more.

As a beginner studying the Japanese language, you don't have to learn all of them at once. It will take time to remember everything. The good news is that you can manage daily life without knowing every counter, which should be a relief.

Why Learn Japanese Counters?

Mastering Japanese counters is crucial in advancing beyond the beginner's stage. So, consider the idea of using counters in Japanese. As you delve deeper into your studies, you'll realize their usefulness.

Embracing the Quirks of Counters!

Counting in Japanese might feel a bit strange because the word you use to count changes depending on what you're counting. For instance, you'll use different words for counting long objects, people, sheets, paper, dogs, and various other things.

We have listed 12 of the most useful Japanese counters on the following pages.

LESSON 1

The counter for people in Japanese is ″人″ (ひと or にん).

Pronounced as "hito" or "nin." When counting people, you typically use ″人″ after the number to indicate the count. Interestingly, all numbers used to count people, except for one and two.

Note:

When counting individuals in Japanese, remember that ″一人″ (ひとり - hitori) means one person, and ″二人″ (ふたり - futari) means two people. These words don't follow the usual pattern, so be careful with their pronunciation.

Hiragana	Kanji	Rōmaji	English
ひとり	一人	hitori	One person
ふたり	二人	futari	Two people
さん にん	三人	san-nin	Three people
よにん	四人	yo-nin	Four people
ごにん	五人	go-nin	Five people
ろく にん	六人	roku-nin	Six people
なな/しち にん	七人	nana/shichi-nin	Seven people
はち にん	八人	hachi-nin	Eight people
きゅう/く にん	九人	kyuu/ku-nin	Nine people
じゅう にん	十人	juu-nin	Ten people

❑ Counting more than 10 people in Japanese follows a pattern. For instance, when you say 11, it's like adding 10 and 1 together. Similarly, for 12, it's like combining 10 and 2, and so on.

十一人	11人	juu ichi nin	十二人	12人	juu ni nin
十三人	13人	juu san nin	十四人	14人	juu yo nin

LESSON 2

Long Cylindrical Objects

Counting long, cylindrical objects in Japanese is simple with the counter ″本″ (ほん-hon). This counter is used for various things such as pens, bottles, umbrellas, neckties, trees, films, chimneys, trains, sashes, telephone poles, cylindrical batteries, ribbons, cacti, soda cans, and more.

You might know ″本″ (ほん-hon) can also mean "book," but when used as a counter, it takes on a different role. Books aren't counted with ″本″ (ほん-hon); instead, they are counted with ″冊″ (さつ-satsu), a counter specifically for bound objects. We'll explain that as well.

The Japanese word for one (long, cylindrical object) is ″一本″ (いっぽん-ippon).

Notes:

❏ Be careful! The ending sound changes to a p-sound in the number one; ″一本″ is **not** spoken as (いちほん-ichihon).

❏ When counting long, cylindrical objects, all of the numbers end in -hon except the number 3 (which ends in-bon), and the numbers 1, 6, 8, and 10 (which end in-pon).

1	一本	いっぽん		6	六本	ろっぽん
2	二本	にほん		7	七本	ななほん
3	三本	さんぼん		8	八本	はっぽん
4	四本	よんほん		9	九本	きゅうほん
5	五本	ごほん		10	十本	じゅっぽん

にほんか
Example: ネクタイを二本買いました。(nekutai wo ni-hon kai mashita.)
I bought two neckties.

LESSON 3

Flat Objects

To count flat objects in Japanese, you can use the counter 〝枚〟(まい-mai).
For example things like sheets of paper, stamps, plates, photos, cards, t-shirts, and even walls!

Kanji	Hiragana	Rōmaji	English
一枚	いち まい	ichi-mai	One flat objects
二枚	に まい	ni-mai	Two flat objects
三枚	さん まい	san-mai	Three flat objects
四枚	よん まい	yon-mai	Four flat objects
五枚	ご まい	go-mai	Five flat objects
六枚	ろく まい	roku-mai	Six flat objects
七枚	なな/しち まい	nana/shichi-mai	Seven flat objects
八枚	はち まい	hachi-mai	Eight flat objects
九枚	きゅう まい	kyuu-mai	Nine flat objects
十枚	じゅう まい	juu-mai	Ten flat objects

❑ To count more than 10 of these flat objects, just follow this pattern:
  For example: 11 is 10 and 1, 12 is 10 and 2, and so on.

十一枚　（じゅういちまい）　juu ichi mai　11 flat objects

十二枚　（じゅうにまい）　juu ni mai　12 flat objects

十三枚　（じゅうさんまい）　juu san mai　13 flat objects

十四枚　（じゅうよんまい）　juu yon mai　14 flat objects

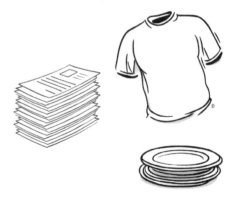

　　　　　　あたら　　　　　さんまいか
Example:　新しいシャツを三枚買いました。(atarashii shatsu wo san-mai kaimashita.)
　　　　　　I bought three new shirts.

LESSON 4 🔊

Small Animals

To count small animals in Japanese, you can use the counter "匹" (ひき-hiki).
This counter is used for various animals like dogs, cats, monkeys, fish, prawns, shrimps, lobsters, wolves, frogs, snails, crabs, tortoises, turtles, octopuses, insects, and more.

Kanji	Hiragana	Rōmaji	English
一匹	いっ ぴき	i-ppiki	One animal
二匹	に ひき	ni-hiki	Two animals
三匹	さん びき	san-biki	Three animals
四匹	よん ひき	yon-hiki	Four animals
五匹	ご ひき	go-hiki	Five animals
六匹	ろっ ぴき	ro-ppiki	Six animals
七匹	なな/しち ひき	nana/shichi-hiki	Seven animals
八匹	はち ひき/はっ ぴき	hachi-hiki/ha-ppiki	Eight animals
九匹	きゅう ひき	kyuu-hiki	Nine animals
十匹	じゅっ ぴき	ju-ppiki	Ten animals

Counting small animals in Japanese, most numbers end with -ひき (-hiki), except for the number 3, which ends in -びき (-biki), and numbers 1, 6, 8, and 10, which end in -ぴき (-piki).

Here are some extra points to remember:

- Rabbits and birds are counted using a different counter, "羽" (わ - wa).
- Larger animals like horses or cows are usually counted using the counter "頭" (とう - tou).

ねこ さんびき か
Example: 猫を三匹、飼っています。(neko wo san-biki, katte imasu.)
     I own three cats.

LESSON 5

Large Animals

You can use the Japanese counter "頭" (とう-tou) to count large animals such as horses, cows, camels, tigers, or elephants!

Kanji	Hiragana	Rōmaji	English
一頭	いっ とう	i-ttou	One (Large) animal
二頭	に とう	ni-tou	Two (Large) animals
三頭	さん とう	san-tou	Three (Large) animals
四頭	よん とう	yon-tou	Four (Large) animals
五頭	ご とう	go-tou	Five (Large) animals
六頭	ろく とう	roku-tou	Six (Large) animals
七頭	なな とう	nana-tou	Seven (Large) animals
八頭	**はち とう/はっ とう**	**hachi-tou/ha-ttou**	**Eight (Large) animals**
九頭	きゅう とう	kyuu-tou	Nine (Large) animals
十頭	じゅっ とう	ju-ttou	Ten (Large) animals

When you want to count more than 10 large animals in Japanese, you can follow a pattern similar to other types of counting. Just remember that 11 is 10 and 1, 12 is 10 and 2, and so on.

十一頭 　　(じゅういち**とう**)　　 juu ichi tou　　 11th (Large) animals

十二頭 　　(じゅうに**とう**)　　 juu ni tou　　 12th (Large) animals

十三頭 　　(じゅうさん**とう**)　　 juu san tou　　 13th (Large) animals

Example: ぞうが、三頭います。(zou ga san-tou imasu.)
　　　　さんとう
　　　　There are three elephants.

202

LESSON 6

Rabbits and Birds

Rabbits and birds are counted using a special counter in Japanese, which is different from the ones we learned earlier. Let's learn how to use the Japanese counter "羽" (わ-wa) to count birds and rabbits.

Kanji	Hiragana	Rōmaji	English
一羽	いちわ	ichi-wa	One bird/rabbit
二羽	にわ	ni-wa	Two birds/rabbits
三羽	さんわ	san-wa	Three birds/rabbits
四羽	よんわ	yon-wa	Four birds/rabbits
五羽	ごわ	go-wa	Five birds/rabbits
六羽	ろくわ	roku-wa	Six birds/rabbits
七羽	ななわ	nana-wa	Seven birds/rabbits
八羽	はちわ	hachi-wa	Eight birds/rabbits
九羽	きゅうわ	kyuu-wa	Nine birds/rabbits
十羽	じゅうわ	juu-wa	Ten birds/rabbits

To count more than 10 birds or rabbits, you can follow a similar pattern that we've seen before. Just remember that 11 is 10 and 1, 12 is 10 and 2, and so on.

十一羽　　　　（じゅういちわ）　　　juu ichi wa　　　　11th birds/rabbits

十二羽　　　　（じゅうにわ）　　　　juu ni wa　　　　12th birds/rabbits

十三羽　　　　（じゅうさんわ）　　　juu san wa　　　　13th birds/rabbits

とり　ろくわ
Example:　鳥が六羽います。(tori ga roku-wa imasu.)
　　　　　There are six birds.

203

LESSON 7

Let's study the names of different Japanese animals from the following vocabulary list.

Kanji	Hiragana	Rōmaji	English
動物	どうぶつ	dou butsu	Animal
猫	ねこ	neko	Cat
犬	いぬ	inu	Dog
兎	うさぎ	usagi	Rabbit
牛	うし	ushi	Cow
馬	うま	uma	Horse
鹿	しか	shika	Deer
山羊	やぎ	yagi	Goat
羊	ひつじ	hitsuji	Sheep
豚	ぶた	buta	Pig
麒麟	きりん	kirin	Giraffe
駱駝	らくだ	rakuda	Camel
子犬	こいぬ	koinu	Puppy
-	（ハムスター）	hamusutā	Hamster
鳥	とり	tori	Bird
白鳥	はくちょう	hakuchou	Swan
鷹	たか	taka	Falcon
猿	さる	saru	Monkey
虎	とら	tora	Tiger
-	（ライオン）	raion	Lion
狐	きつね	kitsune	Fox
熊	くま	kuma	Bear

LESSON 8

Books and Magazines

Counting books and magazines in Japanese, you use the word, "冊" (さつ-satsu).
This word is just for things with covers, like books and magazines.

Kanji	Hiragana	Rōmaji	English
一冊	いっ さつ	i-ssatsu	One book
二冊	に さつ	ni-satsu	Two books
三冊	さん さつ	san-satsu	Three books
四冊	よん さつ	yon-satsu	Four books
五冊	ご さつ	go-satsu	Five books
六冊	ろく さつ	roku-satsu	Six books
七冊	なな さつ	nana-satsu	Seven books
八冊	はっ さつ	ha-ssatsu	Eight books
九冊	きゅう さつ	kyuu-satsu	Nine books
十冊	じゅっ さつ	ju-ssatsu	Ten books

To count more than 10 of them, it's like saying 10 and then adding the regular numbers.

十一冊	(じゅういっさつ)	juu i ssatsu	11 books/magazines
十二冊	(じゅうにさつ)	juu ni satsu	12 books/magazines
十三冊	(じゅうさんさつ)	juu san satsu	13 books/magazines

ほん　にさつか
Example: 本を二冊買いました。(hon wo ni-satsu kaimashita.)
I bought two books.

205

LESSON 9

Machines and Appliances

To count machines and appliances in Japanese, you use a counter word: 〝台〞（だい-dai).
This word is used for things like cars, computers, televisions, and other machines.

Kanji	Hiragana	Rōmaji	English
一 台	いち だい	ichi-dai	One machine
二 台	に だい	ni-dai	Two machines
三 台	さん だい	san-dai	Three machines
四 台	よん だい	yon-dai	Four machines
五 台	ご だい	go-dai	Five machines
六 台	ろく だい	roku-dai	Six machines
七 台	なな だい	nana-dai	Seven machines
八 台	はち だい	hachi-dai	Eight machines
九 台	きゅう だい	kyuu-dai	Nine machines
十 台	じゅう だい	juu-dai	Ten machines

To count more than 10 cars or machines, it's like saying 10 and then adding the regular numbers.

十一台　（じゅういちだい）　juu ichi dai　11 machines

十二台　（じゅうにだい）　juu ni dai　12 machines

十三台　（じゅうさんだい）　juu san dai　13 machines

> **Note:**
> Counting train cars: When talking about counting train cars or compartments.
> 〝号車〞（ごうしゃ）refers to the different cars or compartments within a train. Each car is numbered with a specific 〝号〞（ごう）which means 〝car number〞 or 〝compartment number〞.
>
> To count multiple trains in Japanese, you can use the counter 〝本〞（ほん）along with the number.

わたし　とう　　くるま にだいも
Example: 私のお父さんは車を 二台 持っています。
　　　　　（watashi no o-tou-san wa kuruma wo ni-dai motte imasu.
　　　　　My dad has two cars.

LESSON 10 🔊

Number of Times Something Happens, or Frequency

You can use the Japanese counter '回' (かい, 'kai') to indicate the number of times something happens or the frequency of an action. Simply use '回' to express the repetition of an action several times.

Kanji	Hiragana	Rōmaji	English
一回	いっ かい	i-kkai	Once
二回	に かい	ni-kai	Twice
三回	さん かい	san-kai	Three times
四回	よん かい	yon-kai	Four times
五回	ご かい	go-kai	Five times
六回	ろっ かい	rok-kai	Six times
七回	なな かい	nana-kai	Seven times
八回	**はち/はっ かい**	**hachi/hak-kai**	**Eight times**
九回	きゅう かい	kyuu-kai	Nine times
十回	じゅっ かい	ju-kkai	Ten times

❑ To count more than 10 times, refer to the numbers below. Same as with other types of Japanese counting.

十一回　　　（じゅういっ**かい**）　　juu i kkai　　　11 times

十二回　　　（じゅうに**かい**）　　juu ni kai　　　12 times

十三回　　　（じゅうさん**かい**）　　juu san kai　　13 times

　　　　　　せいと　　さんかいれんぞく　じゅぎょう
Example: その生徒は、三回連続して授業をサボった。
　　　　　（sono seito wa, san-kai renzoku shite jugyou wo sabotta.）
　　　　　The student missed class three times in a row.

Counting the Floors of a Building

When you want to count the floors of a building in Japanese, you use the word: ″階″
(かい - kai) this is the counter for floors, like the first floor, second floor, and so on.

Kanji	Hiragana	Rōmaji	English
一階	いっ かい	i-kkai	Floor 1
二階	に かい	ni-kai	Floor 2
三階	さん がい	san-gai	Floor 3
四階	よん かい	yon-kai	Floor 4
五階	ご かい	go-kai	Floor 5
六階	ろっ かい	rok-kai	Floor 6
七階	なな かい	nana-kai	Floor 7
八階	はち かい/はっ かい	hachi-kai/ha-kkai	Floor 8
九階	きゅう かい	kyuu-kai	Floor 9
十階	じゅっ かい	ju-kkai	Floor 10

To count more than 10 floors, add the regular numbers like 1, 2, 3, and so on.

十一階　　　（じゅういっかい）　　　juu i kkai　　　11th floor

十二階　　　（じゅうにかい）　　　juu ni kai　　　12th floor

十三階　　　（じゅうさんかい）　　　juu san kai　　　13th floor

　　　　　　にかい
Example: トイレは、二階です。(toire wa, ni-kai desu.)
　　　　　　The bathroom is on the second floor.

■ **LESSON 12** 🔊

Counting Money

In the first place, please remember that the official Japanese currency is Yen ″円″ [えん] (It is pronounced 'en' and not 'yen'). The term "yen" in Japanese is derived from the character (kanji) ″円″ (えん, en). That has a literal meaning round, (o-kane) = "Money" in Japanese Kanji: お金/おかね. In Japan, there are 1,000 yen, 2,000 yen, 5,000 yen, as well as 10,000 yen banknotes in circulation nowadays, There are also coins in the denominations of one yen, 5 yen, 10 yen, 50 yen, 100 yen, and 500 yen.

How to Count From 100 to 1,000!

Counting in Japanese from 100 to 1,000 using "hyaku" for certain numbers and special readings for others:

Clarify: (100, 200, 400, 500, 700, and 900) for those numbers use ″百 hyaku.″

Special Readings: 300, 600, 800 have "san byaku," "roku ppyaku" "nana ppyaku".

Kanji	Hiragana	Rōmaji	English
百	ひゃく	hyaku	100
二百	に ひゃく	ni-hyaku	200
三百	さん びゃく	san-**byaku**	300
四百	よん ひゃく	yon-hyaku	400
五百	ご ひゃく	go-hyaku	500
六百	ろっ ぴゃく	ro-**ppyaku**	600
七百	なな ひゃく	nana-hyaku	700
八百	はっ ぴゃく	ha-**ppyaku**	800
九百	きゅう ひゃく	kyuu-hyaku	900
千	せん	sen	1000

- 300: san byaku
- 600: roku ppyaku
- 800: hachi ppyaku   ■ 1,000: 千 sen refers to "One thousand"

LESSON 12 🔊

How to Count From 1,000 to 10,000

Counting from 1,000 to 10,000 in Japanese follows a similar pattern to what we learned earlier, with special readings assigned to certain numbers.

❖ There are some exceptions for reading, such as 3000, and 8000.

Format: Numbers like 1,000, 2,000, 4,000, 5,000, 6,000, 7,000, and 9,000 + "sen."

3,000: The term "zen" is used for 3,000. This is a special case where "zen" is used instead of the typical "san sen."

8000: Pronounced as "hassen" instead of "hachi".

Kanji	Hiragana	Rōmaji	English
千	せん	sen	1000
二千	に せん	ni-sen	2000
三千	さん ぜん	san-zen	3000
四千	よん せん	yon-sen	4000
五千	ご せん	go-sen	5000
六千	ろく せん	roku-sen	6000
七千	なな せん	nana-sen	7000
八千	はっ せん	ha-ssen	8000
九千	きゅう せん	kyuu-sen	9000
一万	いち まん	ichi-man	10000

LESSON 12 🔊

Counting More than 10,000

Numbers	Kanji	Hiragana	Rōmaji	Literal reading in Japanese
10,000	万	まん	man	10,000
100,000	十万	じゅう まん	juu-man	10, 10000
1,000,000	百万	ひゃく まん	hyaku-man	100, 10000
10,000,000	千万	せん まん	sen-man	1000, 10000

❑ When dealing with big numbers, we often use a mix of Arabic numerals and Kanji characters. For example, 5万 (go-man), 4千万 (yon-sen-man), 100億 (hyaku-oku), 3兆 (san-chou), and so on.

How to Say Prices in Japanese

Talking about prices in Japanese is quite straightforward, you just combine the numbers with "en." Generally, Arabic numerals are used for indicating prices.

Numbers + Yen	Kanji	Hiragana	Rōmaji
1 Yen	一円	いち えん	ichi-en
5 Yen	五円	ご えん	go-en
10 Yen	十円	じゅう えん	juu-en
100 Yen	百円	ひゃく えん	hyaku-en
1000 Yen	千円	せん えん	sen-en
5000 Yen	五千円	ご せん えん	go-sen-en

Example: その靴の値段はいくらですか。(sono kutsu no nedan wa ikura desu ka?)
What is the price of those shoes?

Answer: それは五千円です。(sore wa go-sen-en desu.) That's 5000 yen.

■ **LESSON 13**

Getting to Know Japanese Yen (Banknotes)

There are several distinct markings on Japanese banknotes and coins. We have compiled a brief overview here for your reference.

On the 10,000 yen bill, you'll see a picture of Yukichi Fukuzawa, a samurai from the late 1800s. He was not just a samurai, but also an intellectual and educator in Japan during that time.

The 5,000 yen bill has a purple color and shows Ichiyou Higuchi, who was Japan's first well-known female writer. She was known for her short stories and poems.

The 1,000 yen bill features Noguchi Hideyo, a renowned Japanese bacteriologist and physician who made significant contributions to medical research.

■ Japan will have new banknotes in 2024. In the first half of fiscal year 2024 April to September, new banknotes will be issued for the first time in approximately 20 years. Eiichi Shibusawa, Umeko Tsuda, and Shibasaburo Kitasato were to appear on the new banknotes.

Eiichi Shibusawa: (10,000 yen note) founded many companies, including the Daiichi National Bank.
Umeko Tsuda: (5,000 yen note) was the founder of Tsuda College and focused on teaching English.
Shibasaburo Kitasato: (1,000 yen note) the father of modern medicine in Japan, made significant contributions to the prevention of infectious diseases.

Getting to Know Japanese Yen (Coins) 1-2

Japanese Yen coins show a mix of old and new, with pictures like cherry blossoms and temples plus numbers. They teach us about Japan's past and present.

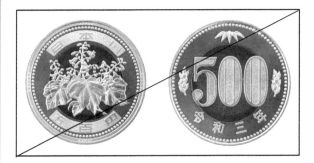

The 500 yen coin is the newest in Japan. It's the largest denomination of yen coins, and you can easily feel its weight when carrying it.

However, In 2021 The Ministry of Finance issued new 500-yen coins. The new coin combines three different metal materials while inheriting the size and design on the front and back. The jagged grooves on the sides are more complicated to enhance anti-counterfeiting.

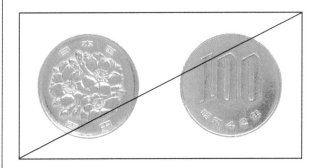

The 100 yen coin is the most commonly used coin for everyday transactions and has various purposes in daily shopping. The coin's back features a design with cherry blossoms.

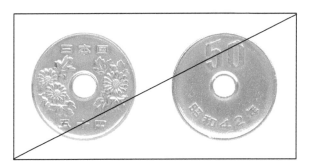

When the 50-yen coins were initially introduced, they didn't have holes in the center. But to make it simpler to tell them apart from 100 yen coins quickly, holes were added to the design. The coin's back features a design with the chrysanthemum flower.

Getting to Know Japanese Yen (Coins) 2-2

Japanese Yen coins show a mix of old and new, with pictures like cherry blossoms and temples plus numbers. They teach us about Japan's past and present.

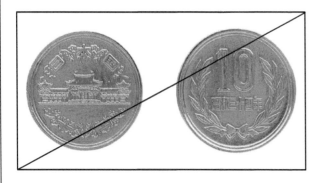

The bronze, 10-yen coin showcases the Phoenix Hall at Byodouin Temple, in Uji, Kyoto prefecture, a UNESCO World Heritage Site, with the Kanji for ″日本 Japan″ and ″十円 Ten Yen″ and the other side shows the number "10" and the date of release written in Kanji, encircled by bay laurel leaves.

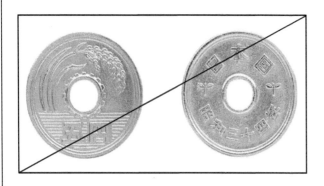

On one side of the five yen coin, you can see a rice plant emerging from the water, and there's the writing for "five yen" in Kanji. The other side has "Japan" and the year of issue also in Kanji, with little tree sprouts in between. Like the 50-yen coin, this one also has a hole in the center. What makes it unique is that it doesn't use Arabic numbers.

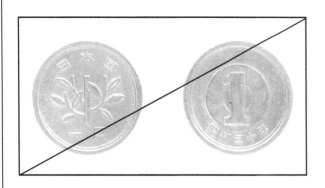

The smallest unit of Japanese currency is the 1-yen coin, known as "Ichi-en kouka." This coin is made from pure aluminum and is very lightweight. On one side, there's an image of a young tree (not any particular plant), with "State of Japan" above it and "1 Yen" in Kanji below. On the other side, there's the number "1" inside a circle, along with the year of issue in Kanji.

UNIT 11

じ かん

時間
Time

- Hours.
- Minutes.
- General Time Reference of the Day.

GUIDE

Knowing how to tell time in Japanese is crucial for everyday life. Whether you're catching a train or scheduling an appointment, expressing the time in Japanese will be helpful during your visit to Japan.

Let's understand how to express periods in Japanese using numbers. It's easy to talk about time in Japanese once you get familiar with their numbers.

To tell the hour, you just add ″時″ (ji) after the number. For minutes, you add ″分″ (fun or pun) depending on the number. It's the same for seconds, where you add ″秒″ (byou) to the number. But, usually, mentioning the seconds isn't needed in most cases.

■ **LESSON 1** 🔊

In this lesson, we'll introduce the basic vocabulary and phrases for telling time in Japanese.

How to Ask for the Time

➤ Here's an example of the most typical phrases for asking about time in Japanese:

いま なんじ
1. 今、何時ですか。
   ima, nan-ji desu ka?
      What time is it now?

いま なんじ
2. すみません、今、何時ですか。
   sumimasen, ima nan-ji desu ka?
      Excuse me, what time is it now?

いま なんじ
3. 今、何時か わかりますか。
   ima, nan-ji ka wakarimasu ka?
      Do you know the time now?

なんじ つ
4. 何時に着きますか。
   nan-ji ni tsukimasu ka?
      What time will you arrive?

➤ And the answer for a correct time expression is something like.

ご じ よんじゅうご ふん
五 時 四十五 分 です。(go-ji yon-juu-go-fun desu.)
   Meaning: It's 5:45.

ごぜん   ごご
☐ When using the twelve-hour clock, add ″午前″(gozen) meaning "a.m." or ″午後″(gogo) meaning "p.m." to clarify.

じ
☐ To tell the hour in Japanese, you just need to append ″時″(ji) to the number.

☐ Similarly, to tell the minute in Japanese, you just need to append ″分″(fun or pun) depends on different numbers) to the numbers.

■ LESSON 2

In this lesson, we'll introduce the basic vocabulary and phrases for telling time in Japanese (hours).

Hours

You should add the Japanese hours ″時″(ji), meaning "hours" or "o'clock", after the numbers Keep in mind that Arabic numbers are commonly used.

Kanji	Hiragana	Rōmaji	English
一時	いちじ	ichi-ji	1 o'clock
二時	にじ	ni-ji	2 o'clock
三時	さんじ	san-ji	3 o'clock
四時	よじ	yo-ji	4 o'clock
五時	ごじ	go-ji	5 o'clock
六時	ろくじ	roku-ji	6 o'clock
七時	しち/ななじ	shichi/nana-ji	7 o'clock
八時	はちじ	hachi-ji	8 o'clock
九時	くじ	ku-ji	9 o'clock
十時	じゅうじ	juu-ji	10 o'clock
十一時	じゅういちじ	juu ichi-ji	11 o'clock
十二時	じゅうにじ	juu ni-ji	12 o'clock

❑ The table above shows the readings for hours, take note of the different pronunciations
   required for the highlighted hours.

   Four o'clock is pronounced as よじ (yo-ji), **not** よんじ (yon-ji).
   Nine o'clock is pronounced as くじ (ku-ji), **not** きゅうじ (kyuu-ji).

あした　あさしちじ　き
Example: 明日の朝七時に来てください。(ashita no asa shichi-ji ni kite kudasai.)
　　　　　 Please come at seven o'clock tomorrow morning.

LESSON 3 🔊

The Japanese counter for hours is "じかん-時間" (jikan).

Kanji	Hiragana	Rōmaji	English
一時間	いちじかん	ichi-jikan	One hour
二時間	にじかん	ni-jikan	Two hours
三時間	さんじかん	san-jikan	Three hours
四時間	よじかん	yo-jikan	Four hours
五時間	ごじかん	go-jikan	Five hours
六時間	ろくじかん	roku-jikan	Six hours
七時間	しち/ななじかん	shichi/nana-jikan	Seven hours
八時間	はちじかん	hachi-jikan	8 hours
九時間	くじかん	kyuu-jikan	9 hours
十時間	じゅうじかん	juu-jikan	10 hours
十一時間	じゅういちじかん	juuichi-jikan	11 hours

➢ Follow the same pattern as other counters do.

Example: この映画は二時間です。(kono eiga wa ni-jikan desu.)
えいが　にじかん
This movie is 2 hours long.

LESSON 4

"分"(fun) or (pun) meaning "minute" is always added after the numbers when telling minutes in Japanese.

Kanji	Hiragana	Rōmaji	English
一分	いっ ぷん	i-ppun	1 minute
二分	に ふん	ni-fun	2 minutes
三分	さん ぷん	san-pun	3 minutes
四分	よんぷん	yon-pun	4 minutes
五分	ご ふん	go-fun	5 minutes
六分	ろっ ぷん	ro-ppun	6 minutes
七分	なな ふん	nana-fun	7 minutes
八分	はち ふん/はっ ぷん	hachi-fun/ha-ppun	8 minutes
九分	きゅう ふん	kyuu-fun	9 minutes
十分	じゅっ ぷん	ju-ppun	10 minutes
二十分	にじゅっ ぷん	ni-ju-ppun	20 minutes
三十分	さんじゅっ ぷん	san-ju-ppun	30 minutes
四十分	よんじゅっ ぷん	yon-ju-ppun	40 minutes

Example: ここから大阪までは車で三十分です。
（おおさか くるま さんじゅっぷん）

(koko kara Oosaka made wa kuruma de san-ju-ppun desu.)

It takes thirty minutes by car from here to Osaka.

■ **LESSON 5** 🔊

Some essential Japanese words for describing time are listed below.

Kanji	Hiragana	Rōmaji	English
午前	ごぜん	gozen	AM
午後	ごご	gogo	PM
朝	あさ	asa	Morning
早朝	そうちょう	souchou	Early morning
日の出	ひので	hinode	Sunrise
正午	しょうご	shougo	Noon
日中	にっちゅう	nicchuu	Midday
夕方	ゆうがた	yuugata	Early evening
日没	にちぼつ	nichibotsu	Sunset
夜	よる	yoru	Evening / night
深夜	しんや	shin'ya	Midnight

Example 1: 明日の夜八時に、夕食を食べましょう。
(ashita no yoru hachi-ji ni, yuushoku wo tabemashou.)
Let's have dinner at eight o'clock tomorrow evening.

Example 2: 私の飛行機は、深夜、十二時三分に出発します。
(watashi no hikouki wa, shin'ya, juu ni-ji san-pun ni shuppatsu shimasu.)
My flight departs at 12:03, at midnight.

UNIT 12

わたし　　　いち　にち
私の一日
My everyday Life

- Daily life (Morning till night).
- Breakfast.
- My Favorite.
- Vocabulary lists.

■ LESSON 1

> The purpose of this lesson is to teach you how to pick up essential **vocabulary** that will be useful in social and real-life situations.

The daily life of (Yukina) 1-2

いちにち
ゆきなの一日

わたし かいしゃいん
私は会社員です。
　watashi wa kaishain desu.
　I am an office worker.

あさ　　　　　　ろく じ はん　お
朝は、いつも、六時半に起きます。
　asa wa, itsumo, roku-ji-han ni oki masu.
　I always get up at 6:30 in the morning

　　　　さんじゅっぷん
そして、三十分くらいジョギングをします。
　soshite, san-jyu-ppun kurai jogingu wo shimasu.
　Then I go jogging for about 30 minutes.

　　　　あさ　　　た　　　　　　　　た　　　　　の
それから、朝ごはんを食べます。サンドイッチを食べてジュースを飲みます。
　sorekara, asagohan wo tabe masu. sandoitchi wo tabete jūsu wo nomi masu.
　Then I have breakfast. Eat sandwiches and drink juice.

　　あいち けん　　　　　　　かいしゃ　なごや
うちは愛知県にあります。会社は名古屋にあります。
　uchi wa Aichi ken ni arimasu. kaisha wa Nagoya ni arimasu.
　I am in Aichi prefecture. The company is in Nagoya.

　　　なごや　　でんしゃ いちじかん
うちから名古屋まで電車で一時間です。
　uchi kara Nagoya made densha de ichi-jikan desu.
　It takes 1 hour by train from our house to Nagoya.

LESSON 1 🔊

The purpose of this lesson is to teach you how to pick up essential vocabulary that will be useful in social and real life situations.

The daily life of (Yukina) 2-2

しごと　　くじ　はじ　　　　　　　　　しごとなかま さんにん　　ひる はん た
仕事は、九時に始まります。たいてい、仕事仲間と三人で、お昼ご飯を食べます。

shigoto wa, ku-ji ni hajimari masu. taitei, shigoto nakama to san'nin de o-hiru gohan wo tabemasu.
Work starts at 9 o'clock. I usually eat lunch with my colleagues.

しごと　　　　　　　ごじ　お　　　　　　ろくじころ いえ　　かえ
仕事は、たいてい五時に終わります。そして 六時頃に家 に帰ります。

shigoto wa, taitei go-ji ni owari masu. soshite roku-ji koro ni ie ni kaerimasu.
Work usually ends at 5 o'clock. And I will go home around 6 o'clock.

　　ばん はんつく　　　　　　　あと　すこ　　　　　み
すぐに晩ご飯を作ります。晩ご飯の後は、少しテレビでニュースを見ます。

sugu ni bangohan wo tsukuri masu. bangohan no ato wa, sukoshi terebi de nyūsu wo mimasu.
I'll make dinner right away. After dinner, I watch news on TV.

　　　　　　　　　　　　　　じゅうじ　　　ね
それから、うちでメールをチェックします。たいてい、十時ごろに寝ます。

sorekara, uchi de mēr u wo chekku shimasu. taitei, juu-ji goro ni nemasu.
Then check my email at home. I usually go to bed around 10 o'clock.

Kanji	Hiragana	Rōmaji	English
会社員	かいしゃいん	kaishain	Employee
何時も	いつも	itsumo	Always
朝ごはん	あさ ごはん	asa gohan	Breakfast
電車	でんしゃ	densha	Train
会社	かいしゃ	kaisha	Company
作ります	つくります	tsukuri masu	To make
終わります	おわります	owari masu	End
家	いえ	ie	House
少し	すこし	sukoshi	Little

LESSON 1 🔊

The purpose of this lesson is to teach you how to pick up essential **vocabulary** that will be useful in social and real-life situations.

The daily life of (Shuu)

いちにち
しゅうの一日

わたし
私は、フリーライターです。
  watashi wa, furīraitā desu.
    I am a freelance writer.

あさ　　　　じゅうじ　　　お
朝は、いつも、十時ごろに起きます。
asa wa, itsumo, juu-ji goro ni okimasu.
  I always get up around 10 o'clock in the morning.

　　からだうご　　　　　　あさ　　　　た
かるく体を動かしてから、朝ごはんを食べます。
  karuku karada wo ugokashite kara asagohan wo tabemasu.
    Exercise lightly before eating breakfast.

しごと　　　　　　　　ごじ　　お
仕事は、たいてい五時に終わらせます。
  shigoto wa, taitei go-ji ni owarasemasu.
    Work usually ends at 5 o'clock.

　　　　さんぽ　で　　　　　　あと　　　　　　い　か　もの
そして、散歩に出かけます。その後すぐに、モールに行って買い物をします。
  soshite, sanpo ni dekakemasu. sono ato sugu ni, mōru ni itte kaimono wo shimasu.
    Then go for a walk. Immediately after that, I will go to the mall and shop.

ばん はん あと　かぞく いっしょ　　　　かいわ
晩ご飯の後は、家族と一緒にたくさん会話をします。
  bangohan no ato wa, kazoku to issho ni takusan kaiwa wo shimasu.
    After dinner, we have a lot of conversations with our family.

かいわ たの　　　　しんや　はな　　　　　　しんやいちじ　　ね
会話が楽しくていつも深夜まで話しています。そして、深夜一時ごろに寝ます。
  kaiwa ga tanoshikute itsumo shin'ya made hanashite imasu. soshite, shin'ya ichi-ji goro ni nemasu.
    The conversation is fun and I always talk until midnight. And I go to bed around 1 am.

■ LESSON 2 🔊

In this lesson about vocabulary, you'll come across the most usual Japanese words for "breakfast." We'll understand their meanings and English translations and learn how to write them in Hiragana and Kanji. Let's start with the basic term "asagohan."

Kanji: 朝ご飯
Hiragana: あさごはん

The two common words to express "breakfast" in Japanese are "asagohan" (朝ご飯) and "choushoku" (朝食). "asagohan" is the informal version, often used in daily life and casual talks. On the other hand, "choushoku" sounds more formal and might be suitable for official settings.

❑ It's made up of "asa" (朝), which means "morning," and "gohan" (ご飯), which refers to "meal" or "cooked rice." So, literally, it translates to "morning meal."

　　　　　　　　　わたし あさ はん　た
Example 1:　私は朝ご飯を食べました。
　　　　　　　　(watashi wa asagohan wo tabemashita.)
　　　　　　　　　I had breakfast.

"choushoku" (朝食) is another common but more formal word for "breakfast" in Japanese. It consists of the kanji character for morning (朝) and the kanji character for food or meal (食).

Kanji: 朝食
Hiragana: ちょうしょく

　　　　　　　　　わたし ちょうしょく た
Example 2:　私は朝食を食べました。
　　　　　　　　(watashi wa choushoku wo tabemashita.)
　　　　　　　　　I had breakfast.

Since the word "朝食"(choushoku) sounds rather formal and polite it is mostly used in formal situations. Use this word instead of "朝ご飯" asagohan whenever you have to talk more respectfully.

■ **LESSON 3** 🔊

The purpose of this lesson is to show you how to say "breakfast" in Japanese, and how to use it with examples.

Advanced Japanese Phrases

あさ はん た
Casual　1. 朝ご飯を食べる。(asagohan wo taberu.) I eat breakfast.

Polite　2. 朝ご飯を食べます。(asagohan wo tabemasu.) I eat breakfast.

"朝ご飯" means breakfast, "wo"（を）is the object particle, and "tabemasu"（たべます）. is the polite verb form used to say "to eat". Informal situations, you can use the more casual "taberu"（食べる）instead of the polite verb form "tabemasu"（食べます）.

```
masu form affirmative   たべます
masu form negative      たべません
masu past affirmative   たべました
masu past negative      たべませんでした
```

あさ はん　　　た
Example 1:　朝ご飯にたまごを**食べる**。(asagohan ni tamago wo **taberu**.)　　(Casual)
　　　　　　I eat egg for breakfast.

Example 2:　朝ご飯にたまごを**食べます**。(asagohan ni tamago wo **tabemasu**.) (Polite)
　　　　　　I eat egg for breakfast.
わたし　にく た
Example 3:　私は、肉を**食べません**。(watashi wa, niku wo **tabemasen**.)　　(Negative)
　　　　　　I don't eat meat.

Breakfast question: (How to ask someone).

あさ はん た
Example 1:　朝ご飯を**食べた**(?)。(asagohan wo **tabeta**?)　　　　　(Casual)
　　　　　Did you eat breakfast?

Example 2:　朝ご飯を**食べました**か。(asagohan wo **tabemashita ka**?)　　(Polite)
　　　　　Did you eat breakfast?

Note: The final particle "か" indicates that the sentence is a question, so that can be seen as the question mark in Japanese.

■ **LESSON 4** 🔊

The daily breakfast of Ami.

➤ あみです。

わたし　まいにち　あさ　　　　た
私は、毎日、朝ごはんを食べます。　　　　　を indicates object of the action
　watashi wa, mainichi, asa gohan wo tabemasu.　　　I eat breakfast every day.

いつも、トーストを食べます。　　　　I always eat toast.
　itsumo, tōsuto wo tabemasu.

　　　やさい　　　　　　　だいす
チキンと野菜のサンドイッチが大好きです。　I love chicken and vegetable sandwiches.
　chikin to yasai no sandoitchi ga daisuki desu.

たまご　　　　　　た
卵とサラダとフルーツも食べます。　　も is close equivalent to "also"
　tamago to sarada to furūtsu mo tabemasu.　　I also eat eggs, salads and fruits.

　　まいあさ　　　　　　　の
そして、毎朝、オレンジジュースを飲みます。　And every morning, I drink orange juice.
　soshite, maiasa, orenjijūsu wo nomimasu.

ときどき　　　の
時々、ミルクも飲みます。
　tokidoki, miruku mo nomimasu.　　Sometimes I also drink milk.

■ **LESSON 5** 🔊

The daily breakfast of Chris

➤ クリスです。

たいてい、卵とチーズのサンドイッチを食べます。 I usually eat egg and cheese sandwiches.
  taitei, tamago to chīzu no sandoitchi wo tabemasu.

┌─────────────────────────────────┐
│ が indicates object of preferences │
└─────────────────────────────────┘

私は、チーズが大好きです。   I like cheese.
  watashi wa, chīzu ga daisuki desu.

┌─────────────────────────────┐
│ や is close equivalent to "or" │
└─────────────────────────────┘

時々、ベーグルやサンドイッチも食べます。   Sometimes I also eat bagels and sandwiches.
  tokidoki, bēguru ya sandoitchi mo tabemasu.

朝ご飯のときは、いつも、コーヒーを飲みます。   Whenever I have breakfast, I drink coffee.
  asa gohan no toki wa, itsumo, kōhī wo nomimasu.

そして、一日に二・三回 コーヒーを飲みます。   And I drink coffee 2.3 times a day.
  soshite, ichi-nichi ni ni-san-kai kōhī wo nomimasu.

紅茶は、あまり好きではありません。   I don't really like black tea.
  koucha wa, amari suki dewa arimasen.

LESSON 6

Expressing your likes in Japanese is quite simple. Start with the noun of the thing you like, and add "が すきです" (ga suki desu) at the end.

"すき"(suki) can be written in kanji "好き"

Sentence pattern:

_____が 好きです。   ⇒   I like _____.

"すき" (suki), which can be written as "好き" in kanji, is a handy word in Japanese to express things you like. If you want to emphasize that you like something, you can use "大好き" (daisuki). "好き" (suki) is useful for indicating your favorite food, music, sport, and more. However, there's an important point to remember: "好き" (suki) can also mean "I love you."

❖ When you want to find out if someone likes something, you can use this pattern:
"....が好きですか。" It's similar to a regular sentence, but with a "か" (ka) at the end, which means a question mark.

To respond, you start with either "yes" (はい) or "no" (いいえ), and then you can add more to explain how much you like or don't like it.

Different degrees of liking things

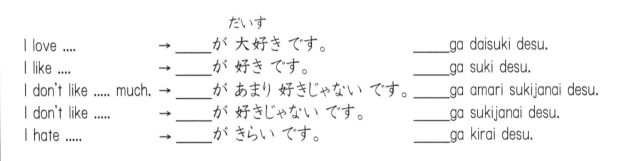

I love	→ ____が 大好き です。	____ga daisuki desu.
I like	→ ____が 好き です。	____ga suki desu.
I don't like ..... much.	→ ____が あまり 好きじゃない です。	____ga amari sukijanai desu.
I don't like	→ ____が 好きじゃない です。	____ga sukijanai desu.
I hate	→ ____が きらい です。	____ga kirai desu.

❑ It is rare for a Japanese person to say that they hate something. Their response is far more likely to be that they do not like it. (The word hate has a strong impact on people.)

LESSON 7

My Favorite Food (Ayaka)

➤ あやかです。

_{わたし}　　　　　　　_{だいす}
私は、フルーツが大好きです。
watashi wa, furūtsu ga daisuki desu.
I like fruits.

_{いちばんす}
ぶどうとオレンジとマンゴーが一番好きです。
budou to orenji to mangō ga ichiban suki desu.
I like grapes, oranges and mangoes the most.

_{もも}　_す
りんごや桃も、好きです。
ringo ya momo mo, suki desu.
I also like apples and peaches.

_{あやか}
彩花の一日

_{にほん} _{もも}
日本の桃は、とてもおいしいです。
Nihon no momo wa, totemo oishii desu.
Japanese peaches are very delicious.

_す
チョコレートとケーキも好きです。
chokorēto to kēki mo suki desu.
I also like chocolates and cakes.

_{わたし あま}　　　　　_す
私は、甘いものが好きです。
watashi wa, amai mono ga suki desu.
I like sweets.

_た
でも、あまりたくさん食べません。
demo, amari takusan tabemasen.
But I don't eat much.

_{ひる} _{はん}　　　　_{わたし いちばんす}　　　　　_{すし}　_{とく}　　　　　　　　_{だいす}
昼ご飯のときは、私が一番好きなのは寿司で、特にマグロやサーモンが大好きです。
hiru gohan no toki wa, watashi ga ichiban sukina nowa sushi de, tokuni maguro ya sāmon ga
daisuki desu. For lunch, my favorite food is sushi, especially tuna and salmon.

_{よる}　　　　　　　　　　_{だいす}　　_{ときどき じぶん つく}
夜ご飯では、カレーライスが大好きで、時々、自分で作ることもあります。
yoru gohan dewa, karēraisu ga daisuki de, tokidoki, jibun de tsukuru koto mo arimasu.
For dinner, I love curry and rice, and sometimes I make it myself.

LESSON 8

My Favorite Sport (Tarou)

➤ たろうです。

たろう
太郎の一日

わたし　　　　　　だいす
私は、スポーツが大好きです。　　　　　　　　I like sports.
 watashi wa, supōtsu ga daisuki desu.

とく　　　　　　す
特に、サッカーが好きです。　　　　　　　　I especially like soccer.
 tokuni, sakkā ga suki desu.

　　　ともだち
よく、友達とサッカーをします。　　　　　　I often play soccer with my friends.
 yoku, tomodachi to sakkā wo shimasu.

　　　　　　　　み
そして、テレビでサッカーを見ます。　　　　Then watch soccer on TV.
 soshite, terebi de sakkā wo mimasu.

　　　　　　　　　す
バスケットボールも、好きです。　　　　　　I like basketball too.
 basukettobōru, mo suki desu.

ちゅうがくせい
中学生のときは、バスケットボールクラブにいました。　　When I was in junior high school,
 chuugakusei no toki wa, basukettobōru kurabu ni imashita.　 I was with basketball club.

ベースボールもします。　　　　　　　　　I also play baseball.
 bēsubōru mo shimasu.

つき いち にかい やま い
月に一・二回、山に行きます。　　　　　　I go to the mountains 1.2 times a month.
 tsuki ni ichi-ni-kai, yama ni ikimasu.

■ **LESSON 9**

My Favorite Music (Tarou)

➤ たろうです。

わたし　おんがく　す
私は、音楽が好きです。　　　　　　　　I like music.
watashi wa, ongaku ga suki desu.

　　　　　　　　　す
クラシックとジャズが好きです。　　　　I like classical music and jazz.
kurashikku to jazu ga suki desu.

どようび　よる　かのじょ　　　　　　おんがく　き
土曜日の夜は、彼女といっしょに、音楽を聞きます。
doyoubi no yoru wa, kanojo to issho ni, ongaku wo kikimasu.
　Saturday night, I listen to music with my girlfriend.

ときどき　えんか　き
時々、演歌も聞きます。　　　　　　　Sometimes I also listen to enka.
tokidoki, enka mo kikimasu.

　　すこ　さけ　の
そして、少しお酒を飲みます。　　　　And I drink a little alcohol.
soshite, sukoshi o-sake wo nomimasu.

☐ **Note:** "enka" is a popular Japanese ballads (Traditional).

233

LESSON 10

Hiragana	Kanji	Rōmaji	English
まいにち	毎日	mainichi	Everyday
あさごはん	朝ご飯	asa gohan	breakfast
たべる	食べる	taberu	Eat
いつも	何時も	itsumo	Always
やさい	野菜	yasai	Vegetable
だいすき	大好き	daisuki	Like
たまご	卵	tamago	Egg
そして	–	soshite	Then
まいあさ	毎朝	maiasa	Every morning
のむ	飲む	nomu	Drink
ときどき	時々	tokidoki	Sometimes
たいてい	大抵	taitei	Usually
とき	時	toki	When
こうちゃ	紅茶	koucha	Black tea
あまり	–	amari	Not much
あります	–	arimasu	Have
ありません	–	arimasu sen	Don't have
とても	–	totemo	Very
おいしい	美味しい	oishii	Delicious
あまい	甘い	amai	Sweets
でも	–	demo	But
たくさん	沢山	takusan	Much

LESSON 10 🔊

Hiragana	Kanji	Rōmaji	English
とくに	特に	tokuni	Especially
よく	-	yoku	Often
ともだち	友達	tomodachi	Friend
します	-	shimasu	Do
テレビ	-	terebi	Tv
みます	見ます	mimasu	Watch
ちゅうがく	中学	chuugaku	Junior high school
しゅう	週	shuu	Week
つき	月	tsuki	Month
やま	山	yama	Mountains
いきます	行きます	ikimasu	to go
どようび	土曜日	doyoubi	Saturday
よる	夜	yoru	Night
すこし	少し	sukoshi	A bit
おさけ	お酒	o-sake	Alcohol
かのじょ	彼女	kanojo	She/girlfriend
おんがく	音楽	ongaku	Music

LESSON 10 🔊

Hiragana	Kanji	Rōmaji	English
ぎゅうにく	牛肉	gyuu niku	Beef
ぶたにく	豚肉	buta niku	Pork
ハム	–	hamu	Ham
とりにく	鶏肉	tori niku	Chicken
さかな	魚	sakana	Fish
えび	海老	ebi	Shrimp
かに	蟹	kani	Crab
たこ	蛸	tako	Octopus
こめ	米	kome	Rice (uncooked)
ごはん	ご飯	go-han	Rice (cooked)
げんまい	玄米	genmai	Brown rice
うどん	饂飩	udon	Wheat noodles
そうめん	素麺	soumen	Thin noodles
そば	蕎麦	soba	Buckwheat noodles

LESSON 10 🔊

Learn some food names in katakana! Be careful with some of the pronunciations since they can sound very different from English words.

Katakana	Rōmaji	English
パン	pan	Bread
サラダ	sarada	Salad
トースト	tōsuto	Toast
フルーツ	furūtsu	Fruit
ヨーグルト	yōguruto	Yogurt
ハンバーガー	hanbāgā	Hamburger
サンドイッチ	sandoitchi	Sandwich
チーズ	chīzu	Cheese
チョコレート	chokorēto	Chocolate
ピザ	piza	Pizza
ラーメン	rāmen	Ramen
カレー	karē	Curry
デザート	dezāto	Dessert
フライドチキン	furaido chikin	Fried chicken
ポテト	poteto	Potatoes
アイスクリーム	aisu kurīmu	Ice cream
スパゲッティ	supagetti	Spaghetti
ステーキ	sutēki	Steak
スープ	sūpu	Soup

LESSON 10 🔊

Learn some fruit's names in katakana / Hiragana! Be careful with some of the pronunciations since they can sound very different from English words.

Hiragana / Katakana	Rōmaji	English
りんご/リンゴ	ringo	Apple
オレンジ	orenji	Orange
バナナ	banana	Banana
すいか / スイカ	suika	Watermelon
いちご/ストロベリー	ichigo/sutoroberī	Strawberry
レモン	remon	Lemon
もも / モモ	momo	Peach
なし	nashi	Pear
マンゴー	mangō	Mango
ドリアン	dorian	Durian
パイナップル	painappuru	Pineapple
ぶどう	budou	Grape
アプリコット	apurikotto	Apricot
チェリー	cherī	Cherry
キウイ	kiui	Kiwi
ココナッツ	kokonattsu	Coconut
グレープフルーツ	gurēpufurūtsu	Grapefruit
ブルーベリー	burūberī	Blueberry
アボカド	abokado	Avocado

UNIT 13

ほう こう
方向

Directions

- Cardinal Directions.
- On the road.
- Asking for directions (Actual Conversations).
- Phrases for giving directions.
- Inside, outside, in front of and behind.
- Preposition Next to, nearby, between.

■ **LESSON 1**

When you're in Japan and need to find your way around, knowing how to ask for directions in Japanese is super helpful. Make sure you learn how to ask politely for help and understand the responses you receive. It'll make navigating the streets and finding your destination a breeze!

1. Cardinal Directions

Here's the basic compass directions in Japanese for reading the map.

Hiragana	Kanji	Rōmaji	English
きた	北	kita	North
みなみ	南	minami	South
にし	西	nishi	West
ひがし	東	higashi	East
ちず	地図	chizu	Map

Example 1: 横浜は、東京の**南**に位置しています。
よこはま　とうきょうみなみ　いち
Yokohama wa Toukyou no **minami** ni ichi shite imasu.
Yokohama is located in the south of Tokyo.

Example 2: 西の空を見てください。
にし　そら　み
nishi no sora wo mite kudasai.
Look at the western sky.

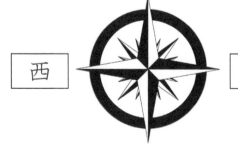

Example 3: 明日、名古屋駅の**北**口に集合しましょう。
あした　なごやえき　きたぐち　しゅうごう
ashita, nagoya eki no **kita** guchi ni shuugou shimashou.
Let's meet at the north exit of Nagoya Station tomorrow.

■ LESSON 2 🔊

Our next set of directions is the intercardinal direction, which mixes the cardinal directions.

2. Additional Cardinal Directions:

Here are the additional compass directions in Japanese.

Hiragana	Kanji	Rōmaji	English
ほくとう	北東	hoku tou	North-East
ほくせい	北西	hoku sei	North-West
なんとう	南東	nan tou	South-East
なんせい	南西	nan sei	South-West

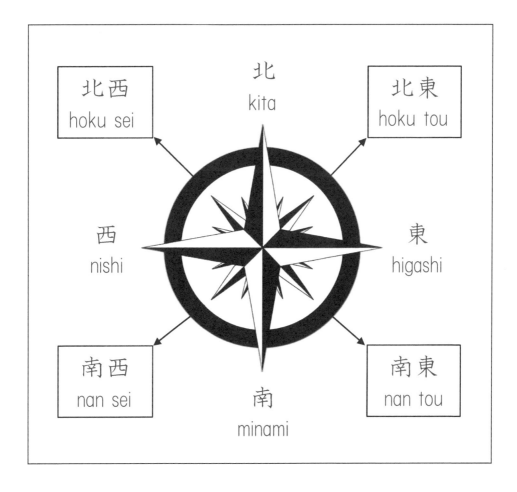

LESSON 3 🔊

Expressing road directions in Japanese, like right and left, is very useful. The vocabulary below is essential for giving and receiving driving directions in Japanese.

3. On The Road

Here are the basic vocabulary directions – On the road.

Hiragana	Kanji	Rōmaji	English
みち	道	michi	Road
みぎ	右	migi	Right
ひだり	左	hidari	Left
まえ	前	mae	Front
うしろ	後ろ	ushiro	Behind
となり	隣	tonari	Next
まっすぐ	真っ直ぐ	massugu	Straight
ここ	此処	koko	Here
あそこ	彼処	asoko	There
とおい	遠い	tooi	Far
ちかい	近い	chikai	Close
わたる	渡る	wataru	Across
かど	角	kado	Corner
こうさてん	交差点	kousaten	Intersection
しんごう	信号	shingou	Traffic light
おうだんほどう	横断歩道	oudan hodou	Crosswalk
はし	橋	hashi	Bridge
たてもの	建物	tatemono	Building

LESSON 3 🔊

1. まっすぐ　massugu　｜.....に いきます。ni ikimasu. － I will go straight.

　｜.....です。desu.　　　－ It is straight.

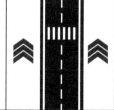

2. みぎ　migi　｜.....に あります。ni arimasu. － It's on the right.

　みぎて　migi te

　みぎがわ　migi gawa　｜.....です。desu.　　　－ It's right.

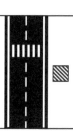

3. みぎ　migi　｜.....の かどにあります。no kado ni arimasu.

　みぎて　migi te　｜ － It is on the right corner.

　みぎがわ　migi gawa　｜.....の かど です。no kado desu. －It is right corner.

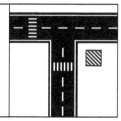

4. ひだり　hidari　｜.....の かどにあります。no kado ni arimasu.

　ひだりて　hidari te　｜ － It is on the left corner.

　ひだりがわ　hidari gawa　｜.....の かど です。no kado desu. －It is left corner.

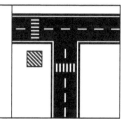

5. みぎ　migi　｜.....に いきます。ni ikimasu.　　　－ I will go right.

　みぎて　migi te

　みぎがわ　migi gawa　｜.....に まがります。ni magari masu. － I turn right.

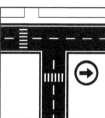

6. ひだり　hidari　｜.....に いきます。ni ikimasu.　　　－ I will go left.

　ひだりて　hidari te

　ひだりがわ　hidari gawa　｜.....に まがります。ni magari masu. － I turn left.

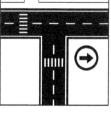
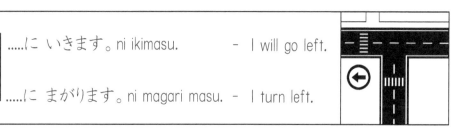

LESSON 3

| 7. つきあたり tsukiatari | .....に いきます。ni ikimasu.
– I go to the end of the street.
.....です。desu. – It is at the end of the street. |  |

| 8. こうさてん kousaten | .....に いきます。ni ikimasu.
– I will go to the intersection.
.....です。desu. – It is the intersection. | 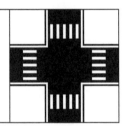 |

| 9. しんごう shingou | .....に いきます。ni ikimasu.
– I will go to the traffic signal.
.....です。desu. – It is the traffic signal. | 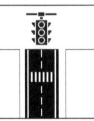 |

| 10. にばんめのかど を ni banme no kado wo
みぎ migi
みぎて migi te
みぎがわ migi gawa | .....に いきます。 ni ikimasu.
– I go right at the second corner.
.....に まがります。ni magari masu.
– I turn right at the second corner. | 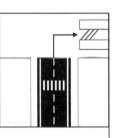 |

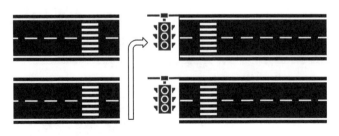

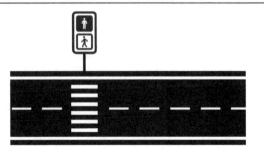

ふた め しんごう ま
二つ目の信号を曲がる
11. (turn at the second traffic light)

みち わた
道を渡る
12. (cross the road)

244

■ LESSON 4 🔊

You'll be able to give directions in Japanese by knowing the basic vocabulary for landmarks and structure.

4. In the City

Here are the basic vocabulary - Landmarks

Hiragana/Katakana	Kanji	Rōmaji	English
くうこう	空港	kuukou	Airport
ぎんこう	銀行	ginkou	Bank
びょういん	病院	byouin	Hospital
ホテル	–	hoteru	Hotel
こうえん	公園	kouen	Park
ちかてつ	地下鉄	chikatetsu	Subway

5. In a Structure/Building

Here are the basic vocabulary - Structure/Building

Hiragana/Katakana	Kanji	Rōmaji	English
もん	門	mon	Gate
かいだん	階段	kaidan	Stairs
エレベーター	-	erebētā	Elevator
いりぐち	入口	iriguchi	Entrance
でぐち	出口	deguchi	Exit
ちゅうしゃじょう	駐車場	chuushajou	Parking lot

■ **LESSON 5** 🔊

Apply the previous vocabulary to actual conversations. 1-2

クリス(Chris): あの、すみません。
　　　　　ano, sumimasen.
　　　　　err... Excuse me.

> **Grammar Structure**
> Sumimasen, **Place** wa doko desu ka?
> **(Place)** wa **(Direction)** desu.

あみ(Ami): はい。hai. Yes.

ゆうびんきょく
クリス(Chris): 郵便局は どこですか。
　　　　　yuu-bin-kyoku wa doko desu ka?
　　　　　Where is the post office?

　　　　　みち ま す い
あみ(Ami): この道を真っ直ぐ行くと、あります。
　　　　　kono michi wo massugu iku to, ari masu.
　　　　　If you go straight down this street, you'll see it.

クリス(Chris): そうですか。あ、それから、このへんにコンビニはありますか。
　　　　　soudesu ka. a, sorekara, kono hen ni konbini wa ari masu ka?
　　　　　Is that so. Oh, and is there a convenience store here?

　　　　　　　　　　しんごう みぎ ま が　　 ま す い　　 つ あ
あみ(Ami): (コンビニは)そこの信号を右に曲って、真っ直ぐ行って突き当たりです。
　　　　　(konbini wa) soko no shingou wo migi ni magatte, massugu itte tsukiatari desu.
　　　　　(Convenience store) Turn right at the traffic light and go straight to the end.

LESSON 5 🔊

Apply the previously vocabulary to actual conversations. 2-2

クリス（Chris）： すみません。それとパールホテルは近くにありますか。
　　　　　　　　 sumimasen. soreto pāruhoteru wa chikaku ni ari masu ka?
　　　　　　　　 Excuse me. And is the Pearl Hotel nearby?

あみ（Ami）： （パールホテルは）そのコンビニから左の信号の交差点を渡って、
　　　　　　　 (Pāruhoteru wa) sono konbini kara hidari no shingou no kousaten wo watatte,
　　　　　　　 (Pearl Hotel) From that convenience store,
　　　　　　　 Cross the intersection of the traffic lights,

　　　　　　　 二番目の角を右に曲ったところにあります。
　　　　　　　 ni-banme no kado wo migi ni magatta tokoro ni arimasu.
　　　　　　　 It's on the second corner to the right.

クリス（Chris）： わかりました。ありがとうございます。
　　　　　　　　 wakarimashita. arigatougozaimasu.
　　　　　　　　 Understood. Thank you very much.

Hiragana	Kanji	Rōmaji	English
どこ	何処	doko	Where
みち	道	mitchi	Road/Street
いく	行く	iku	to go

- に – Particle indicating location or direction.
- の – Particle "の" has many meanings and usage. Here it translates "of".
- Check Unit 2 助詞-Particles.

Here's a list of useful phrases and examples for giving directions 1-2

1	Go Straight	Japanese	Reading
		<ruby>すす</ruby> まっすぐ進みます。	massugu susumi masu.

Example:
<ruby>えき</ruby>　　　<ruby>みち</ruby>　　　<ruby>すす</ruby>
駅へは、この道をまっすぐ進みます。
eki he wa, kono michi wo massugu susumi masu.
Go straight on this road to the station.

2	Go Back	Japanese	Reading
		<ruby>もど</ruby> 戻ります。	modori masu.

Example:
<ruby>とうきょうえき</ruby>　　　　<ruby>みち</ruby>　　　<ruby>しんごう</ruby>　<ruby>もど</ruby>
東京駅へは、この道を、あの信号まで戻ります。
Toukyou eki he wa, kono michi wo, ano shingou made modori masu.
Go back on this road until that traffic light to Tokyo Station.

3	Turn left/right	Japanese	Reading
		<ruby>ひだり</ruby> <ruby>みぎ</ruby> <ruby>ま</ruby> 左 / 右へ曲がります。	hidari / migi e magari masu.

Example:
<ruby>しんごうひだり</ruby> <ruby>ま</ruby>
あの信号を左へ曲がります。
ano shingou wo hidari e magari masu.
Turn left at that traffic light.

■ LESSON 6 🔊

Here's a list of useful phrases and examples for giving directions 2-2

4	Turn left / right at corner / intersection	Japanese: 角 / 交差点を左 / 右へ曲がります。 Reading: kado / kousaten wo hidari / migi e magarimasu.

Example: あの高^{たか}いビルがある交差点^{こうさてん}を右^{みぎ}へ曲^まがります。
ano takai biru ga aru kousaten wo migi e magari masu.
Turn right at the intersection where that tall building is.

5	On Floor	Japanese	Reading
		階^{かい}	kai

Example: トイレは五階^{ごかい}にあります。
toire wa go-kai ni arimasu.
The toilet is on the fifth floor.

6	Keep Going	Japanese	Reading
		このまま行^いってください。	kono mama itte kudasai.

Example: この道^{みち}をこのまま行^いってください。
kono michi wo konomama itte kudasai.
Please keep going on this road.

Describe the position of something in using directions.

Above, Below, Left, Right

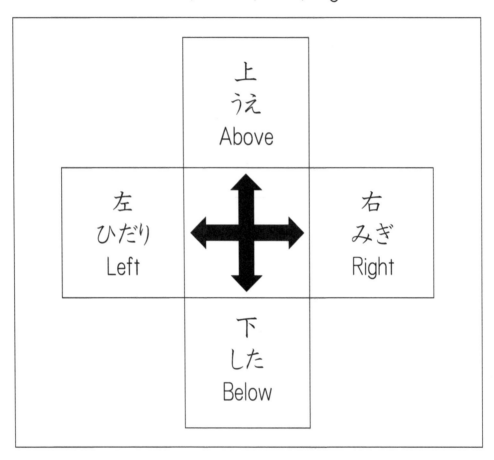

❏   Here are two patterns you can use to describe something or someone's position:

Sentence Patterns:

1. 〜(noun)は〜(noun)の〜(position) に あります／います。

    （〜wa 〜no 〜ni arimasu/imasu.）

2. 〜(noun)の〜(position)に〜(noun) が あります／います。

    （〜no 〜ni 〜ga arimasu/imasu.）

▌ LESSON 7 🔊

---

1. ～(noun)は～(noun)の～(position) に あります／います。

__上: Above/on__

ほん　いす　うえ
Example: 本は椅子の**上**にあります。

hon wa isu no **ue** ni arimasu.

The book is on the chair.

__下: Below/under__

ねこ　　　　　した
Example: 猫はテーブルの**下**にいます。

neko wa tēburu no **shita** ni imasu.

The cat is under the table.

---

2. ～(noun)の～(position)に～(noun) が あります／います。

__左: Left__

ひだり くすり
Example: テレビの**左**に薬があります。

Terebi no **hidari** ni kusuri ga arimasu.

There is medicine to the left side of the TV.

__右: Right__

わたし みぎ くるま
Example: 私の**右**に車がいます。

watashi no **migi** ni kuruma ga imasu.

There is a car on my right.

---

3. Inside, outside, behind, and in front of.

かね　　　　　なか　い
Example 1: お金をかばんの**中**に入れた。

o-kane wo kaban no **naka** ni ireta.

I put the money in my bag.

こどもたち そと あそ　　　い
Example 2: 子供達は**外**に遊びに行った。

kodomotachi wa **soto** ni asobi ni itta.

The children went out to play.

ねこ　と　うし　かく
Example 3: その猫は戸の**後ろ**に隠れていた。

sono neko wa to no **ushiro** ni kakurete ita.

The cat was hiding behind the door.

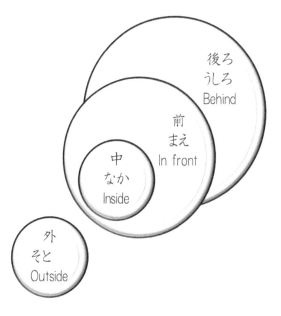

えきまえ　あ
Example 4: 駅**前**で会いましょう。

eki **mae** de aimashou.

Let's meet in front of the station.

■ LESSON 8 🔊

Here's a list of some common Japanese preposition words.

Hiragana	Reading	English
となり	tonari	Next to

Right next to or beside the object you're talking about.

Example: 彼はとなりの家に住んでいる。 kare wa **tonari** no ie ni sunde iru.
かれ　　　　いえ　す
He lives next-door to my house.

Hiragana	Reading	English
ちかく	chikaku	Nearby

Right next to or beside the object you're talking about.

Example: 駅は学校の近くです。 eki wa gakkou no **chikaku** desu.
えき がっこう ちか
The station is near the school.

Hiragana	Reading	English
あいだ	aida	Between

Right next to or beside the object you're talking about.

Example: 名古屋は東京と大阪の間にあります。
なごや　とうきょうおおさか あいだ
Nagoya wa toukyou to Oosaka no **aida** ni arimasu.
Nagoya is in between Tokyo and Osaka.

- ＿＿＿＿＿の + preposition

In many cases you'll put a の (no) before the preposition.
This can allow you to connect a noun to a location word.

- ＿＿と＿＿の + preposition

If you need to attach a location word to two different nouns you can connect them with と (to).
This is especially important for prepositions like ″間″ (aida) or "in between".

UNIT 14

こう つう しゅ だん
交通手段
Transportation

- Transportation facilities.
- Japan Railway's reserved seat (Ticket).
- Vocabulary.

Japan has excellent public transport, whether you are traveling by shinkansen, plane, express train, highway bus, city bus, or ferry, Japan's train, bus, and subway networks are efficient and punctual, and compared with other countries, extremely safe, an extensive and reliable network of railways covers the four major islands of Japan: Honshuu, Hokkaidou, Kyushuu, and Shikoku.

1. Air Travel

Getting around Japan is easy with different airlines offering flights within the country. Two of the main ones are Japan Airlines (JAL) and All Nippon Airways (ANA). They have lots of flights that connect more than fifty airports across Japan.

2. Bullet Trains

Big cities in Japan are well-connected by super-fast trains called "shinkansen." These trains are run by a group called Japan Railways Group (JR Group). They're really impressive because they can go as fast as 320 kilometers per hour. This makes traveling between cities quick and easy.

3. Regular Trains

Most Japanese cities are connected by high-speed "shinkansen" trains, but some areas aren't reached by these. In those cases, people use regular trains to reach their destinations.

4. Highway Buses

If you want to travel affordably over longer distances in Japan, you can take highway buses, sometimes called "kousoku buses." They're a cheaper option compared to trains. These buses are cozy and let you explore different parts of the country without spending too much money.

5. Taxi

Taxis in Japanese cities can be a bit expensive compared to public transportation. But they become really useful after trains and buses stop running, usually around midnight.

6. Ferries

Given its status as an archipelagic nation with over 6,800 islands, Japan boasts a dependable ferry network, providing travelers with a range of amenities and options to explore its diverse regions.

7. Bicycles

Riding a bike is a fun and cheap way to see Japan, especially its cute small towns. Big cities have special areas where you can park your bike near train stations and shopping centers, which makes biking even more attractive.

LESSON 1 🔊

All types of Japanese trains, from shinkansen to local, are typically classified into the following:

はや　　　　　　　　　　　　　　　　　　　　　　おそ
早い hayai (Fast) ←――――――――――――――→ 遅い osoi (Slow)

ジェイアール　　　　　　しんかんせん
JR Jeiāru　　　　　　新幹線　shinkansen bullet train (very high speed)

ジェイアール　　　しんかいそく　　　　　　　　かいそく　　　　　　　　　ふつう
JR Jeiāru　　　　新快速 shinkai-soku　　　快速　kaisoku　　　　　普通 futsuu
　　　　　　　　　Special rapid service　　　Rapid train　　　　　Local

はんきゅう　　　　　とっきゅう　　　　　　　　きゅうこう　　　　　　　ふつう
阪急 Hankyuu　　　特急　tokkyuu　　　　　急行　kyuukou　　　　普通 futsuu
　　　　　　　　　Limited express　　　　　Express　　　　　　Local

Phrases About Transportation

❖　...はどこですか。(...wa doko desu ka?)　　　Meaning: Where is ...?

　　　　　とうきょう　えき
Example 1: JR東京駅はどこですか。　　　JRtoukyou eki wa doko desu ka?
　　　　Where is JR Tokyo Station?

❖　...に行きたい。(...ni ikitai.)　　　Meaning: I want to go to... .

　　　　　しんかんせん おおさか い
Example 2: 新幹線で大阪に行きたいです。　shinkansen de Oosaka ni ikitai desu.
　　　　I want to go to Osaka by bullet train.

❖　どの電車。(dono densha?)　　　Meaning: Which train?

　　　　　きゅうこうでんしゃ の
Example 3: どの急行電車に乗ればいいですか。dono kyuukou-densha ni noreba iidesu ka?
　　　　Which express train should I take?

LESSON 2

When you use Japan Rail, you will have a reserved seat ticket. But the ticket is written in Japanese only. Here is an example with an explanation.

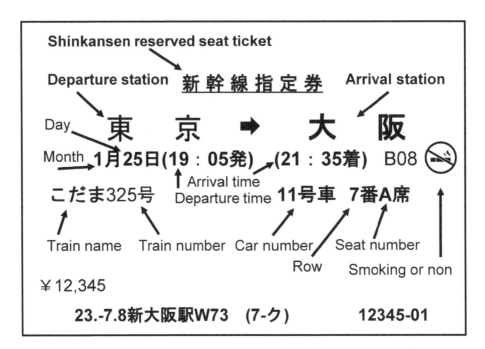

■ The image above displays a reserved seat ticket for the shinkansen (bullet train). The ticket provides the following information:

- Departure station,
- Arrival station,
- Departure time,
- Arrival time,
- Month, Day, Train name, Train number, Car number, Row, Seat number.

LESSON 3 🔊

A list of Japanese transportation vocabulary you will see and hear on trains and at stations, along with sentences in which the vocabulary appears. (1-2)

Hiragana/Katakana	Kanji	Rōmaji	English
のりもの	乗り物	norimono	Transport

"norimono" means vehicle or vehicles, but literally, it means "thing to ride". "乗る"(noru) is the verb "to ride" and "物"(mono) means "thing".

| バスてい | バス停 | basutei | Bus stop |

The Japanese word for bus is basu! It sounds really similar to English! The Japanese word for bus stop is basutei (バス停).

| のりば | 乗り場 | noriba | Platform |

Place for boarding vehicles.
e.g.：バスのりばをおしえてください。basu noriba wo oshiete kudasai.
Please tell me where the bus stop is.

でんしゃ	電車	densha	Electric train
ちかてつ	地下鉄	chikatetsu	Subway train
えき	駅	eki	Station
せん	線	sen	Line
あぶない	危ない	abunai	Dangerous
きけん	危険	kiken	Danger
ごじょうしゃ	ご乗車	go-jousha	Boarding
つぎ	次	tsugi	Next
いき	行き	iki	Destination
ほうこう	方向	houkou	Direction
おつり	お釣り	o-tsuri	Change money

LESSON 3 🔊

A list of Japanese transportation vocabulary you will see and hear on trains and at stations, along with sentences in which the vocabulary appears. (2-2)

Hiragana/Katakana	Kanji	Rōmaji	English
かくえきていしゃ	各駅停車	kakueki teisha	Local train
Train that stops at all stations (local).			
かいそく	快速	kaisoku	Rapid train
Train that stops on selected stations only (rapid).			
とっきゅう	特急	tokkyuu	Limited express trains
Limited express trains stop only at major stations. Depending on the railway company, a limited express fee has to be paid in addition to the base fare in order to ride a limited express.			
くるま	車	kuruma	Car
じてんしゃ	自転車	jitensha	Bicycle
しんかんせん	新幹線	shinkansen	Bullet Train
ふね	船	fune	Ship / Boat
バイク	-	baiku	Motorcycle
きんえん	禁煙	kin-en	No Smoking
のぼり	上り	nobori	Going up
くだり	下り	kudari	Going down
でぐち	出口	deguchi	Exit
いりぐち	入口	iriguchi	Entrance
エレベーター	-	erebētā	Elevator/Lift

UNIT 15

<ruby>買<rt>か</rt></ruby>い<ruby>物<rt>もの</rt></ruby>をする
Shopping

- Irasshaimase.
- Department stores.
- Ayaka-san. (Having a shopping.)
- Shopping expressions.
- Vocabulary.

When shopping in Japan, it's helpful to have some basic Japanese language skills as most local shopkeepers might not know English. Therefore, let's take this opportunity to learn some useful Japanese phrases for shopping in this lesson.

いらっしゃいませ (irasshaimase) means "Welcome!" Or "May I help you?"

If you've ever been to Japan, you've likely heard it multiple times, as store employees frequently use it to greet customers. Unlike the English expression "May I help you?" there is no need to respond to "Irasshaimase."

Another form of this greeting is "Irasshai," which is slightly less formal than "Irasshaimase." While you might not need to use these phrases yourself, you'll encounter them in almost any store you visit in Japan.

The Meaning and Origin of the Word "Irasshaimase."

The word "Irasshaimase" (いらっしゃいませ) is a polite and honorific expression in the Japanese language used to welcome someone. It is a combination of two words:

"Irasshaimasu" (いらっしゃいます): This is the honorific form of the verb "irassharu," which means "to come" or "to go." The "-masu" ending makes it polite.

"-mase" (ませ): This is an auxiliary verb that adds a sense of politeness and respect to the statement.

When combined, "Irasshaimase" essentially means "Please come in" or "Welcome." It is used to greet customers, guests, or anyone entering a place of business or someone's home to show respect and hospitality.

The origin of "Irasshaimase" can be traced back to traditional Japanese hospitality, which places a strong emphasis on providing excellent customer service and making guests feel welcome and appreciated. It is a cultural norm in Japan to use polite language and honorific expressions when interacting with others, especially in a business setting. Therefore, you'll commonly hear this phrase being used by staff members in shops, restaurants, and other establishments across Japan as a way to create a warm and inviting atmosphere for customers.

■ **LESSON 2** 🔊

Department Stores "hyakkaten"（百貨店）

Department store clerks use very polite expressions toward customers. Here are some expressions you are likely to hear, but the term "depaato"（デパート）is more common today.

---

irasshaimase. いらっしゃいませ。	May I help you? or Welcome.
nanika o-sagashi desu ka? なに　　さが 何かお探しですか。	May I help you? Literally means: (Are you looking for something?)
ikaga desu ka? いかがですか。	How do you like it?
kashikomarimashita. かしこまりました。	Certainly.
o-matase itashimashita. 　　ま お待たせいたしました。	Sorry to have kept you waiting.

Common Expressions:

Verbs

To go shopping	-買い物に行きます	/ かいものにいきます	/ kaimono ni ikimasu
To buy	-買います	/ かいます	/ kaimasu
To sell	-売ります	/ うります	/ urimasu
To have	-あります		/ arimasu
To look for	-探します	/ さがします	/ sagashimasu
To match	-合います	/ あいます	/ aimasu

Verbs

Department	-売り場 or 売場	/ うりば	/ araba
Female clothing section	-婦人服売り場	/ ふじんふくうりば	/ fujin-fuku uriba
Male clothing section	-紳士服売り場	/ しんしふくうりば	/ shinshi-fuku uriba
Children's clothing section	-子供服売り場	/ こどもふくうりば	/ kodomo-fuku uriba

LESSON 3 🔊

> **Convenience Stores** "konbini" (コンビニ) – Example Shopping Dialogue.
> Customer word in Japanese is: おきゃくさん (o-kyaku san).
> Staff word in Japanese is: てんいん (tenin).

てんいん: こんにちは！いらっしゃいませ。(konnichiwa! irasshaimase! – Hello! Welcome!)

つぎ きゃく
てんいん: お次のお客さまどうぞ。(o-tsugi no o-kyaku-sama douzo.) Next customer please.

べんとう はし にぜん ねが
おきゃくさん: すみませんが、お弁当に箸を二膳お願いします。
　　　　　(sumimasen ga, o-bentou ni hasi wo ni-zen o-negaishimasu.)
　　　　　Excuse me, I'd like two pairs of chopsticks for my lunch box, please.

てんいん: はい、かしこまりました。(hai, kashikomarimashita.) Yes, certainly.

てんいん: ふくろはいりますか。(fukuro wa irimasu ka?) Do you need a plastic bag?

おきゃくさん: けっこうです。(kekkou desu.) No thank you.

べんとう あたた
てんいん: お弁当は温めますか。(o-bentou wa atatamemasu ka?) Do you want to heat your lunch?

ねが
おきゃくさん: お願いします。(o-negaishimasu) Yes Please!

しょうしょう ま
おきゃくさん: 少々お待ちください。(shoushou o-machi kudasai) Please wait a moment.

せんごひゃくえん
てんいん: 千五百円です。(sen go-hyaku en desu.) That's one thousand five hundred yen.

おきゃくさん: あ、クレジットカードで。(A, kurejittokādo de) Oh, with a credit card.

てんいん: ありがとうございました! (arigatou gozaimashita!) Thank you!

LESSON 4 🔊

Restaurant "resutoran"（レストラン）- Example Dialogue

てんいん： いらっしゃいませ (irasshaimase) !
おふたりさまですか。(o-futari sama desu ka?)
Welcome!   Is it the two of you?

おきゃくさん： いえ、(ie)もうひとり、(mou hitori)あとから きます。(ato kara kimasu)
No, one more person will come later.

てんいん： では、(dewa)ごあんないさせていただきますので、(go-an'nai sasete itadakimasunode)
こちらへどうぞ。(kochira e douzo.)
Now, let me show you around, this way please.

てんいん： ごちゅうもんがおきまりになりましたら、(go-chuumon ga o-kimarini narimashitara,)
そちらのボタンでおよびくださいませ。(sotirano botan de o-yobi kudasai mase.)
When you have decided on your order, please call us using that button.

おきゃくさん：　Aセットをひとつと、(A setto wo hitotsu to)
Bセットをふたつと、(B setto wo futatsu to)
あとでコーヒーをみっつください。(ato de kōhī wo mittsu kudasai,)
Please give us one set A, two sets B, and three coffees later.

てんいん： AとBのセットは、(A to B no setto wa,)
ごはんかパンをえらべますが、(go-han ka pan wo erabemasu ga,)
いかがですか。(ikaga desu ka?)
A and B sets are available with a choice of rice or bread.

おきゃくさん：　ライスでおねがいします。(raisu de o-negai shimasu.)
Rice, please.

てんいん： AセットがおひとつとBセットがおふたつで(A setto ga ohitotsu to B setto ga ofutatsude)
すべてライスですね、(subete raisu desu ne,)
あとでコーヒーをみっつおもちいたします。(ato de kōhī wo mittsu o-motiitashimasu.)
おまちくださいませ。(o-machi kudasaimase.)
One A set and two B sets, all with rice, and I will bring you three coffees later.
Please wait.

LESSON 5 🔊

"Ayaka-san" (Having a shopping.) The purpose of this lesson is to teach you how to pick up essential **vocabulary** that will be useful in social and real-life situations.

わたし どようび　とも　　　　　　　　か もの　い
私は土曜日に、友だちといっしょに、買い物に行きました。
watashi wa doyoubi ni, tomodachi to issho ni, kaimono ni ikimashita.
I went shopping on Saturday with my friends.

彩花さん

　　　　　　　　　　　　　　　　　　　おお
ショッピングモールは、とてもきれいで大きかったです。
shoppingumōru wa, totemo kirei de ookikatta desu.
The shopping mall was very beautiful and big.

"で" is the connective
Ending of an adjective.

　　　　　　　　　　　　　ひと　　　　　　　　　　　　　　　　　　　みせ
ショッピングモールでは、人がたくさんいました。そして、いろいろな店がありました。
shoppingumōru dewa, hito ga takusan imashita. soshite, iroirona mise ga arimashita.
There were a lot of people in the shopping mall. And there were various shops.

わたし　　　　　　　ちい　　　　　ぼうし　　　　　　　　か
私は、スカートと小さくてかわいい帽子とくつと ジーンズを買いました。
watashi wa, sukāto to chiisakute kawaii boushi to kutsu to jīnzu wo kaimashita.
I bought a skirt, a small and cute hat, shoes and jeans.

ともだち　　　　　　　　　　しろ　　　　　　　　　　　か
友達は、ストライプのシャツと白いポロシャツとかわいいポーチを買いました。
tomodachi wa, sutoraipu no shatsu to shiroi poroshatsu to kawaii pōchi wo kaimashita.
My friend bought a striped shirt, a white polo shirt and a cute pouch.

わたし　　　よじかん　　か もの
私たちは、四時間くらい買い物をしました。
watashitachi wa, yo-jikan kurai kaimono wo shimashita.
We shopped about 4 hours.

つか　　　　か もの　　たの
疲れました、でも買い物はとても楽しかったです。
tsukaremashita, demo kaimono wa totemo tanoshikatta desu.
We got tired, But shopping was a lot of fun.

LESSON 6 ◀))

Here are some useful expressions for shopping.

kore wa ikura desu ka? これはいくらですか。	How much is this?
mite mo ii desu ka? 見てもいいですか。	Can I look at it?
~ wa doko ni arimasu ka? 〜はどこにありますか。	Where is ~?
~ (ga) arimasu ka? 〜 (が) ありますか。	Do you have ~?
~ wo misete kudasai. 〜を見せてください。	Please show me ~.
kore ni shimasu. これにします。	I'll take it.
miteiru dake desu. 見ているだけです。	I'm just looking.
dochira ga ii to omoimasu ka? どちらがいいと思いますか。	Which do you think is better?
kono naka de dore ga ichiban ii kana? この中でどれが一番いいかな。	Which one is the best among these?
donna no ga ii deshou ka? どんなのがいいでしょうか。	What do you think is suitable?

Notes:

Decline Politely : すみませんけど、またにします。 sumimasen kedo, mata ni shimasu.
I'm sorry, but some other time.

❑ 客(= kyaku) → (more polite) → お客(= o-kyaku) a customer

❑ お客さん (= o-kyaku san) → (more polite) → お客様(= o-kyaku sama).

❑ Clerks are required to call customers as お客さん (= o-kyaku san)
Or お客様 (= o-kyaku sama).

LESSON 6 🔊

Here are some useful expressions for shopping.

しはら　ほうほう お支払い方法は。 o-shiharai houhou wa?	How to pay?
しはら　かいすう お支払い回数は。 o-shiharai kaisuu wa?	How many payments do you have? (For credit card payment)
も ポイントカードはお持ちですか。 pointo kādo wa o-mochi desu ka?	Do you have a reward card? (In Japan, reward cards are often used.)
こ また、お越しください。 mata, o-koshi kudasai.	Please come again.
き また、来ます。 mata, kimasu.	I will come again.
すこ　やす もう少し安いのは　ありますか。 mou sukoshi yasui no wa ari masu ka?	Is there a little cheaper?
ねが すみません、ラッピングをお願いします。 sumimasen, rappingu wo o-negai shimasu.	Excuse me, please wrap it.
フィッティングルームは どこですか。 fittingurūmu wa doko desu ka?	Where is the fitting room?
これのLサイズはありますか。 kore no eru saizu wa ari masu ka?	Do you have this in size L?
なにいろ 他に何色がありますか。 hoka ni naniiro ga ari masu ka?	How many other colors do you have?
ねが これをお願いします。 kore wo o-negai shimasu.	May I have this.

This phrase is used by store employees

■ LESSON 6 🔊

Here are some useful expressions for shopping.	

<ruby>使<rt>つか</rt></ruby> クレジットカードは 使えますか。 kurejitto kādo wa tsukaemasu ka?	Can I use a credit card?
<ruby>領収書<rt>りょうしゅうしょ</rt></ruby> 領収書をください。 ryoushuusho wo kudasai.	Please give me the receipt.
<ruby>用<rt>よう</rt></ruby> プレゼント用にしてもらえますか。 purezento-you ni shite moraemasu ka?	Can I have this one gift-wrapped?
<ruby>袋<rt>ふくろ</rt></ruby> 袋を、もらえますか。 fukuro wo moraemasu ka?	Can I get a bag?
<ruby>可愛<rt>かわい</rt></ruby> <ruby>小<rt>ちい</rt></ruby> 可愛いですね。でも、ちょっと小さいかな。 kawaiidesu ne. demo, chotto chiisai ka na?	So cute. But is it a little small?
<ruby>二<rt>ふた</rt></ruby> これを二つください。 kore wo futatsu kudasai.	I want two of these.
<ruby>見<rt>み</rt></ruby> あれを見せてくれますか。 are wo misete kuremasu ka?	Can you show me that?
<ruby>安<rt>やす</rt></ruby> 安いですね。 yasui desu ne.	It's cheap.
<ruby>試着<rt>しちゃく</rt></ruby> 試着してもいいですか。 shichaku shite mo ii desu ka?	May I try it on?
<ruby>裾<rt>すそ</rt></ruby> <ruby>直<rt>なお</rt></ruby> 裾を直してもらえますか。 suso wo naoshite morae masu ka?	Can you fix the hem?

LESSON 7

Here are some useful vocabulary for shopping.

Kanji/Katakana	Hiragana	Rōmaji	English
お金	おかね	o-kane	Money
現金	げんきん	genkin	Cash
クレジットカード	くれじっとかーど	kurejittokādo	Credit card
大きい	おおきい	ookii	Big, tall, large
小さい	ちいさい	chiisai	Small
鞄	かばん	kaban	Bag
帽子	ぼうし	boushi	Hat
靴	くつ	kutsu	Shoes
ワンピース	わんぴーす	wanpīsu	One piece
ブラウス	ぶらうす	burausu	Blouse
スーツ	すーつ	sūtsu	Suit
シャツ	しゃつ	shatsu	Shirt
スカート	すかーと	sukāto	Skirt
ズボン	ずぼん	zubon	Pants
ティーシャツ	てぃーしゃつ	tīshatsu	T-shirt
ジーンズ	じーんず	jīnzu	Jeans
ジャケット	じゃけっと	jaketto	Jacket
価格	かかく	kakaku	Price
クーポン	くーぽん	kūpon	Coupon
店	みせ	mise	Shop / Store
花屋	はなや	hana-ya	Florist
魚屋	さかなや	sakana-ya	Fish Dealer
本屋	ほんや	hon-ya	Bookshop

■ LESSON 7 🔊

Here are some useful vocabulary for shopping.

Kanji/Katakana	Hiragana	Rōmaji	English
薬屋	くすりや	kusuri-ya	Pharmacy
パン屋	ぱんや	pan-ya	Bakery
セール	せーる	sēru	Sale
買い物	かいもの	kaimono	Shopping
ネックレス	ねっくれす	nekkuresu	Necklace
指輪	ゆびわ	yubiwa	ring
カメラ	かめら	kamera	Camera
用品	ようひん	youhin	Supplies
化粧	けしょう	keshou	Makeup
電池	でんち	denchi	Battery
傘	かさ	kasa	Umbrella
靴下	くつした	kutsushita	The socks
コート	こーと	kōto	Coat
下着	したぎ	shitagi	Underwear
パジャマ	ぱじゃま	pajama	Pajamas
セーター	せーたー	sētā	Sweater
イヤリング	いやりんぐ	iyaringu	Earring
スカーフ	すかーふ	sukāfu	Scarf
ベルト	べると	beruto	Belt
サンダル	さんだる	sandaru	Sandals
ハイヒール	はいひーる	haihīru	High Heeled Shoes
ブーツ	ぶーつ	būtsu	Boots

UNIT 16

Colors

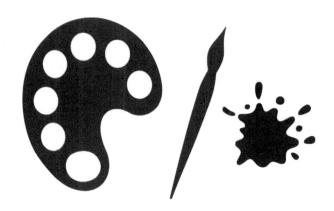

- Colors.
- Colors. – Adjectives.
- Colors. – Vocabulary.

The Japanese word for color is ″色″ (iro) In Japanese, specific colors are expressed using two sets of words, with one set being based on ancient Japanese traditions and aesthetics, such as 'murasaki' (purple) and 'wakakusa' (light green). The other set of words is loan words from English that are written in katakana. However, not all colors have loan word versions, and some loan words are not used as commonly as their Japanese counterparts. The use of each set of words depends on the parts of speech and the context.

Basic Colors in Japanese

Kanji/Katakana	Hiragana	Rōmaji	English
赤/レッド	あか	aka/reddo	Red
橙/オレンジ	だいだい	daidai/orenji	Orange
黄/イエロー	き	ki/ierō	Yellow
緑/グリーン	みどり	midori/gurīn	Green
青/ブルー	あお	ao/burū	Blue
紫/パープル	むらさき	murasaki	Purple
桃/ピンク	もも	momo/pinku	Pink
茶/ブラウン	ちゃ	cha/buraun	Brown
灰/グレイ	はい	hai/gurei	Grey
黒/ブラック	くろ	kuro/burakku	Black
白/ホワイト	しろ	shiro/howaito	White

❑ The above words refer to different colors, so when you're talking about a color of something, you use the particle ″の″ (no).

Example: The basic sentence pattern for describing colors is: color + ″の″ + subject.

Orange flower: ″オレンジ色の花″ (orenji-iro no hana) Orange flowers.

LESSON 2 🔊

Japanese Adjectives to Describe Colors.
Using adjectives, colors can be described in Japanese as well. Interestingly, there are just four colors that turn into adjectives by adding "い" directly to the end.

Exploring Color Basics in Ancient Japanese Language.

Kanji	Hiragana	Rōmaji	English
赤い	あかい	akai	Red
青い	あおい	aoi	Blue
黒い	くろい	kuroi	Black
白い	しろい	shiroi	White

Example of How to Use Japanese Colors: Use directly in front of the subject.

あお うみ
青い海
ao i umi
Blue sea

or

うみ あお
海は 青いです。
umi wa aoi desu.
The sea is blue.

きいろ　　　　ちゃいろ
"黄色い" and "茶色い"

There are two more colors that can function as adjectives: "黄色 and 茶色."
Why aren't they included with the previous four colors?
This is because, even though they mean yellow and brown, "黄" (yellow) and "茶" (brown)
Cannot stand alone when used as colors.

They must be joined with the word "色" (iro – meaning colors) to be color names for yellow and brown. Consequently, when they function as adjectives, they become:
"Yellowish-brown" and "Brownish," rather than "黄い" or "茶い."

きいろ　　　　ちゃいろ　　　　き　　　ちゃ
"黄色い" and "茶色い" instead "黄い" or "茶い"

LESSON 3 🔊

Japanese Adjectives to Describe Colors.
Using adjectives, colors can be described in Japanese as well. Interestingly, there are just four colors that turn into adjectives by adding "い" directly to the end.

Exploring Colors in Ancient Japanese Language.

Kanji	Hiragana	Rōmaji	English
赤色	あかいろ	aka-iro	Red color
青色	あおいろ	ao-iro	Blue color
緑色	みどりいろ	midori-iro	Green color
黄色	きいろ	ki-iro	Yellow color
紫色	むらさきいろ	murasaki-iro	Purple color
黒色	くろいろ	kuro-iro	Black color
白色	しろいろ	shiro-iro	White color
茶色	ちゃいろ	cha-iro	Brown color
紺色	こんいろ	kon-iro	Dark blue color
水色	みずいろ	mizu-iro	Light blue color
金色	きんいろ	kin-iro	Gold color
銀色	ぎんいろ	gin-iro	Silver color
黄緑色	きみどりいろ	kimidori-iro	yellow-green color

❏ Two words for "pink" 桃色 (momoiro) – native Japanese word or ピンク (pinku) borrowed from English.

❏ Two words for "grey" 灰色 (haiiro) – native Japanese word or グレー (gurē) borrowed from English.

❏ Two words for "orange" 橙色 (daidaiiro) – native Japanese word or オレンジ (orenji) borrowed from English.

UNIT 17

よ やく
予約をする

Make a reservation

- Hotel reservation.
- Reservation dialogue. (Over the Phone)
- Japanese phrases related to hotels.
- Counting nights, rooms, and types of rooms.
- Vocabulary.

■ **LESSON 1** 🔊

> When you're in Japan and want a hotel room, it might feel a bit scary to make a reservation, especially if you need to speak Japanese on the phone. But you know what? Even Japanese people feel the same way when they're booking hotels in other countries.
>
> The first time you arrive at the hotel can be a little nerve-wracking. But don't worry, whether you already booked a room or not, there's no need to stress. Japanese hotels are good at helping guests, and checking in is quite simple. They just want to make sure you have a room.
>
> Given the challenges that come with booking a room through a phone conversation in Japanese, this lesson has been thoughtfully designed to equip you with the skills needed to easily reserve a hotel room.

Reservation or booking in Japanese is: よやく

よやく
"予約" (yoyaku) and to book/to make a reservation is "予約をする" (yoyaku wo suru).

りょかん
旅館(ryokan)

A "ryokan" is a traditional Japanese inn or cozy hotel that features tatami floors, futon beds, Japanese-style baths, and local cuisine. These unique accommodations are loved by both Japanese and foreign visitors.

Inside a ryokan guest room

In a usual ryokan guest room, you can anticipate finding:

- "shouji" (sliding paper doors) which separates the agari-kamachi from the room.
- "tatami" mat flooring (reed floor matting).
- "zabuton" (sitting cushions).
- "futon" (sleeping quilts).
- Low wooden tables.

LESSON 2 🔊

Here is an example of dialogue when making a reservation at a hotel over the phone in Japanese.

Clerk: もしもし、大阪ホテルでございます。Hello, it's Hotel Osaka.
(moshi moshi, Oosaka hoteru de go-zaimasu.)

Customer You: 予約を お願いします。I would like to make a reservation.
(yoyaku wo o-negai shimasu.)

Clerk: いつから お泊りになりますか。From when will you be staying?
(itsukara o-tomari ni narimasu ka?)

Customer You: 来週の金曜日から二泊です。Two nights, starting Friday of next week.
(raishuu no kinyoubi kara ni-haku desu.)

Clerk: 何名様でございますか。How many people will there be?
(nan-mei-sama de go-zaimasu ka?)

Customer You: 二人です。It will be 2 people.
(futari desu.)

Clerk: ご一緒でございますか。Will this be one room?
(go-issho de go-zaimasu ka?)

Customer You: いえ、別々のシングルをお願いします。No, I'd like separate singles.
(ie, betsu betsu no singuru wo o-negaishimasu.)

Clerk: お名前を頂けますか。　May I have your name, please?
(o-namae wo itadakemasu ka?)

LESSON 2 🔊

Dialogue when making a reservation at a hotel over the phone in Japanese.

Customer
You: クリスと言います。いくらですか。　　My name is Chris. How much is it?
(Chris to ii masu. ikura desu ka?)

Clerk: クリス様。では、十八日の金曜日から二泊と言うことで、シングルを二部屋

おとりしておきます。三万四千五百円です。
(Chris sama. dewa juu-hachi-niti no kinyoubi kara, ni-haku to iu koto de, singuru wo
huta-heya o-tori-site oki masu. sanman yon sen go hyaku en desu.)
Mr. Chris. OK, three nights, starting Friday the 18th. I'll hold two single rooms.
It will cost 34,500 yen.

Customer
You: 朝食は含まれていますか。(choushoku wa fukumarete imasu ka?) Is breakfast included?

Clerk: 朝食は含まれています。(choushoku wa fukumarete imasu.) Breakfast included.

Customer
You: Wi-Fiは、ありますか。(WI-FI wa, ari masu ka?)　　Is there a WIFI?

Clerk: はい、ございます。(hai, go-zaimasu.)　　　　　Yes, there is.

Customer
You: チェックアウトは何時ですか。(chekku-outo wa nan-ji desu ka?) What time is check-out?

LESSON 2

Dialogue when making a reservation at a hotel over the phone in Japanese.

じゅういちじ
Clerk: チェックアウトは十一時でございます。 Check-out time is 11:00.
(chekku-auto wa juu-ichi-ji de go-zaimasu.)

ねが
Customer
You: よろしく お願いします。(yoroshiku o-negaishimasu.) Thank you.

LESSON 3 🔊

Japanese phrases related to hotels.

よやく
1. すみません、予約をしたいのですが。　　　Excuse me I'd like to make a reservation.
   (sumimasen, yoyaku wo shitai nodesu ga.)

なんじ
2. チェックアウトは、何時ですか。　　　What time is check-out?
   (chekku-auto wa, nan-ji desu ka?)

いっぱく えんちょう
3. 一泊、延長することはできますか。　　　Can I extend my stay by one night?
   (ippaku enchou suru koto wa dekimasu ka?)

にもつ あず
4. 荷物を預けられますか。　　　Can I leave my luggage here?
   (nimotsu wo azukeraremasu ka?)

いちだい よ
5. タクシーを一台、呼んでください。　　　Could you call a taxi for me?
   (takushī wo ichi-dai, yonde kudasai.)

ちょうしょく ばしょ
6. 朝食の場所は、どこですか。　　　Where should I go for breakfast?
   (choushoku no basho wa, doko desu ka?)

なん
7. Wi-Fiのパスワードは、何ですか。　　　What is the WIFI password?
   (waifai no pasuwādo wa, nan desu ka?)

い いちばんはや
8. ダウンタウンまでは、どうやって行くのが一番早いですか。
   (dauntaun made wa, dou yatte iku no ga ichiban hayai desu ka?)
   　　　What's the fastest way to get downtown?

LESSON 4

The following are the most important factors to consider (from one to five) when trying to book a night in a hotel, which will come in handy.

Counting Nights of Stay		Counting Nights		Counting Rooms	
一泊	i-ppaku	一晩	hito-ban	一部屋	hito-heya
二泊	ni-haku	二晩	huta-ban	二部屋	huta-heya
三泊	san-paku	三晩	mi-ban	三部屋	mi-heya
四泊	yon-haku	四晩	yo-ban	四部屋	yon-heya
五泊	go-haku	五晩	itsu-ban	五部屋	go-heya

How Many Nights of Stay?		How Many Nights?		How Many Rooms?	
なんぱく 何泊	nan-paku	いくばん 幾晩	iku-ban	なんへ や 何部屋	nan-heya

Type of Room	Japanese	Rōmaji
Double room	ダブル	daburu
Room with twin beds	ツイン	tsuin
Western-style room	洋間	youma
Japanese-style room	和室	washitsu
Room with a bath	バス付き	basu tsuki

280

LESSON 5 🔊

Here are some useful vocabulary. 1-2

Kanji/Katakana	Hiragana	Rōmaji	English
フロント	ふろんと	furonto	Front desk
予約	よやく	yoyaku	Reservation
部屋	へや	heya	Room
チェックイン	ちぇっくいん	chekkuin	Check-in
チェックアウト	ちぇっくあうと	chekkuauto	Check out
住所	じゅうしょ	juusho	Address
ツインルーム	ついんるーむ	tsuinrūmu	Twin room
シングルルーム	しんぐるるーむ	shingururūmu	Single room
ダブルルーム	だぶるるーむ	dabururūmu	Double room
スイートルーム	すいーとるーむ	suītorūmu	Suite Room
洋室	ようしつ	youshitsu	Western-style room
和室	わしつ	washitsu	Japanese-style room
禁煙	きんえん	kinen	Non-smoking room
喫煙	きつえん	kitsuen	Smoking room
鍵	かぎ	kagi	Key
シングルベッド	しんぐるべっど	shinguru beddo	Single bed
ツインベッド	ついんべっど	tsuinbeddo	Twin bed
クイーンサイズベッド	くいーんさいずべっど	kuīnsaizubeddo	Queen-size bed
キングサイズベッド	きんぐさいずべっど	kingusaizubeddo	King-size bed
予備のベッド	よびのべっど	yobi no beddo	Extra bed
ロビー	ろびー	Robī	Lobby
荷物	にもつ	nimotsu	Luggage

LESSON 5 🔊

Here are some useful vocabulary. 2-2

Kanji/Katakana	Hiragana	Rōmaji	English
シャワー	しゃわー	shawā	Shower
タオル	たおる	taoru	Towel
窓	まど	mado	Window
ソファ	そふぁ	sofa	Sofa
枕	まくら	makura	Pillow
歯ブラシ	はぶらし	haburashi	Toothbrush
シェービング	しぇーびんぐ	shēbingu	shaving
トイレットペーパー	といれっとぺーぱー	toirettopēpā	Toilet paper
ルームサービス	るーむさーびす	rūmusābisu	Room service
セーフティボックス	せーふてぃぼっくす	sēfutibokkusu	Safe box
ドライヤー	どらいやー	doraiyā	Hairdryer
両替	りょうがえ	ryougae	Money exchange
税金	ぜいきん	zeikin	Tax
支払い	しはらい	shiharai	Payment
滞在	たいざい	taizai	Stay
毛布	もうふ	moufu	Blanket
石鹸	せっけん	sekken	Soap
冷房	れいぼう	reibou	Air conditioning
シャンプー	しゃんぷー	shanpū	Shampoo
リンス	りんす	rinsu	Rinse
インターネット	いんたーねっと	intānetto	Internet

■ **LESSON 6** 🔊 Dialogue when checking in at a hotel

Clerk: いらっしゃいませ。(irasshaimase.) Welcome!

Customer
You: こんにちは。チェックイン、おねがいします。 Hello. Please check in.
(kon'nichiwa. chekkuin, o-negaishimasu.)

Clerk: はい、かしこまりました。お名前をお伺いしてよろしいでしょうか。
(hai, kashikomarimashita. o-namae wo o-ukagai shite yoroshiideshou ka?)
Yes, certainly. May I have your name?

Customer
You: 田中です。(Tanaka desu.) I'm Tanaka.

Clerk: 田中様ですね。(Tanaka-sama desu ne.) Mr. Tanaka.

Clerk: 少々お待ちください。(shoushou o-machi kudasai.) Please hold on.

Clerk: 本日から二泊、ご予約いただいております。
(honjitsu kara ni-haku go-yoyaku itadaite orimasu.)
We have your reservation for 2 nights from today.

Clerk: こちらにお名前と電話番号、サインをおねがいします。
(kochira ni o-namae to denwa-bangou, sain wo o-negaishimasu.)
Please write your name, phone number, and signature on this form.

Customer
You: はい。(Hai.) Yes.

Clerk: お部屋は503号室です。(o-heya wa go-maru-san goushitsu desu.) Your room No. 503

Clerk: 明日の朝食は七時から十時までです。Breakfast will be served from 7 to 10 am.
(ashita no choushoku wa shichi-ji kara jyuu-ji made desu.)

Clerk: チェックアウトは十二時までにおねがいします。 Please check out by 12:00 PM.
(chekku auto wa jyuu-ni-ji made ni o-negaishimasu.)

Customer
You: はい、ありがとうございます。(Hai, arigatougozaimasu.) Yes, Thank you.

UNIT 18

からだ　ぶ ぶん
体の部分

Body parts

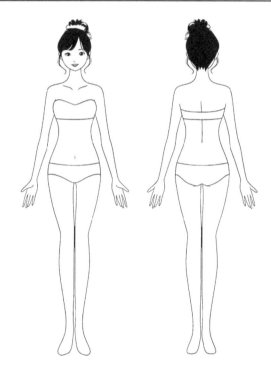

- Body parts.
- How to explain your pain to a doctor.
- Common phrases you might use in normal life.
- Vocabulary.

LESSON 1 🔊

Learning the names of body parts is invaluable in any language, and Japanese is certainly no different, especially if you want to communicate effectively in everyday situations, describe health issues, or seek medical help from Japanese speakers. It can be understanding the names of body parts It is also important in expressing discomfort, pain, or other physical sensations. Imagine that you are in Japan for the first time and need to see a doctor. You can use this vocabulary to accurately describe an area of discomfort.

I understand that remembering all the names of body parts can be difficult. To make things easier, I suggest starting with simpler phrases like ″髪″ (かみ-Hair), ″耳″ (みみ-Ear), and ″目″ (め), for eyes, etc. As you become more familiar with them, you will naturally expand your understanding of these terms, and improve your ability to communicate.

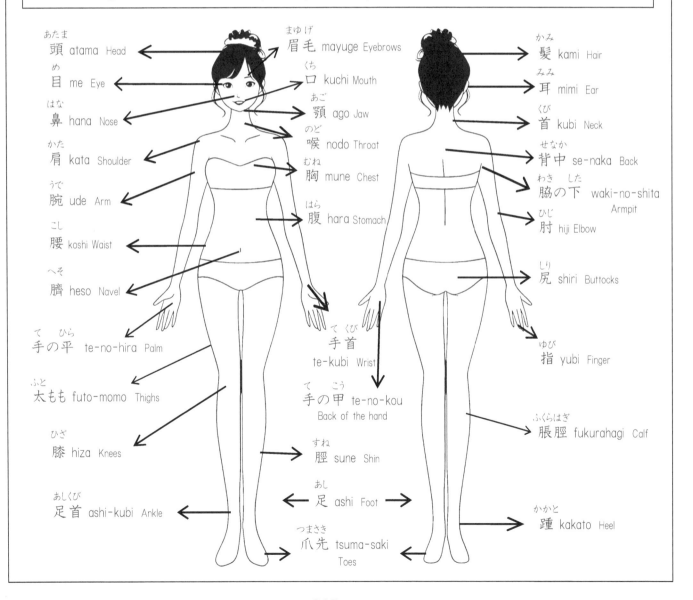

あたま
頭 atama Head

め
目 me Eye

はな
鼻 hana Nose

かた
肩 kata Shoulder

うで
腕 ude Arm

こし
腰 koshi Waist

へそ
臍 heso Navel

て　ひら
手の平 te-no-hira Palm

ふと
太もも futo-momo Thighs

ひざ
膝 hiza Knees

あしくび
足首 ashi-kubi Ankle

まゆげ
眉毛 mayuge Eyebrows

くち
口 kuchi Mouth

あご
顎 ago Jaw

のど
喉 nodo Throat

むね
胸 mune Chest

はら
腹 hara Stomach

て　くび
手首
te-kubi Wrist

て　こう
手の甲 te-no-kou
Back of the hand

すね
脛 sune Shin

あし
足 ashi Foot

つまさき
爪先 tsuma-saki
Toes

かみ
髪 kami Hair

みみ
耳 mimi Ear

くび
首 kubi Neck

せなか
背中 se-naka Back

わき　した
脇の下 waki-no-shita
Armpit

ひじ
肘 hiji Elbow

しり
尻 shiri Buttocks

ゆび
指 yubi Finger

ふくらはぎ
脹脛 fukurahagi Calf

かかと
踵 kakato Heel

■ LESSON 2 🔊

When you need to describe where you feel pain to your doctor, you can fill in the blank 【 】 with the specific body part that hurts and use the following phrase:

Simple Pattern:

　　　　　　　　いた
[Body Part] +が+痛い+です。([Body Part] +ga+ itai+ desu.)

① My【　　　　　】hurt.
　　　　　　いた
【　　　　　】が 痛いです。
【　　　　　】ga itai   desu.

② My【　　　　　】is/are in serious pain.
　　　　　　　　　いた
【　　　　　】が かなり(すごく)痛いです。
【　　　　　】ga kanari(sugoku) itai desu.

③ My【　　　　　】hurts a little.
　　　　　　すこ いた
【　　　　　】が 少し痛いです。
【　　　　　】ga sukoshi itai desu.

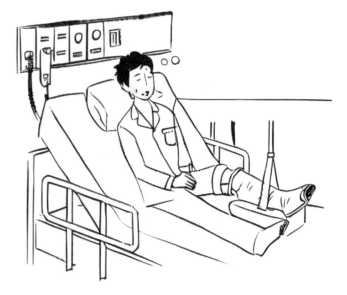

It is helpful to know that when you go to a hospital in Japan, you may not be able to speak Japanese, and you may not know which department to go to, or you may have to wait a long time or make an appointment, or you may have to pay high fees for medical treatment and insurance. Even if you do not speak Japanese, try to communicate with the doctor by gestures.

　　　　　　むね くる
Example 1: 胸が苦しいです。
　　　　　mune ga kurushii desu.
　　　　　I feel tight in my chest.

　　　　　　なか いた
Example 2: お腹が痛い。
　　　　　o-naka ga itai.
　　　　　My stomach hurts.

LESSON 3 🔊

Here are some common Japanese phrases involving body parts. Remembering these phrases can be helpful for everyday conversations.

❖ In formal situations, you can use "ください" at the end of these phrases, but it's not necessary when speaking with close friends or kids.

て あら
Example 1: 手を洗って（ください）！
te wo aratte (kudasai) !
Wash your hands!

ゆび
Example 6: 指をケガしました。
yubi wo kega shimashita.
I hurt my finger.

は みが
Example 2: 歯を磨いて（ください）！
ha wo migaite (kudasai) !
Brush your teeth!

なか いた
Example 7: お腹が痛いです。
o-naka ga itai desu.
I have a pain in my stomach.

はな き
Example 3: 鼻が利くね。(Casual)
hana ga kiku ne.
You have a good nose.

め あ
Example 8: 目を開けて（ください）！
me wo akete (kudasai) !
Open your eyes!

みみ いた
Example 4: 耳が痛い（です）。
mimi ga itai (desu).
That makes my ears burn.

あし あ
Example 9: 足を上げて（ください）！
ashi wo agete (kudasai) !
Raise your legs!

うで
Example 5: それを腕につけて（ください）！
sore wo ude ni tsukete. (kudasai) !
Put it on your arm.

て ひら み
Example 10: 手の平を見せて（ください）！
te-no-hira wo misete (kudasai) !
Show your palm!

LESSON 4

Vocabulary for the Parts of the Human Body (1-2)

Kanji	Hiragana	Rōmaji	English
頭	あたま	atama	Head
顔	かお	kao	Face
髪	かみ	kami	Hair
口	くち	kuchi	Mouth
鼻	はな	hana	Nose
目	め	me	Eye
耳	みみ	mimi	Ear
眉	まゆ	mayu	Eyebrow
瞼	まぶた	mabuta	Eyelid
睫毛	まつげ	matsuge	Eyelash
瞳	ひとみ	hitomi	Iris
首	くび	kubi	Neck
肩	かた	kata	Shoulder
胸	むね	mune	Chest
脇の下	わきのした	waki-no-shita	Armpit
手	て	te	Hand
指	ゆび	yubi	Finger
手首	てくび	tekubi	Wrist
腰	こし	koshi	Waist/hip
腿	もも	momo	Thigh
膝	ひざ	hiza	Knee
脚	あし	ashi	Leg
足	あし	ashi	Foot/Feet

LESSON 4 🔊

Vocabulary for the Parts of the Human Body (2-2)

Kanji	Hiragana	Rōmaji	English
つま先	つまさき	tsuma-saki	Tiptoe
踵	かかと	kakato	Heel
足首	あしくび	ashi-kubi	Ankle
肘	ひじ	hiji	Elbow
腕	うで	ude	Arm
お腹	おなか	o-naka	Stomach
唇	くちびる	kuchibiru	Lips
舌	した	shita	Tongue
爪	つめ	tsume	Nail
歯	は	ha	Teeth
顎	あご	ago	Jaw
喉	のど	nodo	Throat

わたし　かみ　　なが
Example 1: 私は、髪がとても長いです。
　　　　　watashi wa, kami ga totemo nagai desu.
　　　　　I have very long hair.

まいあさ かお あら
Example 2: わたしは毎朝、顔を洗います。
　　　　　watashi wa maiasa, kao wo araimasu.
　　　　　I wash my face every morning.

わたし　　うで こっせつ
Example 3: 私は、腕を骨折した。
　　　　　watashi wa, ude wo kossetsu shita.
　　　　　I broke my arm.

UNIT 19

<ruby>日<rt>に</rt>本<rt>ほん</rt>語<rt>ご</rt></ruby>の<ruby>動<rt>どう</rt>詞<rt>し</rt></ruby>

Japanese Verbs

- Japanese verbs groups.
- Masu form.
- Japanese verbs. – Past tense.
- Japanese verbs. – Present negative.
- Japanese verbs. – Past negative.
- Japanese verbs. – て- form.
- Functions of the 〜 te form.
- Ask permissions.
- Ask question.
- Ask for advice and suggestion.
- Make a request.
- Ask back & ask for help.

Mastering Japanese verbs requires understanding their structures and forms, and it's one of the most essential skills you will need to learn to be fluent in Japanese. Start with the dictionary form to grasp the basic meaning. Move on to the -masu form for polite communication. Learn the -te form for linking actions and the -nai form for negation. Regular practice and real-life application will solidify your command over Japanese verbs.

There are 3 Groups of Verbs in Japanese

Group 1: verbs: Also known as ″う″(u-verbs) or ″五段動詞″(godan doushi). "u-verbs" are verbs that end with the う.

Examples of godan verbs are:

話す (hanasu) → "to speak"
飲む (nomu) → "to drink"
死ぬ (shinu) → "to die"
聞く (kiku) → "to hear"
遊ぶ (asobu) → "to play"
買う (kau) → "to buy"
待つ (matsu) → "to wait"

Group 2: verbs: Also known as る-verbs (ru-verbs) or ″一段動詞″(ichidan doushi), all end in ″いる″ or ″える″.

Examples of ichidan verbs:

食べる (taberu) → "to eat"
見る (miru) → "to see"
出る (deru) → "to leave"
寝る (neru) → "to sleep"
起きる (okiru) → "to get up/wake up"

Group 3: verbs: Also known as **irregular** verbs or ″不規則動詞″(fukisoku doushi). There are only two irregular verbs. And they're so common.

1.する (suru) → "to do"
2.来る (kuru) → "to come"

Examples of irregular verbs : べんきょうする。(benkyou suru.) To study.

Masu Form

The (masu) form (Formal Form).

Add the suffix "ます"(masu) to the dictionary form of a verb to make the sentence polite.

Use this form in situations requiring increased politeness or formality, and it is more appropriate for general use.

~ masu Form	
Group 1	Remove the final ~u, and add ~ imasu (kaku --- kakimasu, nomu --- nomimasu)
Group 2	Remove the final ~ru, and add ~ masu (miru --- mimasu, taberu --- tabemasu)
Group 3	kuru --- kimasu, suru --- shimasu

The verb stem can be found by removing the ~ masu from the ~masu form:

~ Masu Form	Verb Stem
kakimasu	kaki
nomimasu	nomi
mimasu	mi
tabemasu	tabe

Present Tense

Japanese verbs come in two main tenses: present and past. The present tense is used for actions in the future and things you do regularly. The informal present tense looks like the dictionary form. In more formal situations, you can use the ~masu form.

Example: [Informal/Formal]

私は水を飲む。/飲みます。(watashi wa mizu wo nomu. / nomimasu.) I drink water.

LESSON 2 🔊

Masu Form

The (masu) is a polite form of verbs, also known as the "ます"(masu).
Here are some examples of polite non-past verbs:

わたし　　　　　の
Example 1: 私はコーヒーを飲みます。
   watashi wa kōhī wo nomi**masu**.
   I drink coffee.

わたし　さかな　た
Example 3: 私は、魚を食べます。
   watashi wa sakana wo tabe**masu**.
   I eat fish.

みせ　い
Example 2: お店に行きます。
   mise ni iki**masu**.
   I go to the store.

❖   Note: To make the verb negative, we can change the ending "ます" (masu) to "ません" (masen).

e.g. :
いきます   ➡   いきません
iki**masu**   ➡   iki**masen**
go/will go   ➡   don't go/won't go

Affirmative Form: "ます"(masu) Here are some examples:

がっこう　い
Example 1: 学校に行きます。
   gakkou ni iki**masu**.
   I go to school.

"I go to school" (present) or "I will go to school" (future) depending on the context of the sentence.

た
Example 2: おかしを食べます。
   o-kashi wo tabemasu.
   I eat sweets.

(present) or (future) depending on the context of the sentence.

にほんご　べんきょう
Example 3: 日本語を勉強します。
   Nihongo wo benkyou shi**masu**.
   I study Japanese/I will study Japanese.

Past Tense

Creating the past tense in Japanese is quite straightforward. There's only one form for the past tense – no need for variations like "did," "have done," "had done," and so on.

For Group 1 verbs, the way they're conjugated depends on the last sound in their dictionary form. Meanwhile, all Group 2 verbs follow the same conjugation pattern.

Past Tense			
Group 1			
Formal		Replace ～ u with ～ imashita	kaku --- kak**imashita** nomu --- nom**imashita**
Informal	(1)	Verb ending with ～ ku: replace ～ ku with ～ ita	kaku --- ka**ita** kiku --- ki**ita**
	(2)	Verb ending with ～ gu: replace ～ gu with ～ ida	isogu --- iso**ida** oyogu --- oyo**ida**
	(3)	Verb ending with ～ u, ～tsu and ～ ru: replace them with ～ tta	utau --- uta**tta** matsu --- ma**tta** kaeru --- kae**tta**
	(4)	Verb ending with ～ nu, ～bu & ～ mu: replace them with ～ nda	shinu --- shi**nda** asobu --- aso**nda** nomu --- no**nda**
	(5)	Verb ending with ～ su: replace ～ su with ～ shita	hanasu --- hana**shita** dasu --- da**shita**

Group 2		
Formal	Take off ～ru, and add ～ mashita	miru --- mi**mashita** taberu ---tabe**mashita**
Informal	Take off ～ru, and add ～ ta	miru --- mi**ta** taberu --- tabe**ta**

Group 3	
Formal	kuru --- kimashita, suru --- shima**shita**
Informal	kuru --- kita, suru ---**shita**

LESSON 4

Past Tense Change from ます(masu) to ました(mashita)

The polite past form of verbs, end in "ました"(mashita) to change a verb from present to past tense, just change the "ます"(masu) ending to "ました"(mashita).
Here are some examples of (mashita) verbs:

あさ はん た
朝ご飯を食べ<u>ます</u>。
(asa-gohan wo tabe<u>masu</u>.)
I eat breakfast.

朝ご飯を食べ**ました**。
(asa-gohan wo tabe**mashita**.)
I ate breakfast.

Group 2

てがみ か
手紙を書き<u>ます</u>。
(tegami wo kaki<u>masu</u>.)
I write a letter.

手紙を書き**ました**。
(tegami wo kaki**mashita**.)
I wrote a letter.

Group 1

み
わたしはテレビを見<u>ます</u>。
(watashi wa terebi wo mi<u>masu</u>.)
I watch TV.

わたしはテレビを見**ました**。
(watashi wa terebi wo mi**mashita**.
I watched TV.

Group 2

はは はな
わたしは母と話し<u>ます</u>。
(watashi wa haha to hanashi<u>masu</u>.)
I talk with my mother.

わたしは母と話し**ました**。
(watashi wa haha to hanashi**mashita**.)
I talked with my mother.

Group 1

しゅくだい
宿題をし<u>ます</u>。
(shukudai wo shi<u>masu</u>.)
I will do my homework.

宿題をし**ました**。
(shukudai wo shi**mashita**.)
I did my homework.

Group 3

LESSON 5

Present Negative

To make a negative sentence, change the verb ending into the ~nai, negative form.
食べる(taberu) → 食べない(tabenai) Here, 食べ/たべ(tabe) is the verb stem.

All Verbs (Group 1, 2, 3)		
Formal	Replace 〜 masu with 〜 masen	nomimasu --- nomi**masen** tabemasu --- tabe**masen** kimasu ----- ki**masen** shimasu ----- shi**masen**
Group 1		
Informal	Replace the final 〜 u with 〜anai (If verb ending is a vowel + 〜 u, replace with 〜 wanai)	kiku -----kika**nai** nomu-----noma**nai** au ----- awa**nai**
Group 2		
Informal	Replace 〜 ru with 〜 nai	miru ----- mi**nai** taberu --- tabe**nai**
Group 3		
Informal	kuru --- **konai**, suru ---**shinai**	

Examples:

Formal:
わたしあさ　　　　　　た
私は朝ごはんを食べます。
(watashi wa asagohan wo tabe<u>masu</u>.)
I eat breakfast.

→

私は朝ごはんを食べません。
(watashi wa asagohan wo tabe**masen**.)
I don't eat breakfast.

Group 2

Informal:
　　きゅうじつ　なに
わたしは休日に何かをする。
(watashi wa kyuujitsu ni nanika wo <u>suru</u>.)
I do something on my days off.

→

私は休日に何もしない。
(watashi wa kyuujitsu ni nani mo **shinai**.)
I do nothing on my days off.

Group 3

LESSON 6 🔊

Past Negative

To put verbs into the past tense with a formal negative meaning, simply add "でした" (deshita) after the polite present tense form. For Ru-verbs, U-verbs, and irregular verbs, this rule applies. In the informal negative past tense, change "ない" (nai) from the informal present tense form to "なかった" (nakatta).

- This rule works for Ru-verbs, U-verbs, and irregular verbs as well.

Group 1, 2, 3		
Formal	Add 〜 deshita to the formal present negative form	nomimasen − − − nomimasen **deshita** tabemasen − − − tabemasen **deshita** kimasen − − − − − kimasen **deshita** shimasen − − − − −shimasen **deshita**
Group 1, 2, 3		
Informal	Replace 〜 nai with 〜 nakatta	nomanai − − − noma**nakatta** tabenai − − − tabe**nakatta** konai − − − ko**nakatta** shinai − − −shi**nakatta**

Examples:

あさ　　　た
朝ごはんを食べ<u>ません</u>。
(asa gohan wo tabe<u>masen</u>.)
I don't eat breakfast.

➡ 朝ごはんを食べ**ませんでした**。
(asa gohan wo tabe**masen deshita**.)
I didn't eat breakfast.
Formal

あさ　　　た
朝ごはんを食べ<u>ない</u>。
(asa gohan wo tabe<u>nai</u>.)
I don't eat breakfast.

➡ 朝ごはんを食べ**なかった**。
(asagohan wo tabe**nakatta**.)
I didn't eat breakfast.
Informal

What is て Te-form?

The "te-form" is similar to the present progressive tense in English. It's called the "te-form" because you modify verbs to end with "te" (て) or "nde" (んで) in Japanese. The "te-form" is used to create the "ing" form of a verb, like this: "食べる" (taberu) becomes "食べて" (tabete), changing from "I eat" or "I will eat" to "I'm eating."

行く (iku) - to go て-form: 行って (itte) - going

する (suru) - to do て-form: して (shite) - doing

見る (miru) - to see て-form: 見て (mite) - seeing

来る (kuru) - to come て-form: 来て (kite) - coming

書く (kaku) - to write て-form: 書いて (kaite) - writing

読む (yomu) - to read て-form: 読んで (yonde) - reading

食べる (taberu) - to eat て-form: 食べて (tabete) - eating

聞く (kiku) - to listen/ask て-form: 聞いて (kiite) - listening/asking

Notes:

- This form has various uses and is an essential aspect of Japanese grammar. The "te-form" by itself doesn't indicate tense (past, present, etc.).

- Japanese employs the same verb form for both the future and present tenses, as well as for general statements. This can lead to some confusion in distinguishing between "I eat (right now)" and "I will eat (in the future)."

- The te-form is used for various grammatical constructions like connecting verbs, making requests, giving reasons, and more.

LESSON 8

How to Conjugate Te form て-form?

We learned previously that there are 3 groups of Japanese verbs:

1. う-verbs (u-verbs)   **2.** る-verbs (ru-verbs)   **3.** irregular verbs

Group 1

Verbs that end up with the words "う"(u), "つ"(tsu), or "る"(ru), replace these words with "って"(tte). For those verbs which end up with the words "む"(mu), "ぬ"(nu), or "ぶ"(bu), replace the words with "んで"(nde).

Examples:

	Dictionary			Te Form	
To drink	のむ	–	nomu	→	のんで – nonde
To play	あそぶ	–	asobu	→	あそんで – asonde
To die	しぬ	–	shinu	→	しんで – shinde

❑ Group one verbs – U-verbs with final "う", "つ" and "る". "U", "Tsu", and "Ru".

Examples:

	Dictionary			Te Form	
To buy	かう	–	kau	→	かって – katte
To wait	まつ	–	matsu	→	まって – matte
To take	とる	–	toru	→	とって – totte

For group I verbs which end up with the word "く"(ku), change the word to "いて"(ite). For those which end up with the word "ぐ"(gu), change it to "いで"(ide). And for those which end up with the word "す"(su), change it to "して"(shite).

		Dictionary		Te Form
❑ Group one				
❑ U-verbs that end in く – ku		To write かく	→	かいて
❑ U-verbs that end in ぐ – gu	Example >	To swim およぐ	→	およいで
❑ U-verbs that end in す - su		To speak はなす	→	はなして

❖ There is one exception. (In Japanese you always come across many exceptions).
For the Japanese verb "いく"(iku) which means "to go", the te-form is "いって"(itte).

LESSON 8

Group 2

The second group is very easy to conjugate, the verbs always end with the word "る"(ru). You just need to replace "る"(ru) with "て"(te).

Examples:

	Dictionary			**Te Form**	
To eat	食^たべる - tabe<u>ru</u>	→	食^たべて - tabe**te**		
To see	見^みる - mi<u>ru</u>	→	見^みて - mi**te**		

❖ taberu becomes tabete, and miru becomes mite.

Group 3

"Irregular verbs." Verbs the te-form of "する" (suru) is "して" (shite) and the te-form of "くる" (kuru) is "きて" (kite).

Examples:

	Dictionary			**Te Form**	
To do	する - <u>suru</u>	→	して - **shite**		
To come	来^くる - <u>kuru</u>	→	来^きて - **kite**		

Irregular verbs are verbs that have exceptions to the "て form" rules. Instead of simply dropping the ru and adding a te – they each have their own method.

"suru" becomes **shite**, and "kuru" becomes **kite**.

■ **LESSON 9** 🔊

Functions of the 〜 Te form

1. Describe a Habitual Action/ Condition.

2. Request (〜 te form + kudasai).

If you need someone to do something for you, or to ask for a favor, you use て + ください (te + kudasai).

見てください　mite **kudasai.**	<u>Please</u> look.
聞いてください　kiite **kudasai.**	<u>Please</u> listen.
書いてください　kaite **kudasai.**	<u>Please</u> write.
待ってください　matte **kudasai.**	<u>Please</u> wait.

---

3. Present Progressive: 〜 te form + iru or imasu.

あさ はん　た
Example 1: 朝ご飯を食べ<u>ている</u>。　　　　（Casual）
　　　　　asa go-han wo tabete <u>iru.</u>
　　　　　Eating breakfast.

かあ　　でんわ
Example 2: お母さんと電話をして**います**。　（Polite）
　　　　　o-kaasan to denwa wo shite **imasu.**
　　　　　I'm on the phone with my mom.

にほんご べんきょう
Example 3: 日本語を勉強して**います**。　（Polite）
　　　　　Nihongo wo benkyou shite **imasu.**）
　　　　　I'm studying Japanese.

わたし　　ほん よ
Example 4: 私もその本を読ん<u>でいる</u>。　（Casual）
　　　　　watashi mo sono hon wo yonde <u>iru.</u>
　　　　　I'm also reading that book.

4. Ask Permission: (〜 te form + mo ii desu ka)

The phrase "てもいいですか" (te mo ii desu ka) is a polite way to inquire if something is permissible. This structure is used to ask for permission politely. It's important to use it after the te-form of a verb. This pattern closely resembles "Can I" or "May I" in English.

Polite Form: (te-form verb) + もいいですか	**Casual Form:** (te-form verb) + もいい

Example 1:

み
テレビを見てもいいですか。
terebi wo mite mo ii desu ka?
May I watch TV?

Example 1:

ほん か
この本、借りてもいい。
kono hon, karite mo ii?
Can I borrow this book?

Example 2:

ほん よ
この本を読んでもいいですか。
kono hon wo yonde mo ii desu ka?
Can I read this book?

Example 2:

す
ここでたばこを吸ってもいい。
koko de tabako wo sutte mo ii?
May I smoke here?

5. Linking Two Verbs or Verb Phrases Together.

When you're performing two actions simultaneously, you modify the first verb into its te-form, and the second verb according to the required tense (past, present, or negative).

ばん はん つく　おんがく き
Example 1: 晩ご飯を作って音楽を聴いています。(Polite)
　　　　　ban go-han wo tsukutte ongaku wo kiite **imasu.**
　　　　　I'm cooking dinner and listening to music.

ある　はな
Example 2: 歩いて話している。(Casual)
　　　　　aruite hanashite **iru.**
　　　　　I'm walking and talking.

■ LESSON 9 🔊

Let's learn how to ask for permission to do something following a verb. Using て-form (te-form) plus "〜もいいですか" (mo ii desu ka).
Te-form of a few verbs with examples:

Dictionary Form	Te Form	Sample Sentence	Translation
み 観る　　To watch	み 観て　　To watch	テレビを観て**もいい**ですか。	Can I watch TV?
つか 使う　　To use	つか 使って　　To use	パソコンを使って**もいい**ですか。	Can I use this computer?
すわ 座る　　To sit	すわ 座って　　To sit	ここ、座って**もいい**ですか。	Can I sit here?

❖ Important structures of verb te-form, How to make te-form

> 　　te
> 1.〜てください。
> Please.Wait. ➡ まってください。matte kudasai.

> 　　te mo　ii　desu ka
> 2.〜て(も)いいですか。Is it okay...?　May...?
> May I open the window? ➡ まどをあけて**もいい**ですか。mado wo akete mo ii desu ka?

> 　　te imasu.
> 3.〜ています。(be) ...ing [progressive]
> I'm waiting. ➡ まっています。matte imasu.

> 　　te
> 4。〜て、〜...and then...[connective]　(ban gohan wo tabete, uchi ni kaerimasu.)
> I will eat dinner and then go home. ➡ ばんごはんをたべて、うちにかえります。

■ **LESSON 9** 🔊

Let's learn how to ask for permission to do something.

Ask Permissions - Casual

Te-form of a few verbs with examples. (て-form (te-form) plus "いい")

Example 1: トイレに、行っていいですか。
　　　　toire ni, itte ii desu ka?
　　　　May I go to the bathroom?

Example 2: 電話を、かけていいですか。
　　　　denwa wo, kakete ii desu ka?
　　　　Can I make a phone call?

Example 3: 車で、行かせていただいていいですか。
　　　　kuruma de, ika sete itadaite ii desu ka?
　　　　Can I go by car?

Ask Permissions – Formal

You should use this more formal expression:

て-form plus -もよろしいでしょうか　　(mo yoroshii deshou ka?)

Example 1: 明日、来てもよろしいですか。
　　　　ashita, kite **mo yoroshii desu ka**?
　　　　Do you mind if I come tomorrow?

Example 2: ここに座ってもよろしいでしょうか。
　　　　koko ni suwatte **mo yoroshii deshou ka**?
　　　　May I sit here?

LESSON 10 🔊

Ask a question 〝質問する（しつもん）〟 You can ask a question in Japanese by adding the particle 〝か〟 at the end of a declarative sentence. A Japanese particle called "ka" can transform almost any phrase into a question.

Examples (Formal):

すみません！（sumimasen.） excuse me!

1. ちょっと、お聞きしたいんですけど。

    chotto, o-kiki shitain desu kedo.

     May I ask you a question?

2. 駅は、どちらです**か**。

    eki wa, dochira desu **ka**?

    Where is the station?

3. 駅の近くに、コンビニエンスストアはあります**か**。

    eki no chikaku ni, konbiniensusutoa wa ari masu **ka**?

     Is there a convenience store near the station?

Clarification

〝公園に行きます。〟（koen ni iki masu.） Meaning: "I go to the park" Add "ka"(?) to turn it into a question.

☐ 公園に行きます**か**。（koen ni iki masu **ka**?）   "Do you want to go to the park?"

☐ だいじょうぶです。（daijoubu desu.）   "It's okay/I'm okay/You're okay" etc.
            (depending on the context) Add "ka" to turn it into a question.

☐ だいじょうぶです**か**。（daijoubu desu **ka**?）   "Are you okay?" "Is it okay?" etc.
            (Depending on the context).

LESSON 11 🔊

When offering advice or suggestions, you can use the expression "ほうがいいです" (hou ga ii desu) at the end. This is similar to saying "It's better to" or "You should" in English. However, be cautious about the context, as it might sound like you're imposing your opinion. So, think carefully about when to use it, considering the situation of your conversation.

Sentence Patterns

Verb (た-form)	ほうがいいです	→ It's better to ...
Verb (ない-form)	ほうがいいです	→ It's better not to ...

Positive Pattern: Verb (た-form) ほうがいいです。

Negative Pattern: Verb (ない-form) ほうがいいです。

Examples:

Verb (た-form) ほうがいいです。

きょう　あたま　いた
A. 今日は頭が痛いです。(atama ga itai desu.)
   I have a headache.

くすり　の
B. 薬を飲んだ**ほうがいいです**。(kusuri wo nonda **hou ga ii desu.**)
   You had better take some medicine.

Examples:

Verb (ない-form) ほうがいいです。

あした　しけん　う
A. 明日試験を受けます。(ashita shiken wo uke masu.)
   I am taking a test tomorrow.

こんばん　　　　み
B. 今晩、テレビを観**ないほうがいいです**。(konban terebi wo mi**nai hou ga ii desu.**)
   You had better not watch TV tonight.

■ **LESSON 11** 🔊

Depending on the situation, this expression may sound like you are imposing your opinion on the listener. So consider the context of the conversation carefully before using it.

More Examples:

1. お菓子はあまり食べないほうがいいです。 (o-kashi wa amari tabe**nai hou ga ii desu.**)
   You shouldn't eat too many sweets.

2. 暗いから、電気をつけたほうがいいです。 (kurai kara, denki wo tsuketa **hou ga ii desu.**)
   It's dark, so you had better turn on the light.

3. 先生に聞いたほうがいいです。 (sensei ni kiita **hou ga ii desu.**)
   You should ask your teacher.

4. 遅いから、電話をかけないほうがいいです。 (osoikara, denwa wo kake**nai hou ga ii desu.**)
   It's late, so it's better not to call.

5. 気分が悪いので運転しないほうがいい。 (kibun ga warui node unten shi**nai hou ga ii.**)
   I don't feel well so I shouldn't be driving.

LESSON 12 🔊

In this lesson, you'll discover how to politely ask someone to do something by using the te-form of a verb followed by "ください" (kudasai). This helps you make a respectful request.

Making Commands: Using て-form alone.
Making Commands: Using て-form with ください. ("kudasai" similar word "please" in English.)

Examples:

1. 見^みて！(mite!) It means "look!" (**Command**)

2. 聞^きいて！(kiite!) It means "listen!" (**Command**)

3. 見てください！(mite kudasai) means "Please look!" (**Request**)

4. 聞いてください。(kiite kudasai) means "Please listen" (**Request**)

❖ When you use the te-form alone (without kudasai), it becomes a command and is very informal, or even impolite depending on the context and tone. Adding て-form + ください makes it more formal, but it's important to note that it might not be suitable for all situations.

❖ There is a more formal word you can use instead of "ください" (kudasai) is "くれまか。(kuremasu ka?) So if you use "くれますか" Essentially, it is a polite request, equivalent to "Can you please...?"

Examples:

1. 読^よんで**くれますか**。(yonde **kuremasu ka**?) Means "Would you please read?"

2. 聞^きいて**くれますか**。(kiite **kuremasu ka**?) Means "Would you please listen?"

❖ The Japanese language has an intricate system of politeness levels. In various situations, there can be multiple ways to express the same idea.

LESSON 13 🔊

During this lesson, you will learn how to ask back for things you're not sure about.

Ask Back

1. え？ もう一度（いちど）。 (e!? mou ichido.) What! Say it again.

2. どういう意味（いみ）ですか。 (douiu imi desu ka?) What do you mean?

3. もう一度（いちど） ゆっくり お願（ねが）いします。 (mou ichido yukkuri o-negai shimasu.)
Would you please repeat it slowly?

LESSON 14 🔊

The simplest way to express "I need help" in Japanese is by saying "tasukete"（助（たす）けて）, which directly means "Help me." To make it more polite, you can use "tasukete kudasai" （助けてください）, which translates to "Please help me."

Remember, you can use this phrase in both daily situations and emergencies, making it very handy to know.

❑ Here are some common phrases you can use to ask for help.

助けて。	tasukete.	Help me!	Casual
助けてください。	tasukete kudasai.	Please help me!	Polite
助けてくれますか。	tasukete kuremasu ka?	Can you help me?	Polite
手伝っていただけますか。	tetsudatte itadake masu ka?	Could you help Me, please?	Very polite

LESSON 14

In Japanese, you can use different phrases to say "I need help" depending on the situation.

Here are some examples:

きぶん　よ
1. 気分が 良くないです。
(kibun ga yokunai desu.)
I'm not feeling well.

ちか びょういん
2. もっとも 近い病院は どこですか。
(mottomo chikai byouin wa doko desu ka?)
Where is the nearest hospital?

いしゃ　よ
3. 医者を 呼んで ください。
(isha wo yonde kudasai.)
Call the doctor please.

きゅうきゅうしゃ　よ
4. 救急車を 呼んで ください。
(kyuu-kyuu-sha wo yonde kudasai.)
Please call an ambulance.

Although you might not use these phrases often, you've now learned how to ask for assistance in Japanese, just in case.

UNIT 20

<ruby>に ほん ご<rt></rt></ruby>
日本語の動詞
Japanese verb conjugation

JAPANESE VERB CONJUGATION

Verb: 見る (みる) to see, to watch		Class: Godan **Ichidan** Irregular

Sample sentence:
はな み かのじょ じっさい わかみ
離れて見ると、彼女は実際よりずっと若く見える。
hanarete miru to, kanojo wa jissai yori zutto wakakumieru.
From a distance, she looks much younger than she actually is.

Conjunctive Form		見	
Te-form		見て	

		Positive	Negative
Plain Dictionary Form		見る	見ない
Polite Form		見ます	見ません
Past Form	Plain	見た	見なかった
	Polite	見ました	見ませんでした
Potential Form	Plain	見られる	見られない
	Polite	見られます	見られません
Passive Form	Plain	見られる	見られない
	Polite	見られます	見られません
Causative Form	Plain	見させる	見させない
	Polite	見させます	見させません
Conditional Form (Tara Form)	Plain	見たら	見なかったら
	Polite	見ましたら	見ませんでしたら
Conditional Form (Ba Form)		見れば	見なければ
Imperative Form		見ろ	見るな
Volitional Form	Plain	見よう	
	Polite	見ましょう	

- Japanese Verb Conjugation Reference.

LESSON 1

Group 1

Dictionary ending	Masu form ending
〜う 〜u	〜います 〜imasu
〜く 〜ku	〜きます 〜kimasu
〜ぐ 〜gu	〜ぎます 〜gimasu
〜す 〜su	〜します 〜shimasu
〜つ 〜tsu	〜ちます 〜chimasu

Dictionary ending	Masu form ending
〜ぬ 〜nu	〜にます 〜nimasu
〜む 〜mu	〜みます 〜mimasu
〜ぶ 〜bu	〜びます 〜bimasu
〜る 〜ru	〜ります 〜rimasu

❏ Excluding 〜iru and 〜eru endings.

Examples 1-2

Dictionary form	Reading	masu form	Reading	Meaning
かう	kau	かいます	kaimasu	To buy
あう	au	あいます	aimasu	To meet
はらう	harau	はらいます	haraimasu	To pay
かく	kaku	かきます	kakimasu	To write
きく	kiku	ききます	kikimasu	To listen
およぐ	oyogu	およぎます	oyogimasu	To swim
ぬぐ	nugu	ぬぎます	nugimasu	To take off
いそぐ	isogu	いそぎます	isogimasu	To hurry
かす	kasu	かします	kashimasu	To lend
こわす	kowasu	こわします	kowashimasu	To break
けす	kesu	けします	keshimasu	To erase
たつ	tatsu	たちます	tachimasu	To stand

LESSON 2

Group 1 Examples 2-2

Dictionary form	Reading	Masu form	Reading	Meaning
まつ	matsu	まちます	machimasu	To wait
もつ	motsu	もちます	mochimasu	To hold
しぬ	shinu	しにます	shinimasu	To die
よむ	yomu	よみます	yomimasu	To read
のむ	nomu	のみます	nomimasu	To drink
やすむ	yasumu	やすみます	yasumimasu	To rest
とぶ	tobu	とびます	tobimasu	To fly
まなぶ	manabu	まなびます	manabimasu	To learn
あそぶ	asobu	あそびます	asobimasu	To play
すわる	suwaru	すわります	suwarimasu	To sit
わかる	wakaru	わかります	wakarimasu	To understand
はじまる	hajimaru	はじまります	hajimarimasu	To start

Group 2

～る	～ru	～ます	～masu
おきる	okiru	おきます	okimasu
たべる	taberu	たべます	tabemasu

❑ Only ～iru and ～eru endings.

LESSON 3

Group 2 Examples

Dictionary form	Reading	Masu form	Reading	Meaning
いる	iru	います	imasu	To exist
みる	miru	みます	mimasu	To see
きる	kiru	きます	kimasu	To wear
おきる	okiru	おきます	okimasu	To wake up
みせる	miseru	みせます	misemasu	To show
たべる	taberu	たべます	tabemasu	To eat
ねる	neru	ねます	nemasu	To sleep
おしえる	oshieru	おしえます	oshiemasu	To teach

Notes:

1. Although verbs such as kaeru ("to come back"), hairu ("to come in"), kiru ("to cut"), and iru ("to need") end with 〜iru or 〜eru, they are exceptions which still conjugate as Group 1 Verbs.

2. きる(kiru) to wear, its use to clothes above the waist.

Group 3 (Irregular Verbs)

Dictionary form	Masu form	Meaning
する suru	します shimasu	To do
くる kuru	きます kimasu	To come

Welcome to the Exercises
section of the book!

Time to Apply Your Knowledge

You've been learning a lot, and now it's time to put your understanding to the test. This section is all about practicing what you've learned practically.

These exercises are designed to help you gain confidence and improve your Japanese skills step by step. Get ready to engage with the material and see how far you've come in your learning journey!

The Answer Key

The Answer Key is included at the end of the book and organized according to lesson numbers. It allows you to access and refer to the corresponding answers easily.

Evaluating Your Progress

After completing each exercise, be sure to use the review section provided at the end of it. You can rate your performance using the following options:

Review ☐Awesome! ☐Excellent! ☐Good! ☐Average! ☐Poor!

This evaluation assists you in understanding how well you're picking up the language and keeping track of your progress.

Japanese Greetings

LESSONS EXERCISES AND ACTIVITIES

- Draw a line to match the following greetings.

1. Hello. ●		● o-hayou go-zaimasu.
2. I'm sorry. ●		● konbanwa.
3. Good night. ●		● konnichiwa.
4. Thank you. ●		● hisashiburi.
5. Good evening. ●		● hajimemashite.
6. Good Morning. ●		● arigatau go-zaimasu.
7. Nice to meet you. ●		● o-yasuminasai.
8. Long time no see. ●		● gomennasai.

- Write the following Greetings into hiragana and their meaning.

1. o-kaeri. _____ _____

2. tadaima. _____ _____

3. ganbatte. _____ _____

4. gomennasai. _____ _____

5. ki wo tsukete. _____ _____

6. hajimemashite. _____ _____

7. arigatau go-zaimasu. _____ _____

8. o-medetou go-zaimasu. _____ _____

Review ☐Awesome! ☐Excellent! ☐Good! ☐Average! ☐Poor!

Note:

- Circle the correct greetings mean.

1. What does おやすみなさい。(o-yasuminasai) mean?

a. Good evening.

b. Welcome home.

c. Goodnight.

2. What does いってきます (ittekimasu) mean?

a. "ittekimasu" is said after eating.

b. "ittekimasu" is said when you are leaving home to the person staying.

c. "ittekimasu" is said by the person staying home to the person leaving.

3. What does いってらっしゃい。(itterasshai) mean?

a. "itterasshai" is said before eating.

b. "itterasshai" is said when you are leaving home to the person staying.

c. "itterasshai" is said by the person staying home to the person leaving.

4. When you are coming home, what do you say to the person that is already home?

a. o-kaerinasai.

b. hisashiburi.

c. tadaima.

Review ☐Awesome! ☐Excellent! ☐Good! ☐Average! ☐Poor!

Note:

"Kudasai" and "O-negaishimasu"

- Choose the correct phrases using either "kudasai" or "o-negaishimasu".

---

1. How do you tell the taxi driver to take you to Tokyo station?

a. 東京駅まで ください。(Toukyou eki made kudasai.)

b. 東京駅まで おねがいします。(Toukyou eki made o-negaishimasu.)

c. 東京駅は行くお願いします。(Toukyou eki wa iku o-negaishimasu.)

---

2. How to tell someone please wait a moment.

a. ちょっと待ってください。(chotto matte kudasai.)

b. ちょっと待っておねがいします。(chotto matte o-negaishimasu.)

c. ちょっと待ってよろしくおねがいします。(chotto matte yoroshiku o-negaishimasu.)

---

3. When asking to speak to someone on the phone,

a. 田中さんください。(Tanaka-san kudasai.)

b. 田中さんはでんわをおねがいします。(Tanaka-san wa denwa wo o-negaishimasu.)

c. 田中さんお願いします。(Tanaka-san o-negaishimasu.)

---

4. Fill in the blank using either "kudasai" or "o-negaishimasu".

a. しゃしんをとって＿＿＿＿＿＿。(shashin wo totte＿＿＿＿＿＿.) Please take a picture.

b. よやくを＿＿＿＿＿＿。(yoyaku wo ＿＿＿＿＿＿.) I want to make a reservation, please.

c. メニューを＿＿＿＿＿＿。(menyū wo ＿＿＿＿＿＿.) I want to see the menu please.

Review ☐Awesome! ☐Excellent! ☐Good! ☐Average! ☐Poor!

Note:

LESSONS EXERCISES AND ACTIVITIES

- By filling in the blank you can introduce yourself easily. Create your self-introduction.

_____。Hello

_____。Nice to meet to you.

私は_____です。I am ……. (name)

Hello.
Nice to meet you.
My name is …….
I am from …….
I am …… years old.
I am a (student/occupation).
Please treat me well.

_____。 I am from …….

私は_____。I am … years old. (age)

私は(の)_____です。My job is a ……. (Your occupation etc).

_____。Please treat me well.

1. What is the difference between the following two sentences?

a. watashi wa Tanaka desu.

_____.

b. watashi wa Tanaka to mooshimasu.

_____.

2. When would you use the following?

a. hajimemashite. _____.

b. hisashiburi. _____.

Review ☐Awesome! ☐Excellent! ☐Good! ☐Average! ☐Poor!

Note:

■   Write answers to the below questions using the casual and polite form.

---

1. How do you ask someone's age in Japanese? (Write in Hiragana.)

a. Casual _____

b. Polite _____

---

2. What is the difference between the following two sentences?

a. お元気ですか。(o-genki desu ka?)
b. 元気ですか。(genki desu ka?)

_____

---

3.   Which is the more polite use of "大丈夫 (daijoubu-okay)"?

a. この水は大丈夫ですか。(kono mizu wa daijoubu desu ka?)

b. この水、大丈夫？(kono mizu, daijyoubu?)

---

4. How to say (I don't understand) casual and polite form.

a. Casual _____

b. Polite _____

Review □Awesome! □Excellent! □Good! □Average! □Poor!

Note:

- Write out the following numbers in Hiragana and their reading.

No.	Hiragana	Reading	Kanji
1			一
2			二
3			三
4			四
5			五
6			六
7			七
8			八
9			九
10			十

- Write out the following numbers in Hiragana.

No.	Reading	Hiragana
100	hyaku	
1,000	sen	
10,000	man	
100,000	juuman	

- Let's write 2023 in Hiragana.

_____

- Let's write 123456 in Hiragana.

_____

Review ☐Awesome! ☐Excellent! ☐Good! ☐Average! ☐Poor!

Note:

- Match the following days of the week to their correct English meaning.

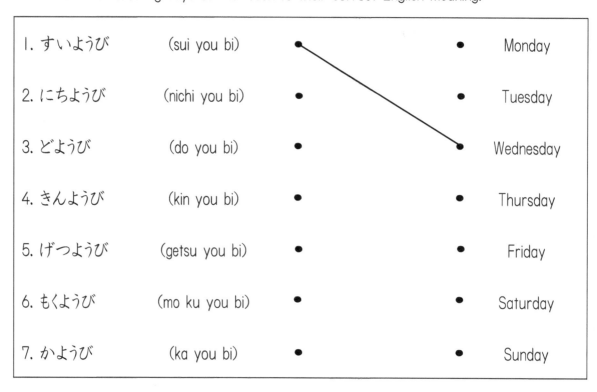

1. すいようび	(sui you bi)	•	• Monday
2. にちようび	(nichi you bi)	•	• Tuesday
3. どようび	(do you bi)	•	• Wednesday
4. きんようび	(kin you bi)	•	• Thursday
5. げつようび	(getsu you bi)	•	• Friday
6. もくようび	(mo ku you bi)	•	• Saturday
7. かようび	(ka you bi)	•	• Sunday

- Write the Kanji for the day(s) of the week.

曜日	曜日	曜日	曜日
Monday	Tuesday	Wednesday	Thursday

曜日	曜日	曜日	曜日
Friday	Saturday	Sunday	What is today?

Review ☐Awesome! ☐Excellent! ☐Good! ☐Average! ☐Poor!

Note:

LESSONS EXERCISES AND ACTIVITIES

- How do you count the weeks in Japanese? Fill in the blank below.

Hiragana	Kanji	Reading	English
いっしゅうかん	一週間	isshuu kan	One week
	二週間		Two weeks
	三週間		Three weeks
	四週間		Four weeks
	五週間		Five weeks

- Match the correct Hiragana of weeks to the correct English and reading.

こんしゅう ●　　　　　● Last week　　　　● ● saraishuu

さらいしゅう ●　　　● The Week after Next ●　　● raishuu

せんしゅう ●　　　　　● Next Week　　　● ● konshuu

らいしゅう ●　　　　　● This Week　　　● ● senshuu

- Write the following sentences into Hiragana.

a. I'm going to America next week. _____

b. I'm going to Tokyo this week. _____

Review ☐Awesome! ☐Excellent! ☐Good! ☐Average! ☐Poor!

Note:

■ Match the following days of the month to their correct English meaning.

1. みっか ●	● (mikka) ●	● 9th
2. ここのか ●	● (koko no ka) ●	● 7th
3. むいか ●	● (mui ka) ●	● 1st
4. ついたち ●	● (tsuitachi) ●	● 3rd
5. なのか ●	● (na no ka) ●	● 5th
6. いつか ●	● (itsuka) ●	● 4th
7. ふつか ●	● (futsu ka) ●	● 6th
8. ようか ●	● (you ka) ●	● 8th
9. よっか ●	● (yokka) ●	● 2nd
10. とおか ●	● (to o ka) ●	● 10th

■ Write the Hiragana for the following days of the month.

1) 九月五日 _____

2) 四月二十日 _____

3) 六月十四日 _____

4) 七月七日 _____

Review ☐Awesome! ☐Excellent! ☐Good! ☐Average! ☐Poor!

Note:

- Match the correct Hiragana to the correct English and Kanji.

くがつ ●	● December ●	● 六月
じゅうにがつ ●	● September ●	● 十月
じゅうがつ ●	● October ●	● 九月
ろくがつ ●	● June ●	● 十二月

- Complete the following table writing the correct Hiragana, reading, English, or Kanji.

Hiragana	Kanji	Reading	English
	一月	ichi-gatsu	January
にがつ	二月	ni-gatsu	February
	三月	san-gatsu	
しがつ			
	五月		
ろくがつ			June
	七月		July
はちがつ	八月	hachi-gatsu	August
	九月		
		juu-gatsu	October
じゅういちがつ	十一月		
		juuni-gatsu	

Review ☐Awesome! ☐Excellent! ☐Good! ☐Average! ☐Poor!

Note:

■ Circle the correct answer for the below questions.

1. How do you say "next month" in Japanese?
a. 再来月（さらいげつ- sarai-getsu）
b. 来月（らいげつ- rai-getsu）
c. 今月（こんげつ- kon-getsu）

2. "Six months" in Japanese is?
a. ろっかげつ(rokka-getsu)
b. ろっかがつ(rokka-gatsu)
c. ろっかつ(rokka-tsu)

■ How do you count the months in Japanese? Fill in the blank below.

Hiragana	Kanji	Reading	English
	五ヶ月		Five months
			Six months
			Seven months
			Eight months
			Nine months

Review ☐Awesome! ☐Excellent! ☐Good! ☐Average! ☐Poor!

Note:

LESSONS EXERCISES AND ACTIVITIES

- How do you write these dates in Japanese?

a.   31st August   _____

b.   16th May   _____

c.   5th December   _____

d.   14th September   _____

- How do you write these dates in English?

a.   五月二十七日 _____

b.   十月三日   _____

c.   一月二十五日 _____

d.   七月十三日   _____

- Write your birthday in Japanese.

_____

- Write today's date in Japanese.

_____

- Write how to read this date in Japanese: 2022年5月29日（火曜）

_____

Review ☐Awesome! ☐Excellent! ☐Good! ☐Average! ☐Poor!

Note:

LESSONS EXERCISES AND ACTIVITIES

- Write the following English words into Hiragana / Kanji.

Hiragana

Next year	
Last year	
This year	
Every year	

Kanji

Year	
Next year	
This year	
Every year	

- How do you tell your age in Japanese? Try using casual or polite expressions.

なんさい
Question: 何歳ですか。(nan sai desu ka?)

Answer: _____

- Practice the Kanji: 才 (sai) Age.
  Looks like a person with a walking stick.

Review ☐Awesome! ☐Excellent! ☐Good! ☐Average! ☐Poor!

Note:

- Write the following English words into Hiragana / Romaji.

	Hiragana	Reading	English
1			Sunshine
2			Cloudy
3			Rain
4			Snow
5			Windy

- Write the following sentence in Japanese.

How's the weather today? _____

- Translate these sentences about the seasons and weather into English.

Japanese	English
1.冬 (ふゆ)は寒い(さむい)です。	
2.四月 (しがつ)は春(はる)です。	
3.夏 (なつ)の天気(てんき)は暑い(あつい)です。	
4.十月 (じゅうがつ)は秋(あき)です。	
5.秋 (あき) は涼しい (すずしい)です。	

Review　□Awesome!　□Excellent!　□Good!　□Average!　□Poor!

Note:

■ Circle the correct question words for the below sentences then fill in the blank and write the meaning for each phrase.

1. トイレは【　　　　】ですか。		
a. なに	b. どこ	c. いつ
Meaning:		

Toilet

2. いま【　　　　】じですか。		
a. いつ	b. いくら	c. なん
Meaning:		

3. コーヒーとジュース、【　　　　】が好きですか。		
a. どちら	b. いくつ	c. どう
Meaning:		

■ Write the following English words/questions in Japanese.

How Long		What is this?	
How Much		How about today?	
Which		How much is it?	
Why		How is it?	

Review ☐Awesome! ☐Excellent! ☐Good! ☐Average! ☐Poor!

Note:

LESSONS EXERCISES AND ACTIVITIES

- Write your answer to the following questions in Japanese.
- Write the meaning for each question.

1. あなたのなまえはなんですか。	
Meaning:	
2. おくにはどこですか。	
Meaning:	

3. おしごとはなんですか。	
Meaning:	
4. どちらにすんでいますか。	
Meaning:	

- How do you introduce yourself, state your name, and indicate your language in Japanese in the following situations:

Your name in a **polite** manner.

Your name in a **casual** situation.

What **language** do you speak?

_____   _____   _____

Review ☐Awesome! ☐Excellent! ☐Good! ☐Average! ☐Poor!

Note:

■ Which form of apology is appropriate in the following situations?

1. Which is the appropriate way to ask when you urgently need to report a job to the boss on the phone?

a. ごめんね、ちょっといいかな？ (gomen ne, chotto ii kana?)

b. ごめんなさい、話を聞いて。(gomen'nasai, hanashi wo kiite.)

c. お話中、失礼します。(o-hanashi-chuu, shitsurei shimasu.)

2. Which is the appropriate way to ask when entering the boss's room?

a. 入ります。(hairimasu.)

b. 入っていいかな？ (haitte ii kana?)

c. 失礼します。(shitsurei shimasu.)

3. Which is the appropriate way to say when you finish work and leave before your co-workers?

a. またね。(mata ne.)

b. さようなら。(sayounara.)

c. お先に失礼します。(o-sakini shitsurei shimasu.)

4. What do you say when your wife gets angry because you ate her favorite cake without her permission?

a. 大丈夫。(daijoubu.)

b. 本当にごめんなさい。(hontou ni gomen'nasai.)

c. 申し訳ございません。(moushiwake go-zaimasen.)

Review ☐Awesome! ☐Excellent! ☐Good! ☐Average! ☐Poor!

Note:

LESSONS EXERCISES AND ACTIVITIES

■   Write your answer to the following questions in Japanese.

1. What should you say at the end of a meal in Japan?

_____ 。

2. What should you say at the start of a meal in Japan?

_____ 。

3. How would you say delicious in Japanese?

_____ 。

4. What does umai mean?

_____ 。

■   Translate these phrases into English.

	Japanese	**English**
1	おかわりをください。	
2	おなかがへった。	
3	おなかがすいていますか。	
4	おなかがすいていない。	
5	もうたべられません。	

Review ☐Awesome! ☐Excellent! ☐Good! ☐Average! ☐Poor!

Note:

Family Members

- Match your family members' words to someone else family.

1. はは ●	● むすこさん
2. いもうと ●	● ごしゅじん
3. むすこ ●	● おくさん
4. ちち ●	● おかあさん
5. おっと ●	● おこさん
6. つま ●	● いもうとさん
7. こども ●	● おとうさん

- Complete the table below by filling in the missing words in the blank boxes, the first one has been done as an example.

Hiragana	ROMAJI	ENGLISH
はは	haha	Your mother
	sofu	
おとうと		
		Your grandmother
ちち		
	kazoku	
いもうと		

Review ☐Awesome! ☐Excellent! ☐Good! ☐Average! ☐Poor!

Note:

LESSONS EXERCISES AND ACTIVITIES

Introducing My Family

LESSONS EXERCISES AND ACTIVITIES

- Introduce your family using the same sentence pattern you have learned.
- How many members of your family, age, student, work, what they like, etc.

Challenge!

- Using a lead pencil/pacer, write the kanji symbol in the smaller boxes.
  Trace the symbols to practice. (Your mother and father).

Review ☐Awesome! ☐Excellent! ☐Good! ☐Average! ☐Poor!

Note:

LESSONS EXERCISES AND ACTIVITIES

- Write in Japanese how many people are in the pictures.

_____   _____   _____

- Write in kanji how many people for the below Romaji, The first one has been done as an example.

十一人　　||人　　juu ichi nin　　　　　　　　　　　　　　　juu ni nin
_____   _____

　　　　　　　　nana nin　　　　　　　　　　　　　　　roku nin
_____   _____

　　　　　　　　yo nin　　　　　　　　　　　　　　　juu san nin
_____   _____

　　　　　　　　kyuu nin　　　　　　　　　　　　　　　juu yo nin
_____   _____

- Please answer the following questions in Japanese.

1. ごかぞくはなんにんですか。 _____ 。

2. The Japanese word for two (people) is _____ 。

3. The Japanese word for one (person) is _____ 。

Review ☐Awesome! ☐Excellent! ☐Good! ☐Average! ☐Poor!

Note:

- Write in Japanese how to count umbrellas in the below pictures.

 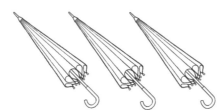 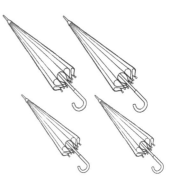

_____   _____   _____

- Write how to count long cylindrical objects in Hiragana or Romaji.

1	一本		6	六本	
2	二本		7	七本	
3	三本		8	八本	
4	四本		9	九本	
5	五本		10	十本	

- Which object can't be used (ほん hon 本) for counting?

Review ☐Awesome! ☐Excellent! ☐Good! ☐Average! ☐Poor!

Note:

- Write in Japanese how many flat objects are in the pictures.

- Complete the following table using the flat objects counter.

Hiragana	Reading	English
ご _____		Five
ろく _____		Six
なな _____		Seven
はち _____		Eight
きゅう _____		Nine
じゅう _____		Ten

Review ☐Awesome! ☐Excellent! ☐Good! ☐Average! ☐Poor!

Note:

- Write in Japanese counting for small and large animals.

Small animals'

一匹	
二匹	
三匹	
四匹	
五匹	
六匹	
七匹	
八匹	
九匹	
十匹	

Large animals'

一頭	
二頭	
三頭	
四頭	
五頭	
六頭	
七頭	
八頭	
九頭	
十頭	

Complete the following table using the birds and rabbits counter.

Kanji	Hiragana	Reading	English
一＿＿＿＿			One
二＿＿＿＿			Two
三＿＿＿＿			Three
四＿＿＿＿			Four
五＿＿＿＿			Five
六＿＿＿＿			Six
七＿＿＿＿			Seven

Review ☐Awesome! ☐Excellent! ☐Good! ☐Average! ☐Poor!

Note:

LESSONS EXERCISES AND ACTIVITIES

- Match the following pictures with their correct counter.

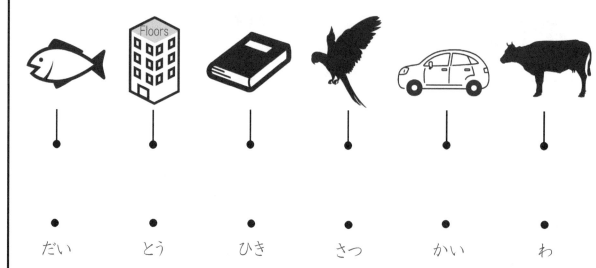

だい　　　　とう　　　　ひき　　　　さつ　　　　かい　　　　わ

- Write down how to count for frequency. Several times an action was repeated.

Hiragana	Reading	English
		Once
		Twice
		Three times

- How to count the following animals?

3 kittens' _____ 。　　　　6 Puppy _____ 。

Review ☐Awesome! ☐Excellent! ☐Good! ☐Average! ☐Poor!

Note:

- Complete the following table using the Money counter.

Kanji	Hiragana	Reading	English
百円	ひゃくえん		100 Yen
			300 Yen
			600 Yen
			800 Yen
			1,000 Yen
			3,000 Yen
			8,000 Yen
一万円			10,000 Yen
十万円	じゅうまんえん		100,000 Yen

- Write out the corresponding Kanji for the following.

Hiragana	Kanji
ごひゃくえん	
にせんえん	
ななひゃくえん	

- What is "One million Yen" in Japanese and how to say it?

_____

- How to say "How much is this" in Japanese?

_____

Review ☐Awesome! ☐Excellent! ☐Good! ☐Average! ☐Poor!

Note:

- Write the price for each item in the following pictures.

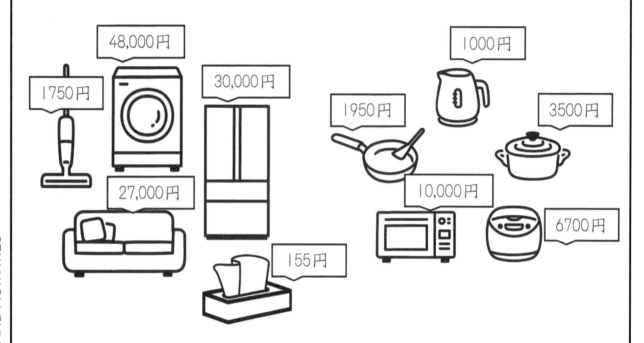

- e.g. 1350円 – せん さん びゃく ご じゅう えん

_____   _____

_____   _____

_____   _____

_____   _____

Review ☐Awesome! ☐Excellent! ☐Good! ☐Average! ☐Poor!

Note:

LESSONS EXERCISES AND ACTIVITIES

■ Match these times expressed in Japanese with the times on the right.

yo-ji juugo-fun ●	●	06:10
hachi-ji niju-ppun ●	●	11:00
ku-ji yonju-ppun ●	●	02:45
shichi-ji ●	●	04:15
roku-ji ju-ppun ●	●	12:05
juu ichi-ji ●	●	08:20
ni-ji yonjuugo-fun ●	●	04:15
juuni-ji go-fun ●	●	7:00
yo-ji juugo-fun ●	●	09:40

Review ☐Awesome! ☐Excellent! ☐Good! ☐Average! ☐Poor!

Note:

Write the time for the clocks below.

いまなんじですか。(ima nanji desu ka?)

| ni-ji sanjuppun (二時三十分) | | |

Review ☐Awesome! ☐Excellent! ☐Good! ☐Average! ☐Poor!

Note:

LESSONS EXERCISES AND ACTIVITIES

- Answer the following questions: What time are you doing these activities?

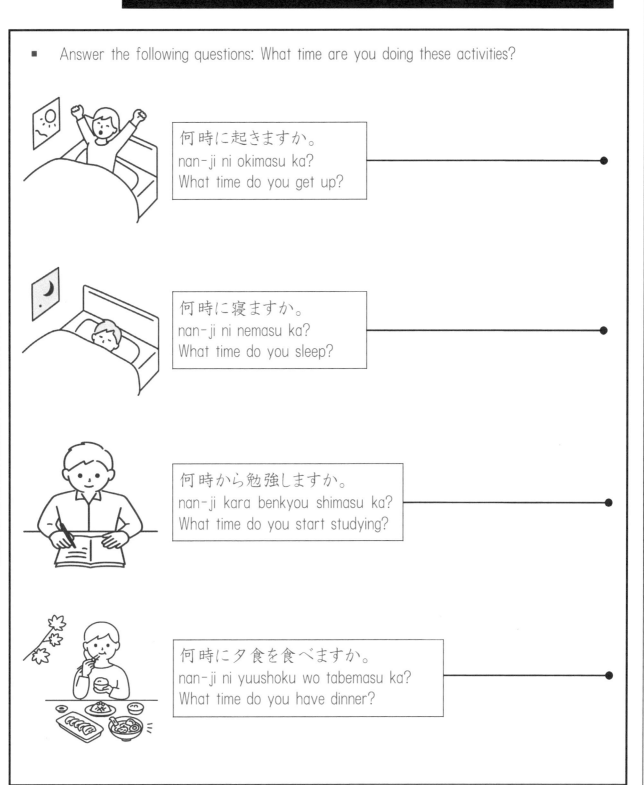

何時に起きますか。
nan-ji ni okimasu ka?
What time do you get up?

何時に寝ますか。
nan-ji ni nemasu ka?
What time do you sleep?

何時から勉強しますか。
nan-ji kara benkyou shimasu ka?
What time do you start studying?

何時に夕食を食べますか。
nan-ji ni yuushoku wo tabemasu ka?
What time do you have dinner?

Review ☐Awesome! ☐Excellent! ☐Good! ☐Average! ☐Poor!

Note:

- Complete the following table using words to describe a time.

Kanji	Hiragana	Reading	English
四時			4 o'clock
	ごじ		5 o'clock
六時			6 o'clock
	しちじ	shichi-ji	7 o'clock
八時			8 o'clock
	くじ		9 o'clock
一分			1 minute
		yon-fun	4 minutes
六分			6 minutes
	よんじゅっぷん		40 minutes
午前			AM
午後			PM
夜		yoru	Night
深夜	しんや		Midnight
朝			Morning
日の出	ひので		Sunrise

Review ☐Awesome! ☐Excellent! ☐Good! ☐Average! ☐Poor!

Note:

- Ask and answer questions about the activities you have done in the past. Such as home, work, school, shopping, etc.

Ask	場所 から場所 まで From place to place	vehicleで、 by vehicle	何時間 How many hours	かかりますか。 Does it take?
Answer	Place から Place まで From place to place	vehicleで、 by vehicle	時間 Hours/Minutes	(ぐらい) かかります。 It takes (about)

LESSONS EXERCISES AND ACTIVITIES

	Place 1	Place 2	Vehicle	Time
Ask e.g.	東京 (Tokyo)(から)	大阪 (Osaka) まで	電車(で)	どれくらいぐらいかかりますか。
Answer e.g.	東京 (Tokyo)(から)	大阪 (Osaka) まで	電車(で)	二時間 三十分ぐらいかかります。
Ask				
Answer				
Ask				
Answer				
Ask				
Answer				

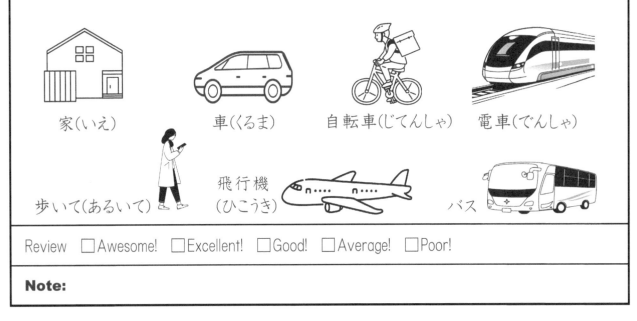

家(いえ)　　　車(くるま)　　　自転車(じてんしゃ)　電車(でんしゃ)

歩いて(あるいて)　飛行機(ひこうき)　　　　　　バス

Review ☐Awesome! ☐Excellent! ☐Good! ☐Average! ☐Poor!

Note:

347

- Describe how your daily life is going using the same pattern of "Yukina" life, from morning till night. (Work, Morning, Sport, breakfast, etc.)

わたし
私は＿＿＿＿＿＿＿＿ です。

Review ☐Awesome! ☐Excellent! ☐Good! ☐Average! ☐Poor!

Note:

- Translate the following words into Japanese.

English	Japanese
Employee	
Always	
Breakfast	
Train	
Company	
Student	
End	
House	
Little	

- Translate the following phrases into Japanese.

1. I ate breakfast. (Formal) _____ 。

2. I didn't eat breakfast. _____ 。

3. I eat breakfast every day. _____ 。

- Write your different degrees of liking things.

I love.....
I like.....
I don't like..... much.
I don't like.....
I hate....etc.

Review ☐Awesome! ☐Excellent! ☐Good! ☐Average! ☐Poor!

Note:

- Using the same pattern as Ami and Chris's daily breakfast, write four sentences:

1. Write two sentences about the food you like.

2. Write two sentences about the food you hate.

_____

_____

_____

_____

_____

_____

_____

- In the same way that "Tarou" wrote his favorite sport, write your favorite sport.

_____

_____

_____

_____

_____

Review ☐ Awesome! ☐ Excellent! ☐ Good! ☐ Average! ☐ Poor!

Note:

LESSONS EXERCISES AND ACTIVITIES

■   Extend your range of vocabulary Circle the correct words for the English meaning.

1.	Always	a. いつも	b. いしも	c. いっも
2.	Breakfast	a. あしごはん	b. あさごはん	c. あさこばん
3.	Egg	a. いまご	b. えまご	c. たまご
4.	Sometimes	a. ときとき	b. どきどき	c. ときどき
5.	Usually	a. たいてい	b. だいてい	c. だいでい
6.	Not much	a. おまり	b. あまり	c. あまい
7.	Delicious	a. あいしい	b. おいしい	c. おいし
8.	Much	a. たくさん	b. たくちん	c. とくさん
9.	Friend	a. ともたち	b. たもだち	c. ともだち
10.	Especially	a. たくに	b. とくに	c. どこに
11.	Saturday	a. どうようび	b. どようび	c. だようび
12.	Music	a. おんかく	b. おんがく	c. あんがく
13.	Beef	a. きゅうにく	b. ぎょうにく	c. ぎゅうにく
14.	Fish	a. ちかな	b. さかな	c. すかな
15.	Vegetable	a. やさい	b. やちい	c. やすい
16.	Employee	a. がいしゃいん	b. かいしゃいん	c. かいしゅいん
17.	Everyday	a. まいにち	b. まいこち	c. まいにさ

Review   ☐Awesome!   ☐Excellent!   ☐Good!   ☐Average!   ☐Poor!

Note:

■ Fill the below boxes with the correct cardinal directions in Japanese.

Japanese	
西	北東
東	南西
北	南東
南	北西

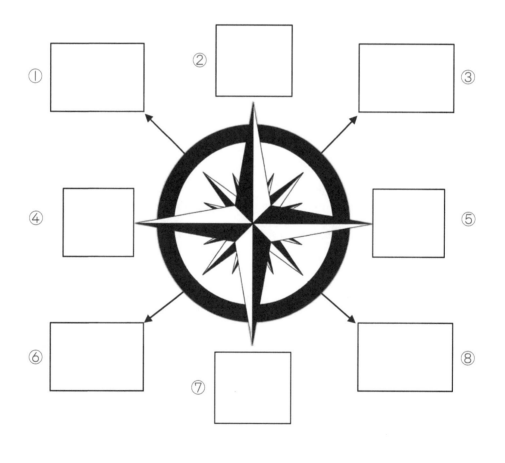

① ② ③
④ ⑤
⑥ ⑦ ⑧

Review ☐Awesome! ☐Excellent! ☐Good! ☐Average! ☐Poor!

Note:

- Test yourself and write the following directions and road words.

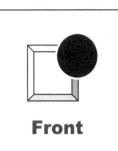

Review ☐Awesome! ☐Excellent! ☐Good! ☐Average! ☐Poor!

Note:

LESSONS EXERCISES AND ACTIVITIES

■ This is a map of the town. Using the road directions you have learned in Japanese, provide walking/driving directions to the bank.

SHOPPING CENTRE

PARKING

DEPARTMENT STORE
デパート

GAS STATION

RESTAURANT

BANK

ぎんこう-銀行

CAFE
カフェ

えき-駅
TRAIN STATION

BOOK STORE
ほんや-本屋

CONVENIENCE STORE
コンビニエンスストア

GYM
ジム

MUSEUM
はくぶつかん
博物館

LIBRARY
としょかん-図書館

PARK

こうえん-公園

HAIR SALON

TRAVEL AGENCY

YOU ARE HERE

HOSPITAL

びょういん
病院

DRUG STORE

BUS STATION
Ⓑ

HOTEL

ホテル

Write here:

Review ☐Awesome! ☐Excellent! ☐Good! ☐Average! ☐Poor!

Note:

- Give directions by filling in the blanks in the following sentences.

1 Go straight on this road to the station.

えき　　　　　　　　　　　　　　すす
駅へは この＿＿＿＿＿ を＿＿＿＿＿＿＿進みます。

eki ewa kono ＿＿＿＿＿wo＿＿＿＿＿＿susumimasu.

2 At the convenience store, turn right and go straight until you reach the end.

コンビニは そこを ＿＿＿＿に＿＿＿＿＿ 、＿＿＿＿行って突き当りです。

konbini wa soko wo＿＿＿＿ ni＿＿＿＿＿ , ＿＿＿＿itte tsukiatari desu.

3 (Pearl Hotel) from that convenience store, cross the intersection of the traffic lights.

パールホテルは その コンビニ から＿＿＿＿ の ＿＿＿＿＿を渡ってください。

Pāruhoteru wa sono konbini kara ＿＿＿＿ no＿＿＿＿＿ wo watatte kudasai.

Review □Awesome! □Excellent! □Good! □Average! □Poor!

Note:

- Write the position words that you have learned.

Above, Below, Left, Right

Behind, In front, Inside, Outside

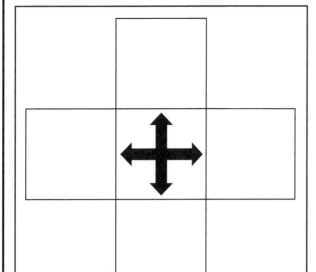

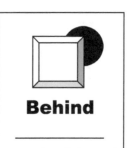

Behind
_____

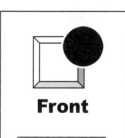

Front
_____

Inside
_____

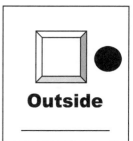

Outside
_____

- Write the following sentences using the position words that you have learned.

1. The book is **on** the chair. _____ ∘

2. The cat is **under** the table. _____ ∘

3. Let's meet in **front** of the station. _____ ∘

4. I put the money **inside** my bag. _____ ∘

5. Keep going. _____ ∘

6. Between. _____ ∘

Review ☐Awesome! ☐Excellent! ☐Good! ☐Average! ☐Poor!

Note:

- Match the transportation word to its correct English meaning.

のりもの ●   ● Dangerous

のりば ●   ● Entrance

しんかんせん ●   ● Destination

きんえん ●   ● Boarding

ちかてつ ●   ● Platform

つぎ ●   ● Bicycl

ふね ●   ● Transport

いりぐち ●   ● Boat

でぐち ●   ● No Smoking

ごじょうしゃ ●   ● Bullet Train

いきさき ●   ● Next

じてんしゃ ●   ● Exit

あぶない ●   ● Subway train

Review ☐Awesome! ☐Excellent! ☐Good! ☐Average! ☐Poor!

Note:

LESSONS EXERCISES AND ACTIVITIES

■ Put the Japanese words that apply to the blanks and read the sentence aloud.
Rearrange the following words to complete the sentence, and try to memorize the sentence.

おきゃくさん： _____ 。(konnichiwa.) Hello.

てんいん： _____ 。(irasshaimase) ! Welcome!

> おきゃくさん： Customer
> てんいん： Salesperson

おきゃくさん：ちょっと、_____ 、でんちはありますか。
　　　　　(chotto, sumimasen denchi wa arimasu ka?) Excuse me Do you have a battery?

てんいん：はい。(hai) ここに、ございます。(kokoni, gozaimasu.) Yes we have in here.

おきゃくさん： ありがとう、(arigatou,)_____ 。(kore wo kudasai.)
　　　　　　　　Thank you,　　　　　　　　Please give me this.

てんいん：はい、かしこまりました。(hai, kashikomar-imashita.) Yes, I got it.

おきゃくさん： _____ 。(o-ikura desu ka?) ! How much is it?

てんいん：ごひゃくえんです。(go-hyaku-en desu.) That's five hundred yen.

おきゃくさん：(The customer paid 1,000 yen.)

てんいん：せんえんをおあずかりします。(sen-en wo o-azukarishimasu.)

_____
(go-hyaku-en no o-kaeshi desu.) 500 yen is your change.

おきゃくさん：ありがとう。(arigatou.) Thank you.

てんいん：どうもありがとうございます、(doumo arigatougo zaimasu,)

_____ 。(mata o-koshi kudasai mase.)
Thank you very much and please come again.

Review ☐Awesome! ☐Excellent! ☐Good! ☐Average! ☐Poor!

Note:

■ Put the Japanese words that apply to the blanks and read the sentence aloud.
Rearrange the following words to complete the sentence, and try to memorize the sentence.

てんいん： いらっしゃいませ (irasshaimase) Welcome!

_____ 。(o-futari sama desu ka?)
　　　　Is it the two of you?

おきゃくさん： いえ、(ie)もうひとり、(mou hitori) _____。(ato kara kimasu.)
　　　　　No, one more person will come later.

てんいん： では、(dewa,)ごあんないさせていただきますので、
　　　　　　　(goan'nai sasete itadakimasunode,)
_____ 。(kochira he douzo.)
Now, let me show you around, this way please.

てんいん： _____(gochuumon ga o-kimarini narimashitara,)
　　　　When you have decided on your order,

そちらのボタンでおよびくださいませ。(sotirano botan de o-yobi kudasai mase.)
Please call us using that button.

■ Questions：(Answer in Japanese.)

1. What did the waiter say when the customer came to the restaurant?

_____

2. How many guests came to the restaurant in total?

_____

3. What did the customer say to the waiter when one of the customers was late?

_____

4. What did the waiter say when he showed the customer to their seat?

Review　□Awesome!　□Excellent!　□Good!　□Average!　□Poor!

Note:

LESSONS EXERCISES AND ACTIVITIES

- Translate the following Japanese colors words into English.

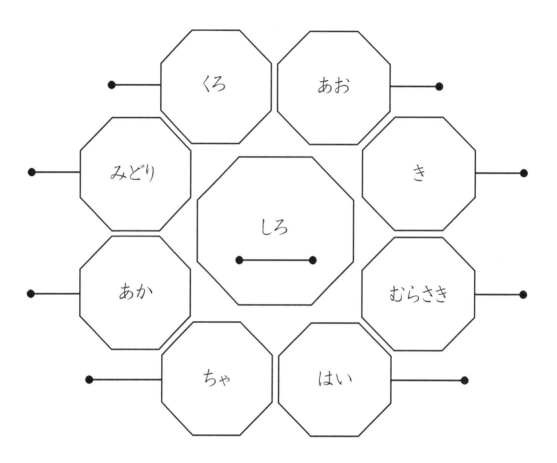

- Translate the following colors words into Japanese.

Pink	_____	Grey	_____
Gold	_____	Light blue	_____
Silver	_____	Dark blue	_____
Orange	_____	Yellow-Green	_____

Review ☐Awesome! ☐Excellent! ☐Good! ☐Average! ☐Poor!

Note:

LESSONS EXERCISES AND ACTIVITIES

■ Complete the following tables for the hotel vocabulary.

Japanese	Reading	English
	furonto	Front desk
		Reservation
		Room
	chekkuin	Check-in
チェックアウト		
		Address
		Non-smoking room
		Smoking room
		Extra bed
		Key
	robii	Lobby
		Luggage

Counting Nights of Stay		Counting Nights		Counting Rooms	
1 night		1 night		2 rooms	
2 nights		3 nights		3 rooms	
5 nights		4 nights		5 rooms	

Review ☐Awesome! ☐Excellent! ☐Good! ☐Average! ☐Poor!

Note:

Hotel Reservation

• Describe how you would make a reservation at a hotel over the phone in Japanese.

1. I would like to make a reservation.
2. Two nights, starting Saturday 28th.
3. For four people
4. Two rooms with twin beds
5. What time is check-out?
6. Is breakfast included?
7. How much is it?
8. Thank you

Customer

1. Hello, it's Plaza hotel
2. From when will you be staying?
3. How many people
4. How many rooms
5. Check-out time is 11:00.
6. Breakfast included.
7. In total it is 50,000 yen.
8. May I have your name, please?

Hotel staff

1._____
2._____
3._____
4._____
5._____
6._____
7._____
8._____

1._____
2._____
3._____
4._____
5._____
6._____
7._____
8._____

Review ☐Awesome! ☐Excellent! ☐Good! ☐Average! ☐Poor!

Note:

Body Parts

- Label the body parts using Hiragana words.

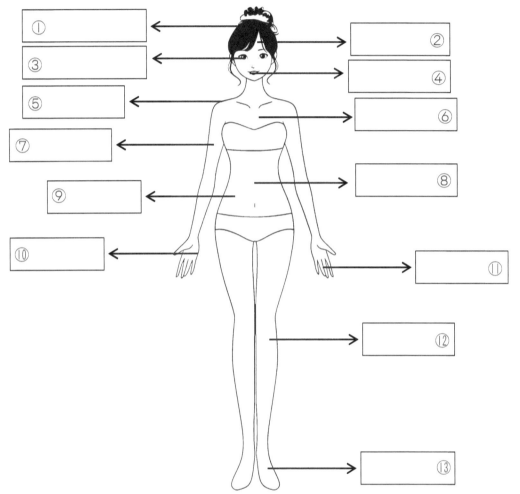

- Translate the following body parts words into Japanese.

⑭ Eyebrows		⑮ Ear	
⑯ Throat		⑰ Nose	
⑱ Neck		⑲ Ankle	

Review ☐Awesome! ☐Excellent! ☐Good! ☐Average! ☐Poor!

Note:

Japanese Verbs Groups

■ 1. What makes a verb a Group Two Verb?

A. All verbs containing an ending character from the "い" column.
B. The verbs are "する(To Do)" and "くる(To Come)".
C. All verbs containing an ending character from the "う" column of the Hiragana Chart.
D. Verbs containing an ending, either with the いる or える sound of the Hiragana Chart.

■ 2. What makes a verb an Irregular Verb?

A. All verbs containing an ending character from the "う" column of the Hiragana Chart.
B. The verbs are "する(To Do)" and "くる(To Come)".
C. Verbs containing an ending, either with the "いる" or "える" sound.
D. Verbs containing an ending character from the "い" column of the Hiragana Chart.

■ 3. What does it mean for a verb to be in MASU form?

A. A form of speaking honorifically in Japanese.
B. A form of speaking politely and neutrally in Japanese.
C. A form of speaking casually and amongst friends.
D. A form of speaking humbly in Japanese

■ 4. Which is stated in present negative MASU Form? (He does not eat sashimi.)

A. 彼は刺身を食べます。(かれはさしみをたべます。)
B. 彼は刺身を食べませんでした。(かれはさしみをたべませんでした。)
C. 彼は刺身を食べました。(かれはさしみをたべました。)
D. 彼は刺身を食べません。(かれはさしみをたべません。)

Review　☐Awesome!　☐Excellent!　☐Good!　☐Average!　☐Poor!

Note:

- Write sentences about **Masako** and **Haruto** using the Japanese verbs you have learned.
- Remember to use 「Topic は Thing を Verb」. (Formal) and (Informal).

Masako

1. I didn't eat breakfast. _____

2. I drink water. _____

3. I'm studying English. _____

Haruto

1. Eating breakfast. _____

2. I eat breakfast every day. _____

3. I don't do anything on a day off. _____

- Fill the below table with the correct Verb Group 1.

Dictionary form	Masu form	Meaning
		To wait
		To buy
		To play
		To read
		To drink
		To rest

Review ☐Awesome! ☐Excellent! ☐Good! ☐Average! ☐Poor!

Note:

Japanese Verbs Groups

- 1. Fill the below table with the correct Verb Group 2.

Dictionary form	Reading	Masu form	Reading	Meaning
				To exist
				To see
				To wear
				To wake up
				To show
				To eat
				To sleep
				To teach

- 2. Fill the below table with the correct Verb Group 3.

Dictionary form	Masu form	Meaning
		To do
		To come

- 3. Fill the below table with the て Te form.

		Please look.
		Please listen.
		Please write.
		Please wait.

Review ☐Awesome! ☐Excellent! ☐Good! ☐Average! ☐Poor!

Note:

- Change the present tense of the verb in the following sentences to the past tense.

あさ はん た
朝ご飯を食べます。
(asagohan wo tabemasu.)
I eat breakfast.

➡

しゅくだいをします。
(shukudai wo shimasu.)
I will do my homework.

➡

- Change the present negative of the verb in the following sentences to the past negative.

きょう がっこう い
今日は学校に行きません。
(kyou wa gakkou ni ikimasen.)
I will not go to school today.

➡

わたし よやく
私はホテルを予約しません。
(watashi wa hoteru wo yoyaku shimasen.)
I don't book hotel.

➡

わたし の
私はワインを飲みません。
(watashi wa wain wo nomimasen.)
I don't drink wine.

➡

Review ☐Awesome! ☐Excellent! ☐Good! ☐Average! ☐Poor!

Note:

- Complete the table by filling up the empty with the correct Japanese verb conjugation.

Group	MASU Form	Dictionary form	TE Form	Meaning
1				To drink
		みる		To see
	かいます		かって	To buy
				To do
				To eat
		かく		To write
	はなします			
3				To come

- Ask for permission using て-form (te-form) plus 〜もいいですか。

1. May I open the window? _____

2. Can I sit here?   _____

- . Ask for permission using て-form (te-form) plus いい.

1. Can I make a phone call?_____

2. May I go to the bathroom?_____

Review ☐Awesome! ☐Excellent! ☐Good! ☐Average! ☐Poor!

Note:

- Change the following verbs from the dictionary form to the TE form.

Dictionary	English	(て)TE Form
よむ	To read	
のむ	To drink	
あらう	To wash	
のる	To get on/ride	
おくる	To send	
かく	To write	
おもう	To think/feel	
ねる	To sleep	
おきる	To wake Up	
くる	To come/arrive	

- Write the group number for the following verbs and translate them into English.

Dictionary	Group	English
おきる		
みる		
する		
はなす		
かう		
くる		

Review ☐Awesome! ☐Excellent! ☐Good! ☐Average! ☐Poor!

Note:

- Highlight the て form of the verb and then take a moment to practice saying the following phrases.

Ask Permissions – Casual & Formal

でんわ
❏ 電話を、かけていいですか。　　(denwa wo, kakete ii desu ka?)
Can I make a phone call?

い
❏ トイレに、行っていいですか。　　(toire ni, itte iidesu ka?)
May I go to the bathroom?

すわ
❏ ここに座ってもよろしいでしょうか。(koko ni suwatte mo yoroshii deshou ka?)
May I sit here?

あした き
❏ 明日来てもよろしいですか。　　(ashita kite mo yoroshii desu ka?)
Do you mind if I come tomorrow?

き
❏ ちょっと、お聞きしていいですか。(chotto, o-kiki shite ii desu ka?)
May I ask you a question?

くるま　い
❏ 車で、行かせていただいていいですか。(kuruma de, ika sete itadaite iidesu ka?)
Can I go by car?

Review ☐Awesome! ☐Excellent! ☐Good! ☐Average! ☐Poor!

Note:

LESSONS EXERCISES AND ACTIVITIES

■ Complete the sentences by filling in the blanks with the correct "Do" verb.

わたし まいにち
私は、毎日べんきょう＿＿＿＿＿＿＿＿。【watashi wa, mainichi benkyou shite imasu.】
I'm studying every day.

かれ
彼は、あまりべんきょう ＿＿＿＿＿＿＿＿。【kare wa, amari benkyou shimasen.】
He doesn't study much.

きのう
あなたは、昨日べんきょう＿＿＿＿＿＿＿＿。【anata wa, kinou benkyou shimashita.】
You studied yesterday.

わたし なに
私は、何もべんきょう＿＿＿＿＿＿＿＿。【watashi wa, nani mo benkyou shimasendeshita.】
I didn't study anything.

あした みせ そうじ
明日、店を掃除 ＿＿＿＿＿＿＿＿。【ashita, mise wo souji shimashou.】
Let's clean the store tomorrow.

か もの
あなたは、買い物を＿＿＿＿＿＿＿＿。【anata wa, kaimono wo shimashita ka?】
Did you go shopping?

わたしふく あら
私は服を洗わ ＿＿＿＿＿＿＿＿。【watashi wa fuku wo arawa nakatta.】
I didn't wash my clothes.

かれ きのう
彼は昨日、ゲームを＿＿＿＿＿＿＿＿。【kare wa kinou, gēmu wo shita.】
He played a game yesterday.

Review ☐Awesome! ☐Excellent! ☐Good! ☐Average! ☐Poor!

Note:

■　Complete the sentences by filling in the blanks with the correct "Come" verb.

はは　わたし　へや
母は、私の部屋に _____ 。【haha wa, watashi no heya ni kimashita.】
My mother came to my room.

かれ
彼は、あなたと _____ 。【kare wa, anata to kimasen.】
He won't come with you.

きのう
あなたは、昨日 _____ 。【anata wa, kinou kimasendeshita.】
You didn't come yesterday.

わたし　べんきょう
私は、勉強しに _____ 。【watashi wa, benkyou shi ni kimashita.】
I came to study.

あさ　わたし　いっしょ
朝、私と一緒に _____ 。【asa, watashi to isshoni kimasen ka?】
Would you like to come with me in the morning?

たぶん
多分、あなたはここへ _____ 。【tabun, anata wa koko e kimasu.】
Maybe you come here.

ともだち　えき
友達は、駅には _____ 。【tomodachi wa, eki niwa kimasendeshita.】
My friend didn't come to the station.

こんど
今度、あなたはここに _____ 。【kondo, anata wa koko ni kimasu ka?】
Will you come here next time?

Review 　☐Awesome! 　☐Excellent! 　☐Good! 　☐Average! 　☐Poor!

Note:

■ Complete the sentences by filling in the blanks with the correct "Speak" verb.

すこ
もう少し、ゆっくり＿＿＿＿＿＿くださいません。【mou-sukoshi, yukkuri hanashite kudasai.】
Please speak a little more slowly.

かれ
彼は、あなたと＿＿＿＿＿＿。【kare wa, anata to hanashimasen.】
He doesn't talk to you.

はは
母は、あなたに＿＿＿＿＿＿。【haha wa, anata ni hanashimashita ka?】
Did your mother talk to you?

わたし かれすべ
私は、彼に全て＿＿＿＿＿＿。【watashi wa, kare ni subete hanashimasendeshita.】
I didn't tell him everything.

あした　　いちど
明日、もう一度＿＿＿＿＿＿。【ashita, mou ichido hanashi mashou.】
Let's talk again tomorrow.

せんせい ほん
先生は、本のことを＿＿＿＿＿＿。【sensei wa, hon no koto wo hanashimashita.】
The teacher talked about books.

みんなで＿＿＿＿＿＿。【minna de hanashimashou ka?】
Shall we talk together?

だれ
誰かがこれを＿＿＿＿＿＿。【dareka ga kore wo hanashimasu ka?】
Does anyone talk about this?

Review ☐Awesome! ☐Excellent! ☐Good! ☐Average! ☐Poor!

Note:

- Complete the sentences by filling in the blanks with the correct "See/Watch" verb.

はは　　　えいが
母はいつも映画を＿＿＿＿＿＿＿＿＿＿。【haha wa itsumo eiga wo mimasu.】
My mother always watches movies.

かれ
彼はテレビを ＿＿＿＿＿＿＿＿＿＿ 。【kare wa terebi wo mimasen.】
He doesn't watch TV.

わたしきのう　うみ
私は昨日、海を＿＿＿＿＿＿＿＿＿＿。【watashi wa kinou, umi wo mimashita.】
I saw the sea yesterday.

ちち　　　やま
父はあの山を＿＿＿＿＿＿＿＿＿＿。【chichi wa ano yama wo mimasendeshita.】
My father doesn't saw that mountain.

あした　　　いちど
明日、もう一度これを＿＿＿＿＿＿＿＿＿＿。【ashita, mou ichido kore wo mimasen ka?】
Would you like to see this again tomorrow.

せんせい　ほん
先生は、本を＿＿＿＿＿＿＿＿＿＿。【sensei wa, hon wo mimasendeshita ka?】
Didn't the teacher look at the book?

　　　　　　　　えいが
みんなであの映画を＿＿＿＿＿＿＿＿＿＿。【minna de ano eiga wo mimashou ka?】
Shall we all watch that movie?

だれ
誰かがこれを＿＿＿＿＿＿＿＿＿＿。【dareka ga kore wo mimashita ka?】
Who saw this?

Review ☐Awesome! ☐Excellent! ☐Good! ☐Average! ☐Poor!

Note:

ANSWER KEY

Exercise 1 Japanese Greetings (Page 316)

1	Hello.-こんにちは。-konnichiwa.	
2	I'm sorry.-ごめんなさい。-gomennasai.	
3	Good night.-おはようございます。-oyasuminasai.	
4	Thank you.-ありがとうございます。-arigatau gozaimasu.	
5	Good evening.-こんばんは。-konbanwa.	
6	Good Morning.-おはようございます。-ohayou gozaimasu.	
7	Nice to meet you.-はじめまして。-hajimemashite.	
8	Long time no see.-ひさしぶり。-hisashiburi.	
1	okaeri.-おかえり。-Welcome home.	
2	tadaima.-ただいま。-I'm home.	
3	ganbatte.-がんばって。-Good luck. / Do your best.	
4	gomennasai.-ごめんなさい。-I'm sorry.	
5	kiwotsukete.-きをつけて。-Take care.	
6	hajimemashite.-はじめまして。-Nice to meet you.	
7	arigatougozaimasu.-ありがとうございます。-Thank you.	
8	omedetougozaimasu.-おめでとうございます。Congratulations.	

Exercice 2 Japanese Greetings (Page 317)

Question 1 → The correct answer is c.
"おやすみなさい" is used in everyday conversation. In more formal situations, such as in business situations, use more polite expressions.

Question 2 → The correct answer is b. "行ってきます" is said to someone staying at home before going out. To show respect, a more polite expression may be used.

Question 3 → The correct answer is c. This is to show respect a more polite expression may also be used. Among family and close friends, the expression "気をつけて行ってらっしゃい"-ki wo tsukete itterasshai.(Take care on your way out) may also be used.

Question 4 → The correct answer is c. It's used in conversations with close people such as family or friends. If the destination of the return is clear, the expression "ただいま帰りました"-tadaima kaerimashita (I have returned home) may also be used.

Exercise 3 "Kudasai" "Onegaishimasu" (Page 318)

Question 1 → The correct answer is b. Another way to say it is "Please go to Tokyo Station", but a more polite expression, if you use honorifics, is "東京駅に行っていただけますか。"

Exercise 3 "Kudasai" "Onegaishimasu" (Page 318)

Question 2 → The correct answer is a. A more polite way to say this is "しばらくお待ちください"-shibaraku o-machi kudasai.-Please wait a moment. but in business situations, you will be instructed to use "少々お待ちください"-shou shou o-machi kudasai.-Please wait a little bit.
Question 3 → The correct answer is b. In Japan, we often use this way of saying because we often respond to phone calls quickly in the business scene.
Question 4 →
a. ください。-kudasai.
b. お願いします。-おねがいします。- o-negaishimasu.
c. お願いします。-おねがいします。- o-negaishimasu.

Exercise 4 Self - Introduction (Page 319)

E.g.
こんにちは。-Kon'nichiwa はじめまして。- hajimemashite
ソフィアと言います。-Sofia to iimasu.
私はフロリダ出身です。-watashi wa Furorida shusshin desu. 22歳です。-nijyuu ni-sai desu.学生です。-gakusei desu.
よろしくお願いします。-yoroshiku o-negai shimasu.
E.g. -More smoother way of expression.
こんにちは、はじめまして、ソフィアと言います。
私はフロリダ出身の22歳で、学生です。
よろしくお願いします。

Question 1 →
a. Formal and less polite.
私は田中です。-わたし は たなか です。-I'm Tanaka.
b. Second sentence is a more polite way.私は田中と申します。わたしは たなか と もうします。-My name is Tanaka.

Question 2 →
a. Hajimemashite-はじめまして。
→ When meeting someone for the first time.
b. Hisashiburi-ひさしぶり。→ When meeting someone after a long time.

Exercise 5 Expressions (Page 320)

Question 1 →
a. Casual→なんさいですか。-nan-sai desu ka?
b. Polite→おいくつですか。-o-ikutsu desu ka?

➤ In situations such as business situations, there are respectful words, "おいくつでらっしゃいますか"
"-o ikutsu de rasshaimasu ka."

Continued on the next page.

ANSWER KEY

Exercise 5 Expressions (Page 320)

Question 2 →
The first sentence a is more polite than the second one.
Question 3 → The correct answer is a.
In recent years, "Daijobu" has been increasingly used to ask or answer others about "necessary/unnecessary," "possible/impossible," "agree/disagree," etc. For example,
"It looks heavy, shall I carry it?"
(unnecessary). " No, I'm fine" (meaning unnecessary), etc.
Question 4
Casual → わからない。(wakaranai.)
Polite → 分かりません。(wakarimasen.)

Exercise 6 Numbers (321)

- Write out the following numbers in Hiragana and their reading.

No.	Hiragana	Reading	Kanji
1	いち	ichi	一
2	に	ni	二
3	さん	san	三
4	し/よん	shi/yon	四
5	ご	go	五
6	ろく	roku	六
7	しち/なな	shichi/nana	七
8	はち	hachi	八
9	きゅう/く	kyuu/ku	九
10	じゅう	juu	十

- Write out the following numbers in Hiragana.

No.	Reading	Hiragana
100	Hyaku	ひゃく
1,000	(Sen)	せん
10,000	(Man)	まん
100,000	(Juuman)	じゅうまん

- Let's write 2023 in hiragana.
にせんにじゅうさん ni sen ni jyuu san
(two thousand twenty-three)

- Let's write 123456 in hiragana.
じゅうにまんさんぜんよんひゃくごじゅうろく
-jyuu ni man san zen yon hyaku go jyuu roku
(one hundred twenty-three thousand four hundred fifty-six)

Exercise 7 Days of The Week (Page 322)

- Match the following days of the week to their correct English meaning.

No.	Kanji	Hiragana	Reading	English
1	水曜日	すいようび	sui you bi	Wednesday
2	日曜日	にちようび	nichi you bi	Sunday
3	土曜日	どようび	do you bi	Saturday
4	金曜日	きんようび	kin you bi	Friday
5	月曜日	げつようび	getsu you bi	Monday
6	木曜日	もくようび	moku you bi	Thursday
7	火曜日	かようび	ka you bi	Tuesday

- Write the Kanji for the day(s) of the week

月	曜日	Monday	literally "moon day"
火	曜日	Tuesday	literally "fire day"
水	曜日	Wednesday	literally "water day"
木	曜日	Thursday	literally "wood day"
金	曜日	Friday	literally "gold day"
土	曜日	Saturday	literally "soil day"
日	曜日	Sunday	literally "sun day"

Exercise 8 Counting Weeks Page (323)

- How do you count the weeks in Japanese? Fill in the blank

	Hiragana	Kanji	Reading	English
1	いっしゅうかん	一週間	isshuu kan	1 week
2	にしゅうかん	二週間	nishuu kan	2 weeks
3	さんしゅうかん	三週間	sanshuu kan	3 weeks
4	よんしゅうかん	四週間	yonshuu kan	4 weeks
5	ごしゅうかん	五週間	goshuu kan	5 weeks

- Match the correct Hiragana of weeks to the correct English and reading.

こんしゅう	今週	konshuu	This Week
さらいしゅう	再来週	saraishuu	The Week after Next
せんしゅう	先週	senshuu	Last week
らいしゅう	来週	raishuu	Next week

Exercise 8 Counting Weeks (Page 323)

■ Write the following sentences into Hiragana.

a. わたしは らいしゅう アメリカ に いきます。
watashi wa raishuu Amerika ni iki masu.
私は来週、アメリカに行きます。

b. わたしは こんしゅう とうきょう に いきます。
watashi wa konshuu Toukyou ni iki masu.
私は今週、東京に行きます。

Exercise 9 Days of The Month (Page 324)

■ Match the following days of the month to their correct English meaning.

Hiragana	Kanji	Reading	English
みっか	三日	mikka	3rd
ここのか	九日	kokonoka	9th
むいか	六日	muika	6th
ついたち	一日	tsuitachi	1st
なのか	七日	nanoka	7th
いつか	五日	itsuka	5th
ふつか	二日	futsuka	2nd
ようか	八日	youka	8th
よっか	四日	yokka	4th
とおか	十日	tooka	10th

■ Write the Hiragana for the following days of the month.
1) 九月 五日 →くがつ いつか -kugatsu itsuka
2) 四月 二十日 →しがつ はつか -shigatu hatsuka
3) 六月 十四日 →ろくがつ じゅうよっか -rokugatsu juuyokka
4) 七月 七日 →しちがつ なのか -shichigatsu nanoka

Exercise 10 Months of The Year (Page 325)

■ Match the correct Hiragana to the correct English and Kanji

Hiragana	Kanji	Reading	English
くがつ	九月	ku-gatsu	Sep.
じゅうにがつ	十二月	juu-nigatsu	Dec.
じゅうがつ	十月	juu-gatsu	Oct.
ろくがつ	六月	roku-gatsu	Jun.

Continue on the top right

Exercise 10 Months of The Year (Page 325)

■ Complete the following table writing the correct hiragana, reading, English, or kanji.

Hiragana	Kanji	Reading	English
いちがつ	一月	ichi-gatsu	January
にがつ	二月	ni-gatsu	February
さんがつ	三月	san-gatsu	March
しがつ	四月	shi-gatsu	April
ごがつ	五月	go-gatsu	May
ろくがつ	六月	roku-gatsu	June
しちがつ	七月	shichi-gatsu	July
はちがつ	八月	hachi-gatsu	August
くがつ	九月	ku-gatsu	September
じゅうがつ	十月	juu-gatsu	October
じゅういちがつ	十一月	juuichi-gatsu	November
じゅうにがつ	十二月	juuni-gatsu	December

■ Write the Kanji for the day(s) of the week

Exercise 11 Months (Page 326)

■ Circle the correct answer for the below questions.

1. How do you say "next month" in Japanese?
The correct answer is b. → 来月 らいげつ –raigetsu

■ Circle the correct answer for the below questions.

2. "Six months" in Japanese is? The correct answer is a.
→ 六か月 ろっかげつ-rokkagetsu

■ How do you count the months in Japanese? Fill in the blank.

Hiragana	Kanji	Reading	English
ごかげつ	五ヶ月	go-ka-getsu	Five months
ろっかげつ	六ヶ月	rokka-getsu	Six months
ななかげつ	七ヶ月	nana-ka-getsu	Sevenmonths
はちかげつ	八ヶ月	hachi-ka-getsu	Eight months
きゅうかげつ	九ヶ月	kyuu-ka-getsu	Nine months

Exercise 12 Date (Page 327)

- How do you write these dates in Japanese?

a. 31st August → 八月三十一日-はち がつ さんじゅう いち にち
  （8月31日）　　（hachi-gatsu-san-juu-ichi-nichi)
b. 16th May → 五月十六日-ご がつ じゅう ろく にち
  （5月16日）　　（go-gatsu-juu-roku-nichi)
c. 5th December → 十二月五日-じゅうに がつ いつか
  （12月5日）　　（juu-ni-gatsu-itsu-ka)
d. 14th September → 九月十四日-く がつ じゅう よっか
  （9月14日）　　（ku-gatsu-juu-yokka)

- How do you write these dates in English?

a. 五月二十七日 → May 27th
b. 十月三日 → October 3rd
c. 一月二十五日 → January 25th
d. 七月十三日 → July 13th

- Write your birthday in Japanese.

E.g.→ 七月八日-しち がつ ようか

- Write today's date in Japanese.

E.g.→ 四月九日-し がつ ここのか

- Write the reading for this date: 2022年5月29日（火曜）

→二千二十二年五月二十九日(かよう-ka you)
→に せん に じゅうに ねん ご がつ に じゅうく にち
  (ni-sen-ni-juu-ni-nen go-gatsu-ni-juu-ku-nichi)

January 1st (ichi-gatsu tsuitachi) is a national holiday in Japan. It was a Sunday and it rained after five days. In Japanese, there are various ways to refer to dates and different readings for the kanji character "日," so let's learn little by little.

Exercise 13 Years Old - Age (Page 328)

- Write the following English words into Hiragana / Kanji

English	Hiragana
Next year	らいねん-rainen
Last year	きょねん-kyonen
This year	ことし-kotoshi
Every year	まいとし-maitoshi
	Kanji
Year	年-nen
Next year	来年-rainen
This year	今年-kotoshi
Every year	毎年-maitoshi

Exercise 13 Years Old - Age (Page 328)

- How do you tell your age in Japanese?

In Japanese, there are several situations and ways to ask someone about their age, including:
➤ When asking someone's age for the first time, it's common to use "年齢はいくつですか。"-nenrei wa ikutsu desu ka or "おいくつですか。"- o-ikutsu desu ka (How old are you?).
➤ It's not common to ask someone's age when talking to someone close to them or close to them, but you can ask them about their birthday or celebrate their age. For example, "誕生日はいつですか。"-tanjyoubi wa itsu desu ka?(When is your birthday?) or "何歳になりましたか。"-nan sai ni narimashita ka? (How old did you turn?).
➤ In a business setting, asking someone about their age is often inappropriate. However, if age-related information is necessary, you may ask about their job title or years of experience.
➤ When asking someone older or in a higher position about their age, you can also ask, "おいくつでらっしゃいますか。"- o-ikutsu de rasshaimasu ka – (How old are you?)

Exercise 14 Weather (Page 329)

- Write the following English words into Hiragana / Romaji.

	Hiragana	Reading	English
1	はれ	Hare	Sunshine
2	くもり	kumori	Cloudy
3	あめ	ame	Rain
4	ゆき	yuki	Snow
5	かぜがつよい	kaze-ga-tsuyoi	Windy

- Write the following sentence in Japanese.

How's the weather today?→ 今日の天気はどうですか。
  (kyou no tenki wa dou desu ka?)

- Translate these sentences about the seasons and weather into English.

	Japanese	Reading
1	冬は寒いです。	It is cold in winter.
2	四月は春です。	April is spring.
3	夏の天気は暑いです。	Summer weather is hot.
4	十月は秋です。	October is autumn.
5	秋は涼しいです。	Autumn is cool.

ANSWER KEY

Exercise 15 Question Words (Page 330)

- Circle the correct question words for the below sentences then fill in the blank and write the meaning for each phrase.

Question 1 → The correct answer is **b.**
トイレは【どこ】ですか。-Where is the restroom?
(toire wa doko desu ka?)

Question 2 → The correct answer is **c.**
いま【なん】じですか-今何時ですか。-What time is it now?
(ima nan ji desu ka?)

Question 3 → The correct answer is **a.**
コーヒーとジュース、【どちら】が好きですか。Which do you prefer, coffee or juice? (kōhī to jūsu, dochira ga suki desu ka?)

- Write the following English words/question in Japanese.

English	Japanese
How Long?	どのくらいですか-donokurai desu ka?
What is this?	これは何ですか。-kore wa nan desu ka?
How Much?	いくらですか。-ikura desu ka?
How about today?	今日はどうですか。-kyou wa dou desu ka?
Which?	どちらですか。-dochira desu ka?
How much is it?	いくらですか。-ikura desu ka?
Why?	なぜですか。-naze desu ka?
How is it?	どうですか。-dou desu ka?

Exercise 16 Basic Questions and Answers (Page 331)

- Write your answer to the following questions in Japanese.
- Write the meaning for each question.

1. あなたのなまえはなんですか。-**What is your name?**
E.g. スティブ (Steve) と言います。-Sutību to ii masu. I am Steve.

2. おくにはどこですか。- **Where are you from?**
E.g. テキサスから来ました。-tekisasu kara kimashita. I'm from Texas.

3. おしごとはなんですか。- **What is your job?**
E.g. エンジニアをしています。-Enjinia wo shite imasu. I'm an engineer.

4. どちらにすんでいますか。-**Where do you live?**
E.g. 東京に住んでいます。-Toukyou ni sunde imasu. I live in Tokyo.

Exercise 16 Basic Questions and Answers (P.331)

- How do you tell your name in Japanese, for the following situations/Your language.

Super polite (Name)
E.g. 私は、エミリーと申します。
watashi wa Emirī to moushi masu.

Casual (Name)
エミリーです。

Your language is?
E.g. 私は英語を話します。
watashi wa eigo wo hanashi masu.

➢ It is easy to make mistakes when using honorific language, particularly distinguishing between honorific and humble language. Even when speaking to someone higher in status, humble language may be used when referring to a specific position or role they hold. Conversely, honorific language may be used when speaking to someone lower in status, to express respect for them.

Exercise 17 Apologizing (Page 332)

- Which form of apology is appropriate in the following situations?

1. Which is the appropriate way to ask when you urgently need to report a job to the boss on the phone?
→ The correct answer is c. お話中、失礼します。

2. Which is the appropriate way to ask when entering the boss's room?
→ The correct answer is c. 失礼します。

3. Which is the appropriate way to say when you finish work and leave before your co-workers?
→ The correct answer is c. お先に失礼します。

4. What do you say when your wife gets angry because you ate her favorite cake without her permission?
→ The correct answer is b. 本当にごめんなさい。

Exercise 18 Expressions Starting Eating/Ending Eating/Hungry/Full (Page 333)

- Write your answer to the following questions in Japanese.

1. What should you say at the end of a meal in Japan?

→ごちそうさまでした。-gochisou sama deshita.

2. What should you say at the start of a meal in Japan?

→いただきます。-itadakimasu.

Exercise 18 Expressions Starting Eating/Ending Eating/Hungry/Full (Page 333)

- Write your answer to the following questions in Japanese.

3. How would you say "delicious" in Japanese?
→ おいしい。 -oishii.

4. What does umai mean? → "Umai" is like a casual way of saying "おいしい" (oishii), which means "delicious."

- Translate these phrases into English.

	Japanese	English
1	おかわりをください。	→ Please refill.
2	おなかがへった。	→ I'm hungry.
3	おなかがすいていますか。	→ Are you hungry?
4	おなかがすいていない。	→ I am not hungry.
5	もうたべられません	→ I can't eat anymore.

Exercise 19 Family Members (Page 334)

- Match your family members' words to someone else family.

	My Family	Someone Else Family
1	はは	おかあさん
2	いもうと	いもうとさん
3	むすこ	むすこさん
4	ちち	おとうさん
5	おっと	ごしゅじん
6	つま	おくさん
7	こども	おこさん

"お母さん"-okaasan is a word used by a child to refer to their mother, or by a third party to refer to someone's mother affectionately.

- Complete the table below by filling in the missing words in the blank boxes, the first one has been done as an example.

	Hiragana	Romaji	English
1	はは	haha	My mother
2	そふ	sofu	Grandfather
3	おとうと	otouto	Younger brother
4	そぼ	sobo	My grandmother
5	ちち	chichi	Father
6	かぞく	kazoku	Family
7	いもうと	imouto	Younger sister

Exercise 20 Introducing My Family (Page 335)

- Introduce your family using the same sentence pattern you have learned.

E.g.
はじめまして、みなさん、こんにちは。
シャーロットと言います。私はフロリダから来ました。家族は父と母、祖母と弟の五人家族です。今、私は日本で看護師をするために日本語を日本の大学で学んでいます。時間があったら日本中を旅行してみたいのでいろいろと教えてください。どうぞ、よろしくお願いします。

Hiragana Ver.
はじめまして、みなさん、こんにちは。
シャーロットと いいます。わたしは フロリダから きました。かぞくは ちち と はは、そぼ と おとうとの ごにんかぞくです。いま、わたしは にほんで かんごし を するために にほんごをにほんの だいがくで まなんで います。じかんが あったら にほんじゅうを りょこうしてみたいのでいろいろと おしえてください。
どうぞ、よろしくおねがいします。

Romaji
hajimemashite, minasan, kon'nichiwa. Shārotto to iimasu. watashi wa Furorida kara kimashita. kazoku wa chichi to haha, sobo to otouto no goninkazoku desu.
ima, watashi wa Nihon de kangoshi wo suru tame ni nihongo wo nihon no daigaku de manande imasu. jikan ga attara Nihonjuu wo ryokou shite mitai node iroiro to oshiete kudasai.
douzo, yoroshiku o-negaishimasu.

English
Nice to meet you, hello everyone.
I am Charlotte and I'm from Florida.
My family comprises five members: my father, mother, grandmother, younger brother, and myself.
I am studying Japanese at a Japanese university to become a nurse in Japan. If I have the time, I would love to travel around Japan, so please tell me about various places to visit. Thank you very much.

❖ If you still find it challenging or confusing, please refer to pages 193-194 in Unit 9.

Exercise 21 Counting People (Page 336)

- Write in Japanese how many people are in the pictures.

1 person → 一人 ひとり- hitori
2 people → 二人 ふたり- futari
3 people → 三人 さんにん- san-nin

- Write in Kanji how many people for the below Romaji. The first one has been done as an example. (From the left column)

Kanji	Kanji with numbers	Reading
十一人	11人	juu ichi nin
七人	7人	nana nin
四人	4人	yo nin
九人	9人	kyuu nin
十二人	12人	juu ni nin
六人	6人	roku nin
十三人	13人	juu san nin
十四人	14人	juu yo nin

- Please answer the following questions in Japanese.

1. ごかぞくなんにんですか。
E.g. → 私の家族は五人です。
　　わたしのかぞくはごにんです。
　　watashi no kazoku wa go-nin desu.
　　I have a family of five.

2. The Japanese word for two (people) is?
　→ 二人-ふたり-futari

3. The Japanese word for one (person) is?
　→ 一人-ひとり-hitori

Exercise 22 Counting Things (Page 337)

- Write in Japanese how to count umbrellas in the below pictures.

1 umbrella → 一本の傘-いっぽんのかさ (ippon no kasa)
3 umbrellas → 三本の傘-さんぼんのかさ (san bon no kasa)
4 umbrellas → 四本の傘-よんほんのかさ (yon hon no kasa)

- Write in Japanese how to count long, cylindrical objects.

1	一本	いっぽん	ippon	1 Piece
2	二本	にほん	ni hon	2 Pieces
3	三本	さんぼん	san bon	3 Pieces
4	四本	よんほん	yon hon	4 Pieces
5	五本	ごほん	go hon	5 Pieces

Exercise 22 Counting Things (Page 337)

- Write in Japanese how to count long, cylindrical objects.

6	六本	ろっぽん	roppon	6 Piece
7	七本	ななほん	nana hon	7 Pieces
8	八本	はっぽん	happon	8 Pieces
9	九本	きゅうほん	kyuu hon	9 Pieces
10	十本	じゅっぽん	juppon	10 Pieces

- Which object can't be used (ほん hon 本) for counting?

The correct answer is: The **book**. In Japanese, the counter for books is "冊" (satsu).

English	Kanji	Hiragana	Counter
Battery	電池	でんち	本/個 -hon/ko
Can	缶	かん	缶-kan/個/本
Book	**本**	**ほん**	**冊** -satsu
Bottle	瓶	びん	本/瓶-bin
Pen	-	ぺん	本-hon

Exercise 23 Counting Flat Objects (Page 338)

- Write how many flat objects are in the picture in Japanese counting.

The correct answer is :
　Stamp → 四枚-よんまい-yon mai-Four stamps.
　T-shirt → 三枚-さんまい-san mai-Three pieces of clothing.

- Complete the following table using the flat objects counter.

English	Kanji	Hiragana	Counter
ごまい	五枚	go-mai	Five flat objects
ろくまい	六枚	roku-mai	Six flat objects
ななまい	七枚	nana-mai	Seven flat objects
はちまい	八枚	hachi-mai	Eight flat objects
きゅうまい	九枚	kyuu-mai	Nine flat objects
じゅうまい	十枚	juu-mai	Ten flat objects

Exercise 24 Counting Small and Large Animals / Rabbits and Birds (339)

- Write in Japanese counting for small and large animals.

Small animals

Kanji	Hiragana	Reading
一匹	いっぴき	ippiki
二匹	にひき	ni-hiki
三匹	さんびき	san-biki
四匹	よんひき	yon-hiki
五匹	ごひき	go-hiki
六匹	ろっぴき	roppiki
七匹	ななひき	nana-hiki
八匹	はっぴき	happiki
九匹	きゅうひき	kyuu-hiki
十匹	じゅっぴき	juppiki

Large animals

Kanji	Hiragana	Reading
一頭	いっとう	ittou
二頭	にとう	ni-tou
三頭	さんとう	san-tou
四頭	よんとう	yon-tou
五頭	ごとう	go-tou
六頭	ろくとう	roku-tou
七頭	ななとう	nana-tou
八頭	はっとう	hattou
九頭	きゅうとう	kyuu-tou
十頭	じゅっとう	juttou

- Complete the following table using the birds and rabbits counter.

一羽	いちわ	ichi-wa	One bird/rabbit
二羽	にわ	ni-wa	Two birds/rabbits
三羽	さんば	san-ba	Three birds/rabbits
四羽	よんわ	yon-wa	Four birds/rabbits
五羽	ごわ	go-wa	Five birds/rabbits
六羽	ろくわ	roku-wa	Six birds/rabbits
七羽	ななわ	nana-wa	Seven birds/rabbits

Exercise 25 Japanese Counters (Page 340)

- Match the following pictures with their correct counter.

English	Hiragana-Counter	Reading
Fish	ひき	hiki
Building floor	かい	kai
Book	さつ	satsu
Bird	わ	wa
Car	だい	dai
Cow	とう	tou

- Write down how to count for frequency. Several times an action was repeated.

Kanji	Hiragana	Reading	English
一回	いっかい	ikkai	Once
二回	にかい	ni-kai	Twice
三回	さんかい	san-kai	Three times

- How to count the following animals?

3 kittens	三匹 の子猫	san-biki-no-ko-neko
6 Puppy	六匹 の子犬	roppiki-no-ko-inu

Exercise 26 Counting Money (Page 341)

- Complete the following table using the Money counter.

Kanji	Hiragana	Reading	English
百円	ひゃくえん	hyaku-en	100 Yen
三百円	さんびゃくえん	sanbyaku-en	300 Yen
六百円	ろっぴゃくえん	roppyaku-en	600 Yen
八百円	はっぴゃくえん	happyaku-en	800 Yen
千円	せんえん	sen-en	1,000 Yen
三千円	さんぜんえん	sanzen-en	3,000 Yen
八千円	はっせんえん	hassen-en	8,000 Yen
一万円	いちまんえん	ichiman-en	10,000 Yen
十万円	じゅうまんえん	juuman-en	100,000 Yen

Exercise 26 Counting Money (Page 341)

- Write out the corresponding Kanji for the following

五百円	ごひゃくえん	gohyaku-en	500 Yen
二千円	にせんえん	nisen-en	2,000 Yen
七百円	ななひゃくえん	nanahyaku-en	700 Yen

- What is "One million Yen" in Japanese and how to say it?
- Answer: 百万円-ひゃくまんえん-hyaku man en.

- How to say "How much is this" in Japanese?
- Answer: これはいくらですか。-kore wa ikura desu ka?

Exercise 27 Counting Money (Page 342)

- Write the price for each item in the following pictures.

Items	Price in Kanji	Price in Hiragana
Vacuum	千七百五十円	せんななひゃくごじゅうえん
Washing Machine	四万八千円	よんまんはっせんえん
Sofa	二万七千円	にまんななせんえん
Refrigerator	三万円	さんまんえん
Tissue	百五十五円	ひゃくごじゅうごえん
Frying Pan	千九百五十円	せんきゅうひゃくごじゅうえん
Microwave	一万円	いちまんえん
Kettle	千円	せんえん
Hot Pot	三千五百円	さんぜんごひゃくえん
Rice Cooker	六千七百円	ろくせんななひゃくえん

Exercise 28 Time (Page 343)

- Match these times expressed in Japanese with the times on the right.

yo-ji juugo-fun	04:15	四時十五分
hachi-ji niju-ppun	08:20	八時二十分
ku-ji yonju-ppun	09:40	九時四十分
shichi-ji	7:00	七時
roku-ji ju-ppun	06:10	六時十分
Juu ichi-ji	11:00	十一時
ni-ji yonjuugo-fun	02:45	二時四十五分
juuni-ji go-fun	12:05	十二時五分
yo-ji juugo-fun	04:15	四時十五分

Exercise 29 Time (Page 344)

- Write the time for the clocks below.

E.g. ni-ji sanjuppun	02:30	二時三十分
shichi-ji juugo-fun	07:15	七時十五分
juu-ji ju-ppun	10:10	十時十分
ku-ji	09:00	九時
juu-ni-ji	12:00	十二時
yo-ji	04:00	四時
go-ji yonjuu-go-fun	5:45	五時四十五分
ichi-ji	01:00	一時
roku-ji sanjuu-go-fun	6:35	六時三十五分

- Answer the following questions: What time are you doing these activities?

- なんじにおきますか。nanji ni okimasu ka.
  What time do you get up?

E.g. Answer: 七時におきます。- shichi-ji ni oki masu.
I get up at seven o'clock.

- なんじにねますか。-nanji ni nemasu ka.
  What time do you sleep?

E.g. Answer: 私はだいたい十一時に寝ます。
watashi wa daitai juu-ichi-ji ni nemasu.
I usually go to bed at eleven o'clock.

- 何時からべんきょうしますか。-nan ji kara benkyou shimasu ka. - What time do you start studying?

E.g. Answer: 朝の十時からべんきょうします。
asa no juu-ji kara benkyou simasu.
I study from ten o'clock in the morning.

- 何時にゆうしょくを食べますか。-nan ji ni yuushoku wo tabemasu ka. -What time do you have dinner?

E.g. Answer: 六時三十分くらいに夕食を食べます。
roku-ji san-juppun kurai ni yuushoku wo tabemasu.
I have dinner at around 6:30.

ANSWER KEY

Exercise 31 Time (Page 346)

- Complete the following table using words to describe a time.

Kanji	Hiragana	Reading	English
四時	よじ	yo-ji	4 o'clock
五時	ごじ	go-ji	5 o'clock
六時	ろくじ	roku-ji	6 o'clock
七時	しちじ	shichi-ji	7 o'clock
八時	はちじ	hachi-ji	8 o'clock
九時	くじ	ku-ji	9 o'clock
一分	いっぷん	ippun	1 minute
四分	よんふん	yon-fun	4 minutes
六分	ろっぷん	roppun	6 minutes
四十分	よんじゅっぷん	yonjuppun	40 minutes
午前	ごぜん	gozen	AM
午後	ごご	gogo	PM
夜	よる	yoru	Night
深夜	しんや	shinya	Midnight
朝	あさ	asa	Morning
日の出	ひので	hinode	Sunrise

Exercise 32 Time (Page 347)

- Pretend you are A and B. Ask and answer questions about activities you have done in the past. Home, work, school, shopping, etc.

いえ　がっこう
E.g. Ask: 家から学校までどのくらいかかりますか。
(ie kara gakkou made dono kurai kakarimasu ka?)
How long does it take from home to school?

いえ　がっこう　ある　じゅうごふん
E.g. Answer: 家から学校まで歩いて十五分かかります
(ie kara gakkou made aruite juu go fun kakarimasu.)
It takes fifteen minutes to walk from home to school.

みせ　えき
E.g. Ask: 店から駅までどのくらいかかりますか。
(mise kara eki made dono kurai kakarimasu ka?)
How long does it take from the store to the station?

みせ　えき　くるま　よんふん
E.g. Answer: 店から駅まで車で四分かかります。
(mise kara eki made kuruma de yonpun kakarimasu.)
It takes four minutes by car from the store to the station.

Exercise 33 Daily Life (Page 348)

- Describe how your daily life is going using the same pattern of "Yukina" life, from morning till night. (Work, Morning, Sport, breakfast, etc.) e.g.

E.g.
わたし　がくせい
私は学生です。watshi wa gakusei desu. –I am a student.

あさ　　　　ごじお　　じぶん　べんとうつ
朝は、いつも五時に起きて、自分のお弁当を作ります。
asa wa itsumo go-ji ni okite jibun no o-bentou wo tsukuri masu.
In the morning, I always wake up at 5 o'clock and make my bento (boxed lunch).

いぬ さんぽ　　あさ
そのあと、犬と散歩してから朝ごはんを食べます。
(sono ato inu to sanpo shite kara asa-gohan wo tabemasu.)
After that, I take a walk with my dog and then have breakfast.

だいがく いえ ある　にじゅうごふん
大学は家から歩いて二十五分のところにあります。
(daigaku wa ie kara aruite nijuugo-fun no tokoro ni arimasu.)
The university is a 25-minute walk from home.

だいがく　え とき　　　　ある　いえ　か
いつも大学から帰る時は、ゆっくり歩いて家まで帰ります。
(itsumo daigaku kara kaeru toki wa yukkuri aruite ie made kaerimasu.)
When I usually return from the university, I walk slowly and go home.

Exercise 34 Daily Life (Page 349)

- Translate the following words into Japanese.

English	Kanji	Hiragana	Reading
Employee	正社員	せいしゃいん	seishain
Always	何時も	いつも	itsumo
Breakfast	朝ご飯	あさごはん	asa-gohan
Train	電車	でんしゃ	densha
Company	会社	かいしゃ	kaisha
Student	学生	がくせい	gakusei
End	終わり	おわり	owari
House	家	いえ	ie
Little	少し	すこし	sukoshi

- The essential N5 Kanji has been highlighted for your reference.

Continued on the next page.

Exercise 34 Daily Life (Page 349)

- Translate the following phrases into Japanese.

1. I ate breakfast (Formal).
Answer:
私は朝食を食べました。
わたし は ちょうしょく を いたべました。
watashi wa choushoku wo tabemashita.

2. I didn't eat breakfast.
Answer:
私は朝食を食べませんでした。
わたし は ちょうしょく を たべません でした。
watashi wa choushoku wo tabemasen deshita.

3. I eat breakfast every day.
Answer:
私は毎日朝食を食べます。
わたし は まいにち ちょうしょく を たべます。
watashi wa mainichi choushoku wo tabemasu.

- Write your different degrees of liking things.

Exercise 35 Breakfast and Favorite Sport or Music (Page 350)

- Using the same pattern as Ami and Chris's daily breakfast, write four

- 1. Write two sentences about the food you like/dislike.

E.g. 私は赤いりんごが大好きです。
Hiragana: わたしは あかい りんごが だいすきです。
Romaji: watashi wa akai ringo ga daisuki desu.
English: I love red apples.

E.g. 私は肉が嫌いです。
Hiragana: わたしは にくが きらいです。
Romaji: watashi wa niku ga kirai desu.
English: I don't like meat.

E.g. 私はあまり牛乳を飲みません。
Hiragana: わたしはあまりぎゅうにゅうをのみません。
Romaji: watashi wa amari gyuunyuu wo nomimasen.
English: I don't drink much milk.

- In the same way that "Tarou" wrote his favorite sport, write your favorite

E.g. 私はバスケットボールが好きです。
Hiragana: わたしはバスケットボールがすきです。
Romaji: watashi wa basuketto booru ga suki desu.
English: I like basketball.

E.g. 私はラップ音楽が好きです。
Hiragana: わたしはラップおんがくがすきです。
Romaji: watashi wa rappu ongaku ga suki desu.
English: I like rap music.

Exercise 36 Vocabulary (Page 351)

- Extend your range of vocabulary Circle the correct words for the English meaning.

English	Answer	English	Answer
Always	a. いつも	Especially	b. とくに
Breakfast	b. あさごはん	Saturday	b. どようび
Egg	c. たまご	Music	b. おんがく
Sometimes	c. ときどき	Beef	c. ぎゅうにく
Usually	a. たいてい	Fish	b. さかな
Not much	b. あまり	Vegetable	a. やさい
Delicious	b. おいしい	Employee	b. かいしゃいん
Much	a. たくさん	Everyday	a. まいにち
Friend	c. ともだち		

Exercise 37 Cardinal Directions (Page 352)

- Fill the below boxes with the correct cardinal directions in Japanese.

①	北西 -hokusei	⑤	東 -higashi
②	北 -kita	⑥	南西 -nansei
③	北東 -hokutou	⑦	南 -minami
④	西 -nishi	⑧	南東 -nantou

Exercise 38 Directions (Page 353)

- Test yourself and write the following directions & road words.

English	Answer	English	Answer
Left	左 -ひだり	Traffic light	しんごう
Right	右 -みぎ	Road	どうろ
Behind	後ろ -うしろ	Bridge	はし
Front	前 -まえ	Far	とおい
Straight	まっすぐ	Close	ちかい
Crosswalk	おうだんほどう	Intersection	こうさてん

The essential N5 Kanji has been highlighted for your reference.

Continued on the next page.

Exercise 39 Directions (Page 354)

- This is a map of the town. Using the road directions you have learned in Japanese, provide walking directions to the bank.

ホテルの<ruby>前<rt>まえ</rt></ruby>のおうだんほどうをわたって、びょういんの<ruby>前<rt>まえ</rt></ruby>をまっすぐ
hoteru no mae no oudan-hodou wo watatte, byouin no mae wo massugu

<ruby>行<rt>い</rt></ruby>きます。<ruby>次<rt>つぎ</rt></ruby>の<ruby>信号<rt>しんごう</rt></ruby><ruby>左<rt>ひだり</rt></ruby>に<ruby>曲<rt>ま</rt></ruby>がります。
ikimasu.　tsugi no shingou wo hidari ni magarimasu.

つきあたりの<ruby>道<rt>みち</rt></ruby>を<ruby>左<rt>ひだり</rt></ruby>に<ruby>曲<rt>ま</rt></ruby>がってヘアサロンの<ruby>前<rt>まえ</rt></ruby>のおうだんほどうを
わたって。tsukiatari no michi wo hidari ni magatte heasaron no mae no
oudan-hodou wo watatte.

<ruby>駅<rt>えき</rt></ruby>の<ruby>前<rt>まえ</rt></ruby>のおうだんほどうもわたります。
eki no mae no oudan-hodou mo watarimasu.

はくぶつかんが<ruby>見<rt>み</rt></ruby>えたら<ruby>左<rt>ひだり</rt></ruby>に<ruby>行<rt>い</rt></ruby>きます。<ruby>本屋<rt>ほんや</rt></ruby>の<ruby>角<rt>かど</rt></ruby>を<ruby>右<rt>みぎ</rt></ruby>に<ruby>曲<rt>ま</rt></ruby>がって、
hakubutsukan ga mietara hidari ni ikimasu. hon'ya no kado wo migi ni
magatte,

<ruby>公園<rt>こうえん</rt></ruby>の<ruby>前<rt>まえ</rt></ruby>のおうだんほどうをわたったら<ruby>銀行<rt>ぎんこう</rt></ruby>に<ruby>着<rt>つ</rt></ruby>きます。
kouen no mae no oudan-hodou wo watattara ginkou ni tsukimasu.

Cross the crosswalk in front of the hotel and go straight in front of the hospital. Turn left at the next traffic light. At the end of the street, turn left and cross the pedestrian crossing in front of the hair salon, then cross the pedestrian crossing in front of the station. When you see the museum, turn left. Turn right at the corner of the bookstore and cross the crosswalk in front of the park to reach the bank.

Exercise 40 Giving Directions (Page 355)

- Give directions by filling in the blanks in the following sentences.

1. <ruby>駅<rt>えき</rt></ruby>へは この<ruby>道<rt>みち</rt></ruby>を<u><ruby>まっすぐ<rt>すす</rt></ruby></u>進みます。
   (eki e wa kono michi wo massugu susumimasu.)
   To get to the station, go straight on this road.

2. コンビニは そこを<u><ruby>右<rt>みぎ</rt></ruby></u>に<u><ruby>曲<rt>ま</rt></ruby>がって</u>、まっすぐ行って<ruby>突<rt>つ</rt></ruby>き<ruby>当<rt>あた</rt></ruby>りです。
   (konbini wa soko wo migi ni magatte, massugu itte tsuki atari desu.)
   The convenience store is to the right, go straight and it's at the end of the road.

3. パールホテルは そのコンビニから<u><ruby>信号<rt>しんごう</rt></ruby></u>の<u><ruby>交差点<rt>こうさてん</rt></ruby></u>を<ruby>渡<rt>わ</rt></ruby>ってください。
   Pāruhoteru wa sono konbini kara shingou no kousaten wo watatte
   kudasai. Cross the traffic light intersection from the convenience store to the Pearl Hotel.

Exercise 41 Position (Page 356)

- Write the position words that you have learned.

Kanji	上	下	右	左	後ろ	前	中	外
Hiragana	うえ	した	みぎ	ひだり	うしろ	まえ	なか	そと
Reading	ue	shita	migi	hidari	ushiro	mae	naka	soto
English	Above	Below	Right	Left	Behind	Front	Inside	Outside

- Write the following sentences using the position words that you have learned.

1. <ruby>本<rt>ほん</rt></ruby>はいすの<ruby>上<rt>うえ</rt></ruby>にあります。-hon wa isu no ue ni arimasu.

2. <ruby>猫<rt>ねこ</rt></ruby>はつくえの<ruby>下<rt>した</rt></ruby>にいます。-neko wa tsukue no shita ni imasu.

3. <ruby>駅<rt>えき</rt></ruby>の<ruby>前<rt>まえ</rt></ruby>で<ruby>会<rt>あ</rt></ruby>いましょう。-eki no mae de aimashou.

4. お<ruby>金<rt>かね</rt></ruby>をかばんの<ruby>中<rt>なか</rt></ruby>に<ruby>入<rt>い</rt></ruby>れました。-okane wo kaban no naka
ni iremashita.

5. つづけてください。-tsudzukete kudasai.

6. <ruby>間<rt>あいだ</rt></ruby>。-あいだ-aida.

Exercise 42 Transportation (Page 357)

- Match the transportation word to its correct English meaning.

のりもの-Transportation
のりば-Platform
しんかんせん-Bullet Train
きんえん-No Smoking
ちかてつ-Subway train
つぎ-Next
ふね-Boat

いりぐち-Entrance
でぐち-Exit
ごじょうしゃ-Boarding
いきさき-Destination
じてんしゃ-Bicycle
あぶない-Dangerous

Exercise 43 Shopping - Convenience Stores (P.358)

- Put the Japanese words that apply to the blanks and read the sentence aloud.

おきゃくさん-こんにちは。-Hello.
てんいん-いらっしゃいませ! -Welcome!
おきゃくさん-すみません。-Excuse me.
おきゃくさん-これをください。-Please give me this.
おきゃくさん-おいくらですか。-How much is it?
てんいん-ごひゃくえんのおかえしです。-500 yen is your
change.
てんいん-またおこしくださいませ。
Thank you very much and please come again.

Exercise 44 Restaurant (Page 359)

- Put the Japanese words that apply to the blanks and read the sentence aloud. Rearrange the following words to complete the sentence, and try to memorize the sentence.

てんいん → お二人様ですか。- o-futari desu ka?
おきゃくさん → 後で来ます。-ato de kimasu.
てんいん → こちらへどうぞ。-kochira he douzo.
てんいん → ご注文がお決まりになりましたら、- go-tyuumon ga o-kimari ni narimashitara,

- Questions: (Answer in Japanese.)

1. いらっしゃいませ!-Welcome!
2. 三人-Three people.
3. いえ、もう一人、後で来ます。–No, one more person will come later.
4. では、ごあんないさせていただきますので、こちらへどうぞ。
   Now, let me show you around, this way, please.

Exercise 45 Colors (Page 360)

- Translate the following Japanese colors words into English.

くろ = Black	あお = Blue	みどり = Green
き= Yellow	あか = Red	しろ = White
むらさき = Purple	ちゃ = Brown	はい = Gray

- Translate the following colors words into Japanese.

Pink: ピンク
Gold: きん
Silver: ぎん
Orange: オレンジ

Grey: グレー
Light Blue: みずいろ
Dark Blue: のうこん
Yellow-Green: きみどり

Exercise 46 Hotel Reservation (Page 361)

- Complete the following tables for the hotel vocabulary.

Kanji	Hiragana	Reading	English
---	(フロント)	furonto	Front desk
予約	よやく	yoyaku	Reservation
部屋	へや	heya	Room
---	(チェックイン)	chekkuin	Check-in
---	(チェックアウト)	chekkuauto	Check out

Continue on the top right

Exercise 46 Hotel Reservation (Page 361)

Kanji	Hiragana	Reading	English
住所	じゅうしょ	juusho	Address
禁煙室	きんえんしつ	kin'en-shitsu	Non smoking room
喫煙所	きつえんじょ	kitsuenjo	Smoking room
---	エキストラベッド	ekisutorabedo	Extra bed
鍵	かぎ	kagi	Key
---	(ロビー)	robī	Lobby
荷物	にもつ	nimotsu	Luggage

Counting Nights of Stay			
English	Hiragana	Kanji	Reading
1 night stay	いっぱく	一泊	ippaku
2 nights stay	にはく	二泊	ni-haku
5 nights stay	ごはく	五泊	go-haku

Counting Nights			
1 night	ひとばん	一晩	hito-ban
3 nights	みばん	三晩	mi-ban
4 nights	よばん	四晩	yo-ban

Counting Rooms			
2 rooms	ふたへや	二部屋	futa-heya
3 rooms	さんへや	三部屋	san-heya
5 rooms	ごへや	五部屋	go-heya

Exercise 47 Hotel Reservation (Page 362)

- Hotel reservation over the phone

- Customer

1.予約したいのですが。
2. 28日（土）から2泊です。
3. 4人分です。
4. ツインベッド2部屋です。
5. チェックアウトは何時ですか。
6. 朝食は付いていますか。
7. 料金はいくらですか。
8. ありがとうございます。

- Hotel staff

1.こんにちは、プラザホテルです。
2.いつから滞在されますか。
3.何名様ですか。
4.何部屋ですか。
5.チェックアウトは11時です。
6.朝食付きです。
7.合計で5万円です。
8.お名前を頂いてよろしいですか。

Exercise 48 Body Parts (Page 363)

- Label the body parts using Hiragana words.

No.	Kanji	Hiragana	Reading	English
①	髪	かみ	kami	Hair
②	顔	かお	kao	Face
③	目	め	me	Eyes
④	口	くち	kuchi	Mouth
⑤	肩	かた	kata	Shoulder
⑥	胸	むね	mune	Chest
⑦	腕	うで	ude	Arm
⑧	腹	はら	hara	Stomach
⑨	腰	こし	koshi	Waist
⑩	手	て	te	Hand
⑪	指	ゆび	yubi	Finger
⑫	膝	ひざ	hiza	Knee
⑬	足	あし	ashi	Foot
⑭	眉毛	まゆげ	mayuge	Eyebrows
⑮	耳	みみ	mimi	Ear
⑯	喉	のど	nodo	Throat
⑰	鼻	はな	hana	Nose
⑱	首	くび	kubi	Neck
⑲	足首	あしくび	ashikubi	Ankle

Exercise 49 Japanese Verbs Groups (Page 364)

1. The correct answer is D.
2. The correct answer is A.
I did. The past tense of "do," a typical irregular verb, is "did." B and D are passive verbs, and C is the polite past tense of "do."

3. The correct answer is B.
A polite and neutral form of speaking in Japanese, the Japanese honorific "masu-cho" is used to express politeness and neutrality. The masu form, which is used in everyday conversation, is used in relatively formal situations, business situations, public speeches, and so on.
4. The correct answer is D. It is negative MASU
"He doesn't eat sashimi."

Exercise 50 Japanese Verbs Groups (365)

- Write sentences about Masako and Haruto (Japanese verbs)

1. 私は朝食を食べませんでした。
watashi wa choushoku wo tabemasendeshita.
Hiragana: わたしはちょうしょくをたべませんでした。

2. 私は水を飲みます。
watashi wa mizu wo nomimasu.
Hiragana: わたしはみずをのみます。

Masako

3. 私は英語を勉強しています。
watashi wa eigo wo benkyou shite imasu.
Hiragana: わたしはえいごをべんきょうしています。

1. 朝食を食べる。
choushoku wo taberu.
Hiragana: ちょうしょくをたべる。

2. 私は毎日朝食を食べます。
watashi wa mainichi choushoku wo tabemasu.
Hiragana: わたしはまいにちちょうしょくをたべます。

Haruto

3. 休みの日は何もしません。
yasumi no hi wa nani mo shimasen.
Hiragana: やすみのひはなにもしません。

Dictionary form	Masu form	Meaning
待つ-matsu	待ちます-machimasu	To wait
買う-kau	買います-kaimasu	To buy
遊ぶ-asobu	遊びます-asobimasu	To play
読む-yomu	読みます-yomimasu	To read
飲む-nomu	飲みます-nomimasu	To drink
休む-yasumu	休みます-yasumimasu	To rest

Exercise 51 Japanese Verbs Groups (Page 366)

Group 2	Reading	Masu form	Reading	Meaning
いる	iru	います	imasu	To exist
見る	Miru	みます	mimasu	To see
着る	kiru	きます	kimasu	To wear
起きる	okiru	おきます	okimasu	To wake
見せる	miseru	みせます	misemasu	To show
食べる	taberu	たべます	tabemasu	To eat
寝る	neru	ねます	nemasu	To sleep
教える	osieru	おしえます	oshiemasu	To teach

ANSWER KEY

(Exercise 51 Japanese Verbs Groups (Page 366)

Group 3	Masu form	Meaning
する-suru	します-shimasu	To do
来る-kuru	来ます-kimasu	To come

- 3. Fill the below table with the て Te form.

With the て Te form	Meaning
見てください。 -mitekudasai	Please look.
聞いてください。-kiitekudasai	Please listen.
書いてください。-kaitekudasai	Please write.
待ってください。-mattekudasai	Please wait.

Exercise 52 Japanese Verbs - Masu Form (Page 367)

- Change the present tense of the verb in the following sentences to the **past tense.**

Present tense	Past tense
朝ご飯を食べます。 -asa gohan wo tabe**masu.** -I will eat breakfast.	朝ご飯を食べました。 -asa gohan wo tabe**mashita.** -I ate breakfast.
しゅくだいをします。 -shukudai wo shi**masu.** -I will do my homework.	しゅくだいをしました。 -shukudai wo shi**mashita.** -I did my homework.

- Change the present negative of the verb in the following sentences to the **past negative.**

Present Negation	Past Negative
今日は学校に行きません。 kyou wa gakkou ni iki**masen.** I am not going to school today.	今日は学校に行きませんでした。 kyou wa gakkou ni iki**masendeshita.** I didn't go to school today.
私はホテルを予約しません。 watashi wa hoteru wo yoyaku shi**masen.** I don't book hotels.	私はホテルを予約しませんでした。 watashi wa hoteru wo yoyaku shi**masendeshita.** I didn't book the hotel.
私はワインを飲みません。 watashi wa wain wo nomi**masen.** I don't drink wine.	私はワインを飲みませんでした。 watashi wa wain wonomi**masendeshita.** -I didn't drink wine.

Exercise 53 Japanese Verbs – Conjugation (Page 368)

- Complete the table by filling up the empty with the correct Japanese verb conjugation.

Group	MASU Form	Dictionary	TE Form	Meaning
1	飲みます (omimasu)	飲む (nomu)	飲んで (nonnde)	To drink
2	見ます mimasu	見る miru	見て mite	To see
1	買います kaimasu	買う kau	買って katte	To buy
3	します shimasu	する suru	して site	To do
2	食べます tabemasu	食べる taberu	食べて tabete	To eat
1	書きます kakimasu	書く kaku	書いて kaite	To write
1	話します hanasimasu	話す hanasu	話して hanasite	To talk
3	来ます kimasu	来る kuru	来て kite	To come

- Ask for permission using て-form plus 〜もいいですか。

1. May I open the window? まどをあけてもいいですか。 mado wo akete mo iidesu ka?	2. Can I sit here? ここにすわってもいいですか。 koko ni suwatte mo iidesu ka?

- Ask for permission using て-form plus いい。

1. Can I make a phone call? 電話をかけていい? denwa wo kakete ii?	2. May I go to the bathroom? トイレに行っていい? toire ni itte ii?

Exercise 54 Verbs Groups – (て) Form (Page 369)

- Change the following verbs from the dictionary form to the て form

Dictionary form	English	(て)TE Form
(読む) よむ -yomu	To read	読んで-yonde
(飲む) のむ -nomu	To drink	飲んで-nonde
(洗う) あらう -arau	To wash	洗って-aratte
(乗る) のる -noru	To ride	乗って-notte
(送る) おくる -okuru	To send	送って-okutte
(書く) かく -kaku	To write	書いて-kaite
(思う) おもう -omou	To think	思って-omotte

Exercise 54 Verbs Groups – (て) Form (Page 369)

（寝る）ねる-neru	To sleep	寝て-nete
（起きる）おきる-okiru	To wake up	起きて-okite
（来る）くる-kuru	To come/arrive	来て-kite

Exercise 54 Verbs Groups – (て) Form (Page 369)

- Write the group number for the following verbs and translate them.

Dictionary form	Group	English
（起きる）おきる-okiru	2	To wake up
（見る）みる-miru	2	To see
する-suru	3	To do
（話す）はなす-hanasu	1	To talk
（買う）かう-kau	1	To buy
（来る）くる-kuru	3	To come/arrive

Exercise 55 Ask Permissions (Page 370)

- Highlight the てform of the verb

❑ でんわを、かけて いいですか。
❑ トイレに、いって いいですか。
❑ ここに すわって よろしい でしょうか。
❑ あした きても よろしい ですか。
❑ ちょっと お-ききして いい ですか。
❑ くるまで、いかせて いただいて いいですか。

Exercise 56 Japanese Verb Conjugation (Page 371)

私は毎日勉強しています。-I'm studying every day.
→ "am studying" indicates the present progressive form.
彼はあまり勉強しません。-He doesn't study much.
→ "doesn't study" is a negative sentence and it's in the present tense of the third person singular, therefore "does" is added.
あなたは、昨日勉強しました。-You studied yesterday.
→ "studied" indicates the past tense.
私は何も勉強しませんでした。-I didn't study anything.
→ "didn't study" is a negative sentence in the past tense and "did" is added.
明日、店を掃除しましょう。-Let's clean the store tomorrow.
→ "Let's" is a contraction of "Let us" and it indicates an invitation.
あなたは買い物をしましたか。-Did you go shopping?
→ "Did you" is a question in the past tense and "did" is added.
私は服を洗いませんでした。-I didn't wash my clothes.
→ "didn't wash" is a negative sentence in the past tense and "did" is added.
彼は昨日ゲームをしました。-He played a game yesterday.
→ "played" indicates the past tense.

Exercise 57 Japanese Verb Conjugation (Page 372)

母は私の部屋に来ました。-My mother came to my room. This sentence uses the past tense verb "came" to indicate that the action of the mother coming to the room has already happened.

彼はあなたと来ません。-He won't come with you.
→ The sentence is a negative statement that uses the future tense to describe the action that will not happen.

あなたは昨日来ませんでした。-The sentence, using the adverb "yesterday," negatively states that the action of not coming occurred within that specific timeframe.

私は勉強しに来ました。-I came to study.
→ This sentence uses the past tense verb "came" to indicate that the action of coming to a place for the purpose of studying has already happened.

朝、私と一緒に来ませんか。
-Would you like to come with me in the morning?
→ The sentence uses the future tense to describe the action that the subject may take if they choose to accept the invitation.

多分、あなたはここへ来ます。-Maybe you come here.
→ The sentence is a simple statement that indicates that the subject may come to the place, but it is not certain.

友達は、駅に来ませんでした。-My friend didn't come to the station, →indicating the past action of not arriving.

今度あなたはここに来ますか。-Will you come here next time?
→ The sentence uses the present tense verb "come" to describe the action the subject may take in the future.

Exercise 58 Japanese Verb Conjugation (Page 373)

- もう少しゆっくり話して（はなして）ください。
- 彼は、あなたと話しません（はなしません）。
- 母は、あなたに話しましたか（はなしましたか）。
- 私は彼に全て話しませんでした（はなしませんでした）。
- 明日、もう一度話しましょう（はなしましょう）。
- 先生は、本のことを話しました（はなしました）。
- みんなで話しましょうか（はなしましょうか）。
- 誰かがこれを話しますか（はなしますか）。

Exercise 59 Japanese Verb Conjugation (Page 374)

- 母はいつも映画を見ます（みます）。
- 彼はテレビを見ません（みません）。
- 私は、昨日海を見ました（みました）。
- 父はあの山を見ませんでした（みませんでした）。
- 明日、もう一度これを見ませんか（みませんか）。
- 先生は、本を見ませんでしたか（みませんでしたか）。
- みんなであの映画を見ましょうか（みましょうか）。
- 誰かがこれを見ましたか（みましたか）。

Made in United States
Troutdale, OR
03/30/2024

18832019R00217